Dancing with Metaphors in the Pulpit

Dancing with Metaphors in the Pulpit

RODNEY WALLACE KENNEDY

CASCADE *Books* • Eugene, Oregon

DANCING WITH METAPHORS IN THE PULPIT

Copyright © 2024 Rodney Wallace Kennedy. All rights reserved. Except for brief quotations in critical publications or reviews, no part of this book may be reproduced in any manner without prior written permission from the publisher. Write: Permissions, Wipf and Stock Publishers, 199 W. 8th Ave., Suite 3, Eugene, OR 97401.

Cascade Books
An Imprint of Wipf and Stock Publishers
199 W. 8th Ave., Suite 3
Eugene, OR 97401

www.wipfandstock.com

PAPERBACK ISBN: 978-1-6667-1228-5
HARDCOVER ISBN: 978-1-6667-1229-2
EBOOK ISBN: 978-1-6667-1230-8

Cataloguing-in-Publication data:

Names: Kennedy, Rodney Wallace, author.

Title: Dancing with metaphors in the pulpit / Rodney Wallace Kennedy.

Description: Eugene, OR: Cascade Books, 2024. | Includes bibliographical references and index.

Identifiers: ISBN 978-1-6667-1228-5 (paperback) | ISBN 978-1-6667-1229-2 (hardcover) | ISBN 978-1-6667-1230-8 (ebook)

Subjects: LCSH: Preaching. | Metaphor—Religious aspects—Christianity. | Rhetoric.

Classification: BV4211.2 K46 2024 (paperback) | BV4211.2 (ebook)

07/29/24

To the memory of my father, Jeff Davis Kennedy,
"Barnabas" to my preaching

Contents

Introduction: Let the Dance Begin		1
Chapter 1	What the Novelists Have to Teach Us	17
Chapter 2	What the Poets Teach Us about Preaching	52
Chapter 3	What the Philosophers Teach Us about Preaching	87
Chapter 4	What the Rhetoricians Teach us about Preaching	125
Conclusion: For God's Sake Feel the Sermon		183
Bibliography		203

Introduction: Let the Dance Begin

As long as you're dancing,
you can break the rules.
Sometimes breaking the rules
is just extending the rules.
Sometimes there are no rules.[1]

—MARY OLIVER

PREACHING DOES NOT DWELL in a land at ease. Those who attempt to preach should heed the words of the prophet Amos: "Woe to those who are at ease in Zion."[2] In particular, it is never easy to live in the sparse land between God and the congregation. We cannot help but be sympathetic with preachers. They are being asked to speak words from God, to preach words that threaten the habits, attitudes, opinions, and existence of the congregation. To preach they must look on death itself as Moses lifted the serpent in the wilderness and said, "Look on death and live."[3] In emotional terms, to preach is to incarnate aspects of the suffering servant of Isaiah 53.

To preach is to writhe and struggle with the harshest existential questions of humanity. I am never far from the words of Habakkuk: "O Lord, how long shall I cry for help, and you will not listen? Or cry to you 'Violence!' and you will not save?"[4] In all that struggle, however, I have a text for what follows. After sixty years, I am unable to write without a biblical text. "I will stand at my watchpost and station myself on the rampart; I will keep watch to see what he will say to me and what he and what he will answer concerning my complaint."[5]

1. Oliver, *Devotions*, 48.
2. Amos 6:1.
3. Num 21:6–9.
4. Hab 1:2.
5. Hab 2:1.

I still have not lost confidence in the power of God to speak hope to humanity. "Though the fig tree does not blossom and no fruit is on the vines; though the produce of the olive fails and the fields yield no food; though the flock is cut off from the fold and there is no herd in the stalls, yet I will rejoice in the Lord; I will exult in the God of my salvation. God, the Lord, is my strength; he makes my feet like the feet of a deer and makes me tread upon the heights."[6] Cue the stringed instruments and let's get this dance started.

The preacher lives his or her life as a rubber band stretched as the galaxies across the universe. This tension distracts or it can be life-giving. Gardner Taylor surmises that the stress of the preacher is "a guilty one telling guilty ones of the judgment upon them."[7] The tension that exists between the preacher and the congregation: the sermon. The key ingredient: empathy. Taylor says that the preacher "enters, actually or vicariously, into the plight and circumstances of human hope and circumstance."[8] Empathy and humanity are the two essential words for the preacher.

The preacher embraces all humanity, all its foibles and failures, all its nightmares and dreams, all the darkness that exists but she can't live there. Harry Crews says, "Most people get away from having to embarrass themselves in front of other people, embarrass themselves to themselves, by simply refusing to think about those things. Let's just not think about it, for God's sake. Let's not talk about it, certainly not in the family where you know Mama and Daddy and little brother, and everybody's body's present."[9] The preacher crosses that line and talks about what people have tried to avoid, bury, or forget. Preachers are the shamans, the medicine men, of the church.

I am not writing for agreement but to create argument. I want disagreement, dissension. I want you to be forced into a corner until you have no choice but to drop the infernal niceness of being a preacher and fight back with stronger arguments, more scholarly debate, and better discernment. I want you on the ropes fighting against everything, questioning everything, as if you are wrestling with the angel who attacked Jacob in the dark. If that works for you, I can work with it.

This is a homiletical handbook intended for preachers. To translate and unpack the arguments that I make in this book, I have employed portions of essays on current social issues to raise questions for reflection and to encourage preachers to research these issues for their own sermons. The

---

6. Hab 3:17–19.
7. Taylor, *How Shall They Preach?*, 31.
8. Taylor, *How Shall They Preach?*, 31.
9. Crews, "Interview," 350.

homiletical principles mix seamlessly with the materials. I provide these "material" examples of gathering material for sermons. The reader will be able to judge her agreement or disagreement with my positions and better consider some of the applications that *Dancing with Metaphors in the Pulpit* raises for the practice of preaching.

A great preacher, like a great novelist, at times visits the land of darkness, but can never stay there or purchase property in that land. The preacher seeks to know the nature of life, including the darkness, but not to the point of being driven to clinical depression. A character in a short story, unable to handle the death of her husband, feels she is being pursued by a group of Christians who only look on the sunny side, says of them: "They refuse to look on the dark side of things, and they want her to blink it away too. If she can smile in the face of loss, grief, and death, so can they. They're like children in a fairy tale, singing songs, holding hands. Never mind the dark wood, the wolves and witches. Or birds that eat up the breadcrumbs."[10] Many preachers try to eliminate the tension, but it is like attempting to remove oxygen from the air we breathe. They work hard at avoiding the natural tension by not preaching the hard texts, the hard issues, the controversial events. They circle warily around politics, money, and sex—all the interesting topics—and then wonder why people find their sermons boring. Pick any of the thinking, writing, and speaking disciplines and you will discover that the great ones welcome the tension, create more tension, and make the air breathe with a healthy tension. James H. Robinson argues that the preacher must preach to "preserve a nation."[11]

There is a dark cloud hovering over those who preach. There's a tentativeness, a lingering timidity for preachers confronted with congregations that do not always share the preacher's deepest commitments. In language that is harsh but honest, George Lakoff asks, "Why are Democrats such wimps?"[12] I ask, "Why are progressive preachers often such wimps?" A wimp is a person who is weak, timid, cowardly, unadventurous. These are the preachers who speak pleasing words so that congregations may experience the drug-like sensation of being pleased with their lives and the state of the nation.

The character, integrity, moral backbone, and courage of the preacher is essential to faithful preaching. The winds of danger, criticism, being unliked, and angry congregations always live in the shadows of our minds.

10. Brown, "New Life," 315.

11. Robinson, *Adventurous Preaching*, chapter 5: "Preaching to Preserve a Nation," 115–42.

12. Lakoff, *Political Mind*, Kindle ed. loc. 143.

Only a preacher with the spirit of boldness, a spirit that covers the entire first forty or so years of Christian preaching in the book of Acts will make the life of preaching the joy it is intended to be. I have been marked for life by a remark of Marney that preachers owned by the culture "become a successful blesser of a successful culture."[13]

Paul, giving instructions in preaching, tells Timothy: "God did not give us a spirit of cowardice but rather a spirit of power and of love and of self-discipline."[14] In the book of Job, Elihu confesses, "I was timid and afraid to declare my opinion to you."[15] Is this not an understandable response in churches that are now more defined by secular political issues than by biblical or theological teaching? The woman of wisdom says, "The timid become destitute."[16] The most direct reminders of the danger of timidity is found in Sirach: "Woe to timid hearts and to slack hands."[17]

Gardner Taylor always claimed that the three temptations of the preacher were to whine, to shine, and to recline.[18] "Fences set on a high place will not stand firm against the wind; so a timid mind with a fool's resolve will not stand firm against any fear."[19] And there's this bold encouragement: "Those who fear the Lord will not be timid or play the coward, for his is their hope."[20]

Preachers have imbibed a gospel predicated on the message "Do not be afraid." We have been formed by histories of bold preachers. In Greek, the word for these preachers is parrhesiastes. Michel Foucault says, "Someone is said to use parrhesia and merits consideration as a parrhesiastes only if there is a risk or danger for him in telling the truth."[21] (I will return to this concept in the conclusion, but right up front my goal is for preachers to merit consideration as true and faithful parrhesiastes of the gospel of Jesus.)

I confess that the first time I read St. Paul saying, "For now we see through a glass, darkly; but then face to face: now I know in part; but then shall I know even as also I am known,"[22] my only thought was walking through the looking glass. For me the preaching life is that kind of adventure,

---

13. Marney, *Priests to Each Other*, 10.
14. 2 Timothy 1:7.
15. Job 32:6.
16. Prov 11:16.
17. Sir 2:12.
18. Taylor, *How Shall They Preach?*, 33.
19. Sir 22:8.
20. Sir 34:16.
21. Foucault, *Fearless Speaking*, 16–17.
22. 1 Cor 13:12.

the Alice in Wonderland, Dorothy in *The Wizard of Oz*, *The Chronicles of Narnia* kind of adventures. Take the leap. Make the step. Always be the seeker, the wild-eyed explorer armed with nothing but the old maps, the allure of potential treasure, with faith and a belief in the power of language. As Gerhard Von Rad puts it, "Good sermons have something of an intellectual adventure about them."[23]

I prefer preachers who possess the soul of Pat Conroy:

> Great teachers had great personalities and . . . the greatest teachers had outrageous personalities. I did not like decorum or rectitude in a classroom; I preferred a highly oxygenated atmosphere, a climate of intemperance, rhetoric, and feverish melodrama. And I wanted my teachers to make me smart. A great teacher is my adversary, my conqueror, commissioned to chastise me. He leaves me tame and grateful for the new language he has purloined from other kings whose granaries are filled and whose libraries are famous. He tells me that teaching is the art of theft: of knowing what to steal and from whom. Bad teachers do not touch me; the great ones never leave me. They ride with me during all my days, and I pass on to others what they have imparted to me. I exchange their handy gifts with strangers on trains, and I pretend the gifts are mine. I steal from the great teachers. And the truly wonderful thing about them is they would applaud my theft, laugh at the thought of it, realizing they had taught me their larcenous skills well.[24]

"Ego integrity," to use Marney's word, is essential for preachers. In Marney's work at Interpreter's House he told Karl Menninger, "From some 8,000 laymen and ministers with whom we have conferred, five principal problems emerge: a loss of nerve, a loss of direction, erosion from culture, confusion of thought, exhaustion. . . . They have become shaken reeds, smoking lamps, earthen vessels . . . spent arrows. They have lost heart. But they can be revived!"[25]

It is vital that the preacher know her values, how to frame and state them clearly. An overall articulation of the preacher's values should align with the values, empathy, and compassion of the gospel of Jesus. If we are to be faithful preachers, it is imperative that speak our values loudly and clearly. A clear moral vision is a part of the values package. There must be a

---

23. Von Rad, *Biblical Interpretations in Preaching*, 17.
24. Conroy, *Lords of Discipline*, 251.
25. Menninger, *Whatever Became of Sin?*, 224.

moral alternative to the moralistic vision of evangelical Christianity with its propensity for excluding, demeaning, and dehumanizing so many Others.

I try to teach my preaching students the art of staying alive and still preach the gospel. When we preach in a temple of the (secular) kingdom (as we do every Sunday) we had better come prepared with the finest of metaphors, the best of analogies, and the most inspiring of stories. Even then, the potential for trouble exists among a people who "will not put up with sound teaching, but, having their ears tickled, they will accumulate for themselves teachers to suit their own desires and will turn away from listening to the truth and wander away to myths."[26]

Centuries ago, a saucy Chaucer growled, "Those shitty shepherds and their shitty sheep."[27] Alcuin wrote sermons for his awful preachers at the bequest of the emperor. It still stings to hear the Wakefield Master's question, "Are we all hand-tamed by these gentry?"[28] H. L. Mencken, his tongue dripped in a potent blend of vitriol and satire, said that the South consists of a "cesspool of Baptists, a miasma of Methodists, snake charmers, phony real estate operators, and syphilitic evangelists."[29] Preachers seem to have been in his mind's eye as he composed this awful depiction.

Still we preach. Dangers, hazards, passive-aggressive church members, angry church members, conflicts, opposition, defeat, misunderstandings—still we preach. Some days it just feels crazy. As novelist Barry Hannah comments, echoing the theology of his own character, "We have all worked in the foyer of the lunatic asylum. Release and deliverance by work is all we know. But we pray and beg for something else across the river and into the shade of the trees. For me, that is where Christ stands."[30] Flannery O'Connor's haunting depiction of a preacher who preaches a church without Christ in *Wise Blood* shows the downside of struggling with Jesus and his message. Hazel Motes, raised badly on bad religion, saw Jesus as a shadow in the trees calling to him, but Motes is an unending train of tragedy on the tracks to destruction and he says, "Listen, get this: I don't believe in anything."[31] Until we struggle with Jesus like Hazel Motes, we haven't even worked up a sweat.

I share what I have learned in this voyage to all the other planets other than theology, biblical studies, ethics, and homiletics. Rhetoric is the chief steward who brings clarity and vividness to truth spoken in metaphor.

---

26. 2 Tim 4:3–4.
27. Quoted in Marney, "Fundaments of a Competent Ministry," 2.
28. Marney, "Fundaments of a Competent Ministry," 2.
29. Mencken, quoted in Ketchin, ed., *Christ-Haunted Landscape*, Kindle ed. loc. 51.
30. Hannah, *Yonder Stands Your Orphan*, 11.
31. O'Connor, *Wise Blood*, 10.

Philosophy is the intellectual underpinning of the house. Writing (novels and short stories) is the outside gardener and can keep the place from blowing up. Poetry is the kitchen stirring up all the images and words that create meaning.

Together, their service faithfully establishes a competent keep in the Christian house, and together, I think, they provide the fundaments of being-in-the-world as a person-in-relation who can preach the truth in love.[32] My task is to assign the homework and expect it to be done. By homework I mean that decades-long process of inquiry, of a growing intellectual appetite, hat in hand, humility actual, begun long before seminary and preaching class, continued forever after as unfinished business, addressed to competent rhetoric, poetry, philosophy, history, drama, art, daily affairs, sociology, science, interpreted by a growing biblical memory, contemporary experience, theological acumen, into some kind of understanding that we have not lost confidence in the power of the gospel proclaimed to a secular but dying world.

No seminary on earth can do in three years or six years or fifteen what it takes to make competent ministry of the Gospel of God, but competent ministry can start there, tools and skills acquired there, resources for the long haul can be identified there, relationships that will undergird the tough times established there, friends and mentors and heroes for the journey, with bread and wine, can come together there. But the other disciplines must accompany the preacher every day of his or her life. As Stanley Hauerwas mentions, seminary teaches us to read and then we read for a lifetime.[33]

Rhetoric, philosophy, poetry, writing, sociology, science will not save us; they are neither salvation nor even evangelism and witness. Like any other discipline, each in turn represents a method. And here those vaunted "orders" come into proper play. They furnish the preacher a place to take hold, allies for disturbing the peace of the principalities and powers. Aided and abetted by the wisdoms of the world, resurrection and Pentecost has granted us the power to stand against these de-humanizers and, wise as serpents, we are loosed on the world to be properly seditious, in the service of all humankind. This is why our marching orders read "plunder the Egyptians."[34]

Kenneth Burke insists that we keep finding words for certain social relationships. By plundering the Egyptians, we are better equipped to "have a word for it." Burke notes that Eskimos have special names for many kinds

---

32. Marney, "Fundaments of a Competent Ministry," 3.
33. Hauerwas, *Working with Words*, 86.
34. Exod 3:22.

of snow because variations in the snow affects their living. In like manner, the preacher must "size" up social situations, which are as varied as snow in Alaska. Burke insists, "We must size up social issues because they greatly affect our living. And we must do so much more accurately than people who are going on emotions alone."[35]

Instead of offering a pretentious view of American Christian righteousness, the preacher should be part of the Christian tradition of finding truth wherever truth exists.[36] Floyd Anderson argues that Augustine produced a synthesis of sacred doctrine and pagan knowledge, representing "probably the most successful synthesis of Hebraism and Hellenism in Western history." Augustine: "Every good and worthy Christians should understand that wherever they may find truth, it emanates from their Lord."[37]

I do not apologize that the preacher, who may frequently really be as harmless as a dove will also at times need the "wisdom of a serpent" to be effective, for the challenge makes for a tough journey. The preacher among the disciplines is incarnating the sermon, filling the sermon with life, energy, passion, seriousness. The sermon informed by the wisdom of the ages is flesh, physical, material, the opposite of the kind of syrupy sentimentalism and sloppy superficiality that often plagues sermons.

After all, the serpent in the garden of Eden invented preaching with one question: "Did God say?"[38] A startling claim, no doubt, but one that I believe is accurate. David S. Cunningham reminds us, "Whenever people attempt to communicate through language, they will eventually find themselves disagreeing with one another; and, when their language concerns God, they may find themselves disagreeing quite frequently . . . . Hence, the enterprise of [preaching] necessarily involves the construction . . . . of arguments."[39] Preachers have been attempting to say what God said from the beginning. Flannery O'Connor says of her writing, "my subject in fiction is the action of grace in territory held largely by the devil."[40] "Did God say?" calls everything into a contestable arena.

Ellen Davis remarks, "It is a sad fact of history that authoritative texts held in common but read differently are less likely to create mutual sympathy than bitter division between religious communities."[41] No wonder so

---

35. Burke, "Literature as equipment for living," 294.
36. Anderson, "Doctrina christiana," 102.
37. Augustine, *On Christian Doctrine*, 2:18:28.
38. Genesis 3:1.
39. Cunningham, *Faithful Persuasion*, xiii.
40. O'Connor, *Mystery and Manners*, Kindle ed. loc. 1091.
41. Davis, "Critical Traditioning," 175.

many preachers can't resist saying, "God says," or "The Bible says," or "I'm just telling you what God says." The tension produced by the devil's question causes some preachers to lose nerve and grasp for the straws of certainty.

Kenneth Burke's idea of the "negative"[42] can be seen in the devil's question, "Did God say?" Burke says this is the "hortatory negative, the negative of command," as with the 'Thou shalt not's' of the Decalogue."[43] The answer of Eve, if she had said, "No," would have ended the charade. But Eve left the question hanging, and preachers attempt to fill in the blanks.

Filling in those blanks is a positive good that has accrued to the church as we have argued over the meaning of biblical texts. The energy derived from these disputes has produced our best theologians and preachers. This may strike some readers as an odd stance, but it is in line with those who in the past have asked why I was so angry. They assumed I was angry because of the attitude and content of my frequent essays. I can only say that upon introspection, I am not angry; I am happy. My writing makes me happy.

Overcoming the idea that preaching is about being simple can be a harrowing experience. The tradition of the church growing into a powerful institution on the preaching of uneducated apostles has always been a strong impetus for certain portions of the church. This is not a criticism of that history. What I am attempting is a recovery of the intellectual firepower of the sermon rooted in a different history, a history that begins with Paul. His CV appears in bits and pieces in his writings. On the summary line of his CV Paul could have written: "If anyone else has reason to be confident in the flesh, I have more: circumcised on the eighth day, a member of the people of Israel, of the tribe of Benjamin, a Hebrew born of Hebrews; as to the law, a Pharisee; as to zeal, a persecutor of the church; as to righteousness under the law, blameless."[44] His major professor was Gamaliel. Paul says, "I am a Jew, born in Tarsus in Cilicia, but brought up in this city at the feet of Gamaliel, educated strictly according to our ancestral law, being zealous for God, just as all of you are today."[45] Gamaliel was a celebrated Pharisee, a Jewish rabbi, a doctor of the law, and member of the Sanhedrin (highest Jewish council) in the early times of Christianity. He bears in the Talmud the surname of "the old man," and is represented as the son of Rabbi Simeon, and grandson of the famous Hillel. He is said to have occupied a seat, if not the presidency, in the Sanhedrim during the reigns of Tiberius, Caligula, and Claudius. He intervened in the trial of Peter and the other apostles. Luke says that he was

---

42. Burke, *Rhetoric of Religion*, 20.
43. Burke, *Rhetoric of Religion*, 20.
44. Philippians 3:4–6.
45. Acts 22:3.

"respected by all the people."[46] He is also represented by the apostle Paul as his early teacher before the conversion of the latter (Acts 22:3). The line of succession is suggestive: Hillel, Simeon, Gamaliel, and Paul.[47] This Jewish connection to the best rabbinical scholarship has not received the attention that it deserves.

The history of preaching has two streams of influence: Peter, uneducated fisherman and country preacher (Nazareth); Paul, educated and cosmopolitan (Jerusalem). The two streams continue to nourish the churches in the world. The Peter stream can be seen and celebrated in frontier preachers in early American history, itinerant Methodists, shopkeepers, farmers, tradesmen. The Paul stream flows from prestigious graduate schools and produces MDiv and PhD graduates. My interest lies in the Pauline succession of preachers.

A cursory review of the history of early preaching makes clear that the church's development and growth in the second to the fifth century was dominated by scholarly preachers educated in pagan schools of philosophy and rhetoric. Origen was an early scholar, ascetic, and theologian who was born and spent the first half of his career in Alexandria. He was a prolific writer who wrote roughly two thousand treatises in multiple branches of theology, including textual criticism, biblical exegesis, and hermeneutics, homiletic, and spirituality. He was one of the most influential and controversial figures in early Christian theology, apologetics, and asceticism. Chrysostom began his education under the pagan teacher Libanius, one of the best documented teachers of higher education in the ancient world. From Libanius, John acquired the skills for a career in rhetoric, as well as a love of the Greek language and literature. Eventually, he became a lawyer. As he grew older, however, John became more deeply committed to Christianity and went on to study theology under Diodora of Tarsus, founder of the reconstituted School of Antioch. According to the Christian historian Sozomen, Libanius was supposed to have said on his deathbed that John would have been his successor "if the Christians had not taken him from us."[48] Chrysostom, the "golden tongued one," is perhaps the greatest preacher in Christian history. His rhetorical training played a role in that preaching excellence.

Augustine was a theologian, philosopher, and the bishop of Hippo Regius in Numidia, Roman North Africa. His writings influenced the

---

46. Acts 5:34.

47. Bible Portal Staff, "Who was Gamaliel in the Bible (Acts 5)?"

48. Sozomen, *Ecclesiastical History of Sozomen*, book VIII, chapter II: "Education, Training, Conduct, and Wisdom of the Great John Chrysostom," 362.

development of Western philosophy and Western Christianity, and he is viewed as one of the most important church fathers of the Latin Church in the patristic period. His many important works include *The City of God*, *On Christian Doctrine*, and *Confessions*.

Clement was a Christian theologian and philosopher who taught at the Catechetical School of Alexandria. Among his pupils were Origen and Alexander of Jerusalem. A convert to Christianity, he was an educated man who was familiar with classical Greek philosophy and literature. As his three major works demonstrate, Clement was influenced by Hellenistic philosophy to a greater extent than any other Christian thinker of his time, and in particular, by Plato and the Stoics. Athanasius of Alexandria was educated with a secular Greek education: philosophy and rhetoric. The combination of scriptural study and of Greek learning was characteristic of the famous Alexandrian School. Basil the Great received a classic Greek education in philosophy, rhetoric, law, and history. Gregory of Nyssa read classical literature, philosophy and perhaps medicine. Gregory himself claimed that his only teachers were Basil, "Paul, John and the rest of the Apostles and prophets." Gregory of Nazianzus is widely considered the most accomplished rhetorical stylist of the patristic age.[6] As a classically trained orator and philosopher, he infused Hellenism into the early church, establishing the paradigm of Byzantine theologians and church officials. Against the grain of "elitist" charges, I propose the philosophical/rhetorical preacher.

Martin Luther argued that the church "comes into being because God's word is spoken."[49] Dietrich Bonhoeffer, like Luther, held a deep belief in preaching. Bonhoeffer's interest in preaching was central to his understanding of worship. Clyde Fant said, "Only [Bonhoeffer's] involvement in Christology could challenge [preaching] for preeminence in his writings, and that question was so closely bound with the other that the two are virtually inseparable."[50] In other words, preaching matters. I argue as passionately and insistently as possible that preaching matters not only for how we live as Christians but how we do biblical studies, theology, and ethics. The subject of the Bible is God, and the subject of preaching is God, and it matters. I am pained that so many seminaries, churches, and preachers do "holy" calisthenics to deny that preaching matters. What would it mean for seminary curriculums if preaching does matter and matter so much that the seminary becomes a school of preaching, where students learn and practice preaching? Hauerwas speaks truthfully of seminaries as "schools of rhetoric, where

---

49. Martin Luther, quoted in Buttrick, *Homiletic*, Kindle ed. loc. 2929.
50. Fant, *Bonhoeffer*, ix.

our bodies, and the tongue is flesh, are subject to disciplines necessary for the tongue to approach perfection."[51]

In league with Luther and Bonhoeffer I will insist that preaching matters. Preachers all live in the big house—a house not made with hands—a kingdom not established in violence, but a house of truth. Like heaven, the house of preaching has many windows. Rather than seeking a final word (a violent quest, at any rate) the question ought to be, "who can respond most profoundly and convincingly to what are ultimately commonly felt dilemmas?"[52]

Those who enter are branded as slaves of truth. The vows taken at the entrance are those of a slave: "I love God. I love the Word of God. I love words. I will not go out free."[53] Only the search for truth matters in the house of truth. Each room is set aside for brothers and sisters of the various tribes of truth-tellers: Theology, History, Rhetoric, Philosophy, Novelists, Scientists, Poets, Epistemologists. Indeed, in the house of truth there are many rooms. Over the front entrance hang words from a poem, "Let us argue with one another."[54]

Here is a metaphorical and biblical description of the work of invention that occurs in the house of preaching: [Preaching] "is like treasure hidden in a field, which a man found and reburied; then in his joy he goes and sells all that he has and buys that field." Again, preaching is like a "merchant in search of fine pearls; on finding one pearl of great value, he went and sold all that he had and bought it." "Again, preaching "is like a net that was thrown into the sea and caught fish of every kind; when it was full, they drew it ashore, sat down, and put the good into baskets but threw out the bad."[55] The preacher is like the master of a house who brings out of his treasure what is new and what is old.[56] Within the family that dwells in the house of preaching, there is a shared intimacy.

One of our permanent residents in the room labeled rhetoric is the illustrious scholar rhetorician/philosopher Kenneth Burke. His description of the parlor in the house of truth has never been exceeded. "Imagine that you enter a parlor. You come late. When you arrive, others have long preceded you, and they are engaged in a heated discussion, a discussion too heated for them to pause and tell you exactly what it is about. In fact, the

51. Hauerwas, *Working with Words*, 87.
52. Taylor, *Secular Age*, 675.
53. Exod 21:5.
54. Isa 1:18.
55. Paraphrase, Matt 13:44–51.
56. Matthew 13:52.

discussion had already begun long before any of them got there, so that no one present is qualified to retrace for you all the steps that had gone before. You listen for a while, until you decide that you have caught the tenor of the argument; then you put in your oar. Someone answers; you answer him; another comes to your defense; another aligns himself against you, to either the embarrassment or gratification of your opponent. However, the discussion is interminable. The hour grows late, you must depart. And you do depart, with the discussion still vigorously in progress."[57]

Lady Wisdom lives here—that magnificent woman who gave us the book of Proverbs. Here's her course description: "For learning about wisdom and instruction, for understanding words of insight, for gaining instruction in wise dealing, righteousness, justice, and equity; to teach shrewdness to the simple, knowledge and prudence to the young—let the wise also hear and gain in learning, and the discerning acquire skill, to understand a proverb and a figure, the words of the wise and their riddles."[58] Take treasures with you back to the land where people walk in darkness and desire the light.

Aristotle, with his classic definition of rhetoric as the discovery of all available resources to persuade others, has lived here, it seems forever. "Rhetoric may be defined as the faculty of observing in any given case the available means of persuasion."[59] The question hovers over all that follows: How do we use all the available resources to persuade people to follow Jesus? How many hear us preach only to say, "Almost thou persuadest me to be a Christian"?[60] How many of the tribe of the Galatians sit in our pews?—"quickly deserting the one who called you in the grace of Christ and are turning to a different gospel—not that there is another gospel, but there are some who are confusing you and want to pervert the gospel of Christ."[61] How many, having abandoned the hearing of sermons, "live in the futility of their minds, darkened in their understanding, alienated from the life of God because of their ignorance and harness of heart"?[62] How many have turned away from the truth to follow silly myths? How many have been "drifted by"[63] as the river of God's truth and purpose move across the land. There's a gallery of the dropouts in the early church. Ephesus left her first love; Pergamum still clung to pagan teaching; Thyatira flirted with Jezebel;

---

57. Burke, *Philosophy of Literary Form*, 110.
58. Proverbs 1:2–6 (NRSV).
59. Aristotle, *Rhetoric*, chapter 2, 6.
60. Acts 26:28 (KJV).
61. Galatians 1:6–7.
62. Ephesians 4:17–18.
63. Hebrews 2:1.

Sardis pretended life but was dead; Laodicea was lukewarm. Corinth was an unmitigated disaster: a church divided into factions, riddled with sexual immorality, embedded still in much pagan superstition, beset by class, economic, and ethnic exclusion, and confusion about if those who spoke in tongues were superior.

I am not offering another technique manual, a how-to book for preachers to imitate. There are a variety of excellent preaching books available for preachers and they offer a veritable feast of methods, ideas, techniques, and principles. I have been immensely enriched by reading and teaching Thomas Long's *The Witness of Preaching*, David Buttrick's *Homiletic*, and Fred Craddock's *Preaching*. I asked professors of homiletics for the textbooks they used. Alyce McKenzie, of Perkins School of Theology, listed her work, *Novel Preaching*. Marvin McMickle's *Shaping the Claim*, Wes Allen's *Determining the Form*, Nora Tisdale's *Pastoral Prophetic Preaching*, Lisa Thompson's *Ingenuity*, and Jared Alcantara's *The Practice of Preaching* are valuable assets. I often use Gardner Taylor, James Forbes, and Jeremiah Wright in my preaching classes. In reading them, I couldn't think of a single addition that I could add to the vast literature of how to preach a sermon. What I offer is the prequel to preaching.

This prequel explores one of Aristotle's five canons of rhetoric—invention. Invention relates to what the preacher says and describes the persuasive, argumentative content of the sermon. Invention captures the essence of Aristotle's definition of rhetoric as "the discovery of all the available means of persuasion."

My interests are in the material the preacher accumulates Sunday after Sunday, year after year, in a lifetime of study, reading, reflection, imagination, and prayer. The focus of this study is the invitation for the preacher to attempt the impossible—be a Renaissance person in an age of specializations. In a culture overwhelmed with an excess of materials, the preacher's task becomes one discovering the best available means. The preacher, through experience, gains a sense of what will "preach" and what needs the mercy of the "delete" button.

J. Barrie Shepherd, a poet, and a preacher, proposed that imagination and creativity are the essential foundations for preaching.[64] This means all kinds of literature, but it also means people, politics, culture, congregations, and the multiple crises that arise in our ministry to and for the people of God. Pat Conroy has a book called *My Reading Life*. Every preacher should write such a book: *My Reading Life*.

---

64. Shepherd, *Whatever Happened to Delight?*, 33.

For example, William Hoffman's short story, "The Question of Rain," brings us eyeball to eyeball with the tension of no rain in a farming community and what the preacher is supposed to do about it. The story opens with a simple request from a church member: "I'd like for you to pray for rain." With lawns "scorched right to the soil," they want Wayland to designate the upcoming Sunday service as a "Special Prayer Day for Rain."[65]

Wayland refuses to make rain the goal of an entire service. He has theological reasons for his resistance to the idea, reasons his congregation fail to grasp. He complains that people would start asking for snow on Christmas or cooling breezes in August. His response is theologically sound, but the people want a rainmaker. What should he do? After much struggle and intense conversations with trusted friends, Wayland comes down from the rock of theological certainty and stands with his people in their common humanity. He prays for the rain they all need. In the story, as the pastor prays, the thunder rolls, the rain falls. Sometimes prayers have vivid, real answers. But whether it rains or not, if people need rain, pray for rain!

Reading, thinking, and writing are essential tasks for preachers. Harry Crews says, "When I'm writing, I'm into it, and I want to get inside it and do something to it because it's on my back like a junkie's needle is on his back. That subject's riding me."[66] Crews says that he sits at his typewriter every day for three hours. "I've been at a typewriter and I don't know what comes next. And what I say to myself is, I say, okay, you don't have to write, just sit here for three hours and you can leave, but you can't write letters, and you can't clean your fingernails, and you can't obviously, look out a window."[67] Crews credits Flannery O'Connor with this practice. He says, "Her statement has that element of mystery in it that I love, because where does all this stuff come from? You think I know? If I did, I'd give it to you because some of you want it, you'd like to have it, and I'd give it to you. Share it. There's enough for everybody. I don't know where it comes from. Here's what O'Connor said: 'I go to the typewriter every day for three hours so that if anything comes, I am prepared to receive it.' Receive it as gift from God, from the muses. Receive it as the blossoming mystery. God bless her heart, hey, that's powerful. Think about it—'receive it.'"[68]

The preacher cultivates the self-criticizing skill to know a bad sermon when it has been written. Instead of visiting the affliction on the

---

65. Hoffman, "Question of Rain," 160–61, 163. Quoted in Ramsey Jr., *Preachers and Misfits*, Kindle ed. loc. 2109–10.

66. Crews, "Interview," 338–39.

67. Crews, "Interview," 338–39.

68. Crews, "Interview," 339.

unsuspecting congregation, offer the bad sermon as a burnt offering to God. Perhaps the pastor's office needs a bona fide altar for burnt offerings. This may feel extreme, exaggerated, but remember the writing of a bad sermon gives experience. Other bad sermons may follow, but bit by painful bit, you will come to love the act of writing, of inventing, of imagining between the lines of your biblical characters and texts. As time passes, fewer bad sermons will dare show their face at the table and your writing will become recreation.

A country song rattles in my head suggesting that they should put warning labels on bad sermons to save people from bad religion. Those unwilling to pay the price of the hard work that precedes the presenting of a sermon should be arrested by the pulpit police. I am interested in the work of preparation—the long hours that take place every week in the life of the preacher. We have so much to learn from novelists, poets, philosophers, and rhetoricians. Let the dance begin!

Chapter 1

What the Novelists Have to Teach Us

Heart, soul, and mind are required to forge the preacher. Knowing the width, length, depth, and height of heaven and earth—this is the preacher's unending task. Here the preacher may learn from the novelists how to work with words. The task each week is to pore over every syllable of the text, frustration, fear, and foreboding notwithstanding, until the preacher can present the word as "some molten words perfected in an oven seven times."[1]

Of all the descriptors used of the preacher, truth-teller remains the one that I cling to forever. The preacher has a responsibility as a truth-teller. Truth-telling is a specific role for preachers. This raises questions like: Who is able to tell the truth? What are the moral, ethical, and the spiritual conditions to be considered as a truth-teller? About what topics is it important to tell the truth? About nature? About the city? About behavior? About humanity? What are the consequences of telling the truth? What are the consequences of not telling the truth?

Preachers who fail to speak the truth may be called "depraved orators."[2] The truth-telling preacher is courageous enough to oppose the cultural and political prejudices of the congregation. He plays a pedagogical role in which he attempts to transform the will of the congregation so that they will serve the interests of the gospel.

Being a truth-teller in a post-truth world presents many challenges for the preacher. Reynolds Price says, "It is a must—writing as truthfully and as lovingly about the whole of the world as I can."[3] Sheila Bosworth

---

1. Osherow, *Dead Man's Praise*, 53; Ps 12:6.
2. Foucault, *Fearless Speech*, 82.
3. Price, "Interview," Kindle ed. loc. 1142–43.

says, "What I feel I am . . . that we're not in this alone, that the truth is that we're all in this human condition together, and that there's hope in the very communal nature of that."[4] Doris Betts: "Stories must deal with matters of ultimate truth and must have meaning."[5] Betts describes the writing process as ultimately concerning nothing less than matters of life and death: "I'm astonished by people who cope with plenty of pain and do so with real grace. To write about that and not sentimentalize, to tell the truth, the tragic truths, is what I'd like to do as a mature writer."[6] Flannery O'Connor goes so far as to insist that the writer's task can be fulfilled "only by the violence of a single-minded respect for the truth."[7]

The education of a preacher begins in apprenticeship to the great novelists. Homiletics professor Alyce McKenzie has paved the way to investigating the impact of novelists on preaching in her book *Novel Preaching: Tips from Top Writers on Crafting Creative Sermons*.[8] The question asked and answered in this chapter: What are the lessons that the preacher learns from great novelists? I want to offer six lessons that I believe the novelists teach the preacher. I list them here as a summary of what will follow: (1) Reading—The Writer's Incubator. (2) Novelists Are in Tune with the Human Condition. (3) Novelists Have a Moral Imperative. (4) Novelists Have Habits and Practices of Writing and Reading. (5) Novelists Have Only Words. (6) Novelists Follow the Fine Art of Wondering, Imagining, Creating.

THE PREREQUISITE FOR PREACHING: READING

The most important room in the metaphorical house of the preacher is the reading room. This is where everything begins. The lifelong reader has at her disposal enough material to last forever. Reading is like living and breathing for the preacher. As Flannery O'Connor puts it, "Anybody who has survived his childhood has enough information about life to last him the rest of his days. If you can't make something out of a little experience, you probably won't be able to make it out of a lot."[9] Stanley Hauerwas argues that a lifetime of reading is required to teach a theologian how to speak Christian. He insists that seminary teaches preachers to read, and the rest of ministry consists of faithful, imaginative reading. Hauerwas also makes

---

4. Bosworth, "Interview," Kindle ed. loc. 2051–52.
5. Betts, "Interview," Kindle ed. loc. 3220.
6. Betts, "Interview," Kindle ed. loc. 3228–30.
7. O'Connor, *Mystery and Manners*, Kindle ed. loc. 758.
8. McKenzie, *Novel Preaching*.
9. O'Connor, *Mystery and Manners*, Kindle ed. loc. 774.

clear the relationship between reading and speaking. "For what you learned to do in seminary is read. By learning to read you have learned to speak Christian. That you have learned to read and speak means you have been formed in a manner to avoid the pitfalls I have associated with the contemporary ministry. For I want to suggest to you that one of the essential tasks of those called to the ministry in our day is to be a teacher. You are called to be a teacher of language."[10]

Those who preach do their present and future congregations a service by reading Hauerwas. The preacher's reading time is a gift to her congregation because the reading introduces the preacher to serious minds who, having already traversed the pilgrim's way, can now serve as expert guides for preacher and congregation. The preacher's reading life is the magic carpet ride of life for the congregation.

Hauerwas also models the philosophical approach to preaching. He notes, "For as I suggested, there is an essential relation between reading and speaking; because it is through reading that we learn how to discipline our speech so that we say no more than needs to be said. . . . To be so habituated requires constant repetition. Without repetition, and repetition is but another word for the worship of God, we are in danger of losing the grammar of the faith."[11]

The reading required in seminary may have felt excessive, but those readings were preparation for the weekly sermon. You have discovered that your life is a life of reading. There may not seem to be much reward from reading. The congregation will not consciously know that reading is hard work. There will be all kinds of distractions, some of busy work, some of it real church work, but the great preacher will find time to keep reading. As Hauerwas makes the connection between the preacher's reading and the good of the congregation, "You must, moreover, help the people you serve recognize that their support of your study is a good the whole people of God have in common."[12]

I recommend that the preacher make a contract with the church that among the usual items of salary, benefits, and vacation, there is a one-month reading/study sabbatical each year. For ten years, I and, I believe, my congregation, benefited from my annual monthly sabbatical. One year, my assigned study subject was the social gospel. Professor Jake Dorn, whose remarkable dissertation on Washington Gladden and the social gospel, loaned

---

10. Hauerwas, *Working with Words*, 86.
11. Hauerwas, *Working with Words*, 87.
12. Hauerwas, *Working with Words*, 92–93.

me twenty-five books for my study. He told me on the Sunday morning before the sabbatical began, "There will be a test when you return."

Larry Brown talks about his own internship in becoming a novelist: "I had always loved books and reading, it was what I cared most about. I figured writing was the only thing I could teach myself to do on my own. I checked out books from the library by the armload . . . I found out I wanted to write 'literature,' the kind of stories that I had read over and over again. At first, I thought it would be simple. It's not."[13]

The first rule of preaching: Read! When confused by all the other rules of preaching, return to Rule Number 1: Read. An autobiographical musing sets the scene for my insistence on the power of reading in the life of the preacher. Intellectual life often grows in the most infertile of conditions. My family came to the pine woods and clay hills of North Louisiana with a wild dream to grow cotton. The ground simply refused the task of producing those giant white bales of money. My grandfather turned, in desperation or thirst, to bootlegging. My father quit school after the sixth grade to plow the mule and help raise his siblings. My mother managed nine grades before she married my father. No one in the family had ever been to college. Then my mother made it her life's mission to make me a scholar. She fed me books to read and taught me to love the library and the bookmobile that brought the magic of reading to our country, dirt-road doorstep. To this day, the two most essential sanctuaries that give me total peace of mind is a church—any church anywhere will suffice—and a public library. When I step into a church, Isaiah speaks for me: "I saw the Lord sitting on a throne, high and lofty; and the hem of his robe filled the temple."[14]

I had not heard of William Blake at nine, but I was walking in his God-saturated steps. At the age of four, Blake saw God "put his head to the window," and at nine, he saw "a tree full of angels."[15] As a grown man-poet, Blake wrote, "The Angel that presided 'oer my birth Said, 'Little creature, form'd of Joy and Mirth, Go love without the help of any Thing on Earth.'"[16]

The first time I enter a church I head straight for the pulpit—I prefer the grand pulpits that are architectural icons—and I stand there in silence while imagining the pews filled with people desiring to hear the gospel. The words of the unknown author of the Epistle to the Hebrews comes easily to my lips in that sacred moment: "You have come to Mount Zion and to the city of the living God, the heavenly Jerusalem, and to innumerable angels

---

13. Brown, "Interview," 133–34.
14. Isa 6:1–3.
15. Blake, "Angel that Presided O'er My Birth."
16. Blake, "Angel that Presided O'er My Birth."

in festal gathering, and to the assembly of the firstborn who are enrolled in heaven."[17]

My childhood passed in obsessive evangelical readings. Fighter jets ripped out the pages of Ezekiel. American tanks rolled from Revelation. The beast from the sea haunted my dreams. It was a literal world, what Charles Taylor would later call an age of naivete and enchantment. "The enchanted world in this sense is the world of spirits, demons, and moral forces which our ancestors lived in."[18] Like Winston Churchill, I thought I had been born at least a century late.

There's one of those hand-wringing disputes in our culture about the danger of books. I find this absurd and revolting. Read everything. The more I read science, the more my faith increased. Lewis Thomas and his *Late Night Thoughts on Listening to Mahler's Ninth Symphony* produced eruptions of "Amen" and "Alleluia." My brain felt it would explode as I read *Full House: The Spread of Excellence from Plato to Darwin*, by Stephen Jay Gould. Later I would be fascinated by David C. Lindberg's *The Beginnings of Western Science*. I return often to Kenneth R. Miller's *Only a Theory* and *The Language of God: A Scientist Presents Evidence for Belief*, by Francis S. Collins.

While Ken Ham and the creationists attempt to deny the age of rocks, I turn often to the story of the resurrection and the rock that was rolled away. Every three years, when John 20 is the lectionary Gospel lesson, I preach a version of my sermon, "God's Second Big Bang." The God that created the universe is the God who raised Jesus from the dead. I listen on Easter Sunday morning, before that sermon, to the Barenaked Ladies sing the theme song for the television situation comedy *The Big Bang*. The scientific insight that our very existence, through evolution, requires a universe of the very size, scale, and age that we see around us implies that the universe, in a certain sense, had us in mind from the very beginning. It is very much, in the memorable words of physicist Freeman Dyson, a "universe that knew we were coming."[19]

The precision, oh my, the precision of creation—it should warm the hearts of engineers and computer scientists. "In Martin Rees's wonderful book *Just Six Numbers*, he demonstrates how slight changes in any of [the universe's beginning conditions] would have made life as we know it literally impossible."[20] A universe capable of generating the chemical diversity that

---

17. Heb 12:18–24.
18. Taylor, *Secular Age*, 25.
19. Miller, *Only a Theory*, 161.
20. Miller, *Only a Theory*, 120.

makes life possible has to get these numbers just right. Our universe has done exactly that. See, I believe that when the writer of Genesis says, "and it was so" and "it was good," he is saying more than he knew. God is saying, "That's just right."

Do you know about the "Goldilocks Principle"? In planetary astronomy, a planet orbiting its sun at just the right distance for liquid water to exist on its surface, neither too hot nor too cold, is referred to as being in the "Goldilocks Zone." Stephen Hawking argued that the existence of life requires that the planetary temperatures be "just right."[21]

Preaching requires an alert, alive, and constantly "on" preacher's imagination. This general preparation for preaching has much to do with our reading habits. The habit of reading—books, articles, movies, people, newspapers, poems, short stories, culture, politics, economics, science—permeates our every waking moment. We may not get four uninterrupted hours for sermon writing during the week, but we have every moment of every day for preparing to preach by listening, interpreting, and being attentive to life as it happens to us. And at every opportunity, the preacher will read. Steal fifteen minutes here, there, and everywhere. Remember that reading is not confined to printed pages. The preacher must read the culture, the people, the human condition, the congregation, the political culture, the community. The preacher not only reads the *New York Times*, but also the times in which the gospel is to be preached.

Congregations should have greater expectations of the preacher's reading life and intellectual development. So much that passes for "church work" is mere busy work and shouldn't be a part of a congregation's expectations. Hauerwas offers excellent advice here: "Many who enter the ministry discover after a few years of doing the best they can to meet the expectations of those they serve, expectations such as whatever else you may do you should always be nice, end up feeling as if they have been nibbled to death by ducks."[22]

Pat Conroy, in *My Reading Life*, not only makes the case for lifelong reading. He also inspires reading as vocational necessity. He recommends the practice of hunting, collecting, and gathering words into a notebook. "Words call out my name when I need them to make something worthy out of language."[23] Conroy suggests that we enter every word that captures our attention in the notebook. Hunt down every analogy, metaphor, interesting phrase—write them all in the notebook. One of my favorite

---

21. Hawking, *Grand Design*, 194.
22. Hauerwas, *Working with Words*, 84–85.
23. Conroy, *My Reading Life*, 51.

lines was written by Allan Gurganus—"when we are fog on a coffin lid."[24] Gurganus uses the metaphor in an interview with Susan Ketchin: "To welcome others into your stories years after you're just so much fog on a coffin lid, that surely constitutes as sweet a state of grace as I can imagine. The moral of all my stories? The moral weight and transforming joy of the Story itself. To the holiness of 'Once upon a time,' yes, I say daily, 'Amen, amen.'"[25]

The fertile ground of reading produces an abundant crop of great writing. The great readers are the ones who planted seeds in good soil and brought forth grain of a hundredfold. The great readers are the black Delta soil of the Mississippi River rather than the desert wasteland of Arizona. Sermons and stories grow from reading.

NOVELISTS ARE IN TUNE WITH THE HUMAN CONDITION

"My humanity is bound up in yours, for we can only be human together."

—Desmond Tutu

"If there is no struggle, there is no progress."

—Frederick Douglass

Richard Lischer says, "If Ezra Pound was right when he claimed that poets are the antennae of the race, William Butler Yeats had his antennae out early. He is our first alert. He sounds the first modern alarm that whoever has a serious vocation in language and proposes to communicate from depth to depth will be in trouble."[26] Like poets, novelists and short story writers have their antennas out and in tune with the human condition. Even writers that have moved as far from faith as the east is from the west, there is this amazing religious sensibility.

Toni Morrison may have the largest antennae of all. Cornel West pays tribute to the democratic spirit of Morrison. "The most sophisticated exploration of this black enactment of dialogue, resistance, and hope is found in the magisterial corpus of Toni Morrison. She is the towering democratic artist and intellectual of our time. Morrison's texts embody and enact forms of deep democratic energies unparalleled in America's long struggle with

---

24. Gurganus, "Interview," 395.
25. Gurganus, "Interview," 395.
26. Lischer, *End of Words*, Kindle ed. loc. 37.

the dark side of its democracy. She highlights the strong will and potential promise of democratic individuals. Ordinary people taking back their power sit at the center of her artistic vision."[27]

West offers testimony from Morrison: "The slaveholders have won if this experience is beyond my imagination and my powers. It's like humor: you have to take the authority back; you realign where the power is. So, I wanted to take the power. They were very inventive and imaginative with cruelty, so I have to take it back—in a way that I can tell it."[28]

One of Morrison's most vivid characters, Sethe in *Beloved*, explains why she killed her daughter, named Beloved, when a fugitive-slave hunter came to take them all back to their Southern slave owners. Sethe says: "That anybody white could take your whole self for anything that came to mind. Not just work, kill, or maim you, but dirty you. Dirty you so bad you couldn't like yourself anymore. Dirty you so bad you forgot who you were and couldn't think it up. And though she and others lived through and got over it, she could never let it happen to her own. The best thing she was, was her children. Whites might dirty her all right, but not her best thing, her beautiful, magical best thing—the part of her that was clean."[29]

James Baldwin offers a new vision for all preachers in his books *Nobody Knows My Name* and *No Name in the Street*. He wrote in his essay "The Creative Process": "The artist cannot and must not take anything for granted but must drive to the heart of every answer and expose the question the answer hides. We know, in the case of the person, that whoever cannot tell himself the truth about his past is trapped in it, is immobilized in the prison of his undiscovered self. This is also true of nations."[30]

Baldwin's single-minded vision about the power of "name" speaks volumes for all the nameless ones of history. They rise up like ghosts out of the swamps of the South, the nation, and the world. Nameless, but not shamed. Nameless, but not rejected. Once you had no name, but now you have a name. Nothing matters as much as "naming." "Your name shall be . . ." First Peter 2:10—"Once you were not a people, but now you are God's people; once you had not received mercy, but now you have received mercy." "Call me Mr. Tibbs." Naming calls the world into existence and the metaphors that name the world are the most powerful creators of reality in all of language.

Preaching is naming. Not theological words. Not political words. Naming persons to give them dignity, respect, freedom, standing. The primal cry

---

27. West, *Democracy Matters*, 93.
28. West, *Democracy Matters*, 93–94.
29. Morrison, *Beloved*, 295.
30. Baldwin, "Creative Process," 16.

of the nobodies is found down in Egypt where the people suffered oppression. They were slaves and they had no names. Then the name came into existence. God told Moses the name and then God's people were named and claimed by God. First the divine name and then everyone gets a name.

Baldwin issues a challenge to all preachers to be an "incorrigible disturber of the peace."[31] Baldwin shows the preacher the road to truth: "The role of the artist, then, precisely, is to illuminate that darkness, blaze roads through that vast forest; so that we will not, in all our doing, lose sight of its purpose, which is, after all, to make the world a more human dwelling place."[32] And he adds:

> The artist is distinguished from all other responsible actors in society—the politicians, legislators, educators, scientists, et cetera—by the fact that he is his own test tube, his own laboratory, working according to very rigorous rules, however unstated these may be, and cannot allow any consideration to supersede his responsibility to reveal all that he can possibly discover concerning the mystery of the human being. Society must accept some things as real; but he must always know that the visible reality hides a deeper one, and that all our action and all our achievement rests on things unseen.[33]

Baldwin demands a loyalty to one's self that frightens even the stronghearted. He notes the gap between what we think of ourselves and the truth about ourselves. He says, "If we understood ourselves better, we would damage ourselves less."[34] He explains that there are forces within us that threaten our precarious securities.

> The forces are there and we cannot will them away. All we can do is learn to live with them. And we cannot learn this unless we are willing to tell the truth about ourselves, and the truth about us is always at variance with what we wish to be. The human effort is to bring these two realities into a relationship resembling reconciliation. The human beings whom we respect the most, after all—and sometimes fear the most—are those who are most deeply involved in this delicate and strenuous effort: for they have the unshakeable authority that comes only from having looked on and endured and survived the worst. That nation is healthiest which has the least necessity to distrust or ostracize

---

31. West, *Democracy Matters*, 80.
32. Baldwin, "Creative Process," 16.
33. Baldwin, "Creative Process," 16.
34. Baldwin, "Creative Process, 17.

or victimize these people—whom, as I say, we honor, once they are gone, because, somewhere in our hearts, we know that we cannot live without them.[35]

Our best novelists always take us out to the deepest of the deeps. They are exploring the width, length, height, and depth of human experience. Flannery O'Connor says, "All my stories are about the action of grace on a character who is not very willing to support it, but most people think of these stories as hard, hopeless and brutal."[36] "The writer operates at a peculiar crossroads where time and place and eternity somehow meet. His problem is to find that location."[37] "I have found, in short, from reading my own writing, that my subject in fiction is the action of grace in territory largely held by the devil. I have also found that what I write is read by an audience which puts little stock either in grace or the devil. You discover your audience at the same time and in the same way that you discover your subject, but it is an added blow."[38]

Reading the stories of novelists opens the preacher to the hearts and minds of the congregation. Lee Smith, for example, says of her short story, "Tongues of Fire," that it "is truly one of the most autobiographical stories I have ever written. The character Karen is absolutely the way I was as a child, including the obsessive reading, and the obsessive religion."[39] Speaking for more people than she can imagine, Smith says, "I believe in God, I've just never been able to find a way to act on that without having it take me over. I need to find a church somewhere, some way to be able to act on it more without feeling I'll be engulfed."[40]

If there is a novelist where the preacher needs to pull up a chair, share a bottle of bourbon, and stay for a long while, that writer is Reynolds Price. He has suggested that the novel comes closer than anything else to being a truly Judeo-Christian form. Sounding more like a pastor than a novelist, at one point Price says, "I think one of my purposes as a writer is simply to understand as much of creation as possible to as large an audience as possible."[41] "The whole point of learning about the human race is presumably to give it mercy."[42] The preacher needs to cultivate an eclectic reading strategy that

---

35. Baldwin, "Creative Process," 17.
36. O'Connor, *Habit of Being*, 275.
37. O'Connor, *Mystery and Manners*, Kindle ed. loc. 1091–99.
38. O'Connor, *Mystery and Manners*, Kindle ed. loc. 1091.
39. Quoted in Ketchin, ed., *Christ-Haunted Landscape*, 45.
40. Quoted in Ketchin, ed., *Christ-Haunted Landscape*, 50.
41. Price, "Interview," 75.
42. Price, "Interview," 79.

includes fiction, especially novels and short stories. Price insists, "Christian churches seem to be too busy getting vengeance on and sacrificing other Christians, not with mercy and forgiveness."[43]

bell hooks says that she links dialogue "to regular communion service in the Black church at Yale where we would often stand in a collective circle and sing, 'Let Us Break Bread Together on Our Knees,' and the lines in the song which say, 'When I Fall on My Knees with My Face to the Rising Sun, Oh Lord Have Mercy on Me.' I liked the combination of the notion of community which is about sharing and breaking bread together, of dialogue as well as mercy because mercy speaks to the need we have for compassion, acceptance, understanding, and empathy."[44]

In a discussion of his writing, Price says, "My purpose. . . is really to elicit understanding of and mercy toward as much creation as I can present, and you, the reader, can manage."[45] Reading fiction along with the Scripture will trigger powers of imaginative interaction. My purpose is to teach my students about people who know how to create with words. Words are all we have and how we use them is the practice of a lifetime of work.

Deeply moved by the stories of the novelists, the preacher should genuflect, make the sign of the cross, or whisper, "Amen." If there's a subject begging to be preached over and over, it has to be mercy.

Larry Brown speaks to all preachers when he says, "I just believe that my fiction, anybody's fiction, is simply supposed to illuminate the human condition, tell us something about ourselves."[46] A sermon that shines the light on the human condition—the good, the bad, and the ugly—allows the gospel to be heard in flesh and blood. Brown speaks directly to a pastor's heart when he reminds us, "Some people just have harder lives than others. Some people have such a harder time than other people do, some people have to pay more in life, I don't know why."[47] Preachers need to be careful with the difficulties people experience. It is so easy to become a scold, a high and mighty judge. People often need the balm of the gospel to heal the wounds. There are novelists who at times sound like policemen rounding up all the evil people. There are preachers who seem hellbent on making sure that everybody that's got it coming, gets it in the end. They consign all these evil people to the fires of hell. "E. M. Forster and Flannery O'Connor give this sense that she's arresting some of her characters and punishing them. In

---

43. Price, "Interview," 79.
44. hooks and West, *Breaking Bread*, 1–2.
45. Price, "Interview," 80.
46. Brown, "Interview," 128.
47. Brown, "Interview," 128.

Forster this always means having to marry the wrong girl, the unimaginative, plain woman. Hell in O'Connor means being one of those people in Georgia who has to sit down and listen to your mother talk to you all day and all night, and you're ugly and peg-legged."[48]

And there's this to warm a preacher's heart from Brown: "My fiction is about people surviving, about people proceeding out from calamity. I write about loss. These people are aware of their need for redemption. We all spend our time dealing with some kind of hurt and looking for love. We are all striving for the same thing, for some kind of love. But love is a big word. It covers a lot of territory. I try to tell it in a fresh, new way, to be innovative."[49] The preacher who struggles with issues of survival, calamity, redemption, hurt, and love will be a godsend to any congregation.

The preacher may be tempted by satire, but satire, like sarcasm, has no place in the pulpit if its source is meanness and hatred toward the congregation. It's compassion that reaches out to embrace the suffering that matters. The preacher's path is more that of touching lepers than it is condemning folks to hell. When the preacher's sermons reveal meaning rather than pat moral preachments there's redemption. The most basic value of the preacher is empathy. George Lakoff could have been speaking to preachers: "Behind every progressive policy lies a single moral value: empathy."[50]

Harry Crews has said that he feels matters of life and death, and suffering and meaning, so deeply that he has to write about them in his fiction, sort out these emotions through his characters. "The characters themselves start talking to him about their struggles."[51] Larry Brown says, "Yeah, I've seen other writers that are doing it, too. Cormac McCarthy's got a couple of lines—this preacher is travelling around, doing this talking, and he said, 'A blind feller hollered out one day and said, "Look at me" (and he only had one leg). He said, "Look at me, legless and everything; I reckon you think I ought to love God." And the feller said, "Yeah," said, "I reckon you ought. An old blind mess and legless fool is a flower in the garden of God.""[52]

A MORAL IMPERATIVE

There's a moral imperative in the great novels. The novelist deals with these ultimate questions of good and evil. When I read a great novel that makes

48. Price, "Interview," 75.
49. Brown, "Interview," 129.
50. Lakoff, *Political Mind*, Kindle ed. loc. 780.
51. Brown, "Interview," 136.
52. Brown, "Interview," 136.

me cry and laugh as well as struggle and suffer, I remember why I have no patience with sermons that sound like pop psychology. There are these preachers populating the internet with these series of sermons that all sound more like Ted Talks than preaching. They preach popular series designed to help people feel better about themselves and handle the emotional struggles. These preachers no longer consider it necessary to speak to the biblical text. They are caught up in the need to be popular and there's a lot of ego involved in these productions—the preacher's personal spiritual or ethical musings. They seem more informed by the latest bestseller the preacher has read in pop psychology or self-improvement or positive thinking.

As Lauren Berlant asserts, "The [evangelical] emotion machine delivers feeling ok, acting free."[53] There's little sense in these exhortations that the preachers are dealing with the steady "pressure of the Church's experience of Scripture."[54] I can't tell if I'd rather suffer through an Episcopal priest explaining the latest article from *The Atlantic* or a megachurch evangelical telling me how I can live my best life now, but given my theological assumptions, I would rather suffer with the Episcopalian. At least there, I'd have the sacrament of Holy Communion and not leave church hungry and thirsty.

A major component in sermons designed to make congregations "feel good" is the reversal of the dynamics of shame. Megachurches populated with an overwhelming majority of whites tend to be warriors in the culture wars that plague American religion and politics. They are the previous masters of shame where they poured out the harsh judgment and condemnation on African Americans, gays, immigrants, and other minorities. Since these groups have all experienced a "rights" movement, and the pedagogy of shame has shifted to the liberal/progressive side, the previous masters of shame are now shamed for their judgment. But they have not responded well. They have refused to be shamed and they are pushing back.

The evangelical pastor who takes the side of whites who have been confronted with their complicity in centuries of appalling abuse, even murder, of women, Jews, slaves, colonized peoples, homosexuals, takes his congregation by the hand and leads them to the comfortable promised land. He assures them that rather than feeling ashamed, they should feel proud, and they should take revenge on the liberals who have sought to challenge their sense of being at ease in Zion. Here the pulpit is skillfully converted into a rhetorical weapon of war, an affective battlefield, mobilizing political power

---

53. Berlant, "Trump, or Political Emotion."
54. Davis and Hays, eds., *Art of Reading Scripture*, 165.

and feeling good power.[55] Such preaching may be emotionally satisfying to preach and to hear, but all of this emotional firepower is not the gospel.

There's a moral imperative in fiction, that is, that it must deal with these ultimate questions of good and evil, life and death. I believe this is also true of the sermon. The simplest construct is either to be good or to be bad. It's comes down to good vs. evil, and in the Bible, this is a cosmic warfare that makes *Star Wars* look like a Sunday school outing. In order to be good you have to fight evil. Hauerwas argues that we need to keep the cosmic nature of our faith and to have Christians tough enough to stand up to the beast kings of the earth. This sounds apocalyptic but this isn't a *Left Behind* appeal. "There is no genre in Scripture," says Hauerwas, "that seems more ready for a little demythologizing than apocalyptic literature."[56]

Brown notes, "So those are the issues that most of my characters are struggling with. They are struggling to be good people. They know the difference between good and bad, and right and wrong. They don't always do what's right, because they're imperfect, like all of us. Like all people. And I try to give my characters those human traits that we all recognize, and all have and all feel."[57]

In a good sermon there is always something going on: either they are not satisfied with their life, or they have some major problem that's disrupting their life. I mean if you go along happy-go-lucky, one scene to another, nothing ever happens, there's never any trouble, everybody in the world is nice and treats everybody with kindness—that's not representative of the real world, and it's not representative of a real sermon, either. It's got to be a major struggle.

In his short story "Roadside Resurrection," Brown produces a real faith healer, someone who really heals the afflicted. He says the story is "all about faith and trust, where they come from. This famous healer has lost his faith, but no one knows it yet. It has humor in it, too. There's an ex-Elvis impersonator who needs healing."[58] People think that Brown is mocking their faith, but he insists, "I'm not. I have a strong belief in God."[59]

The most inspirational words from Brown spoke directly to my preaching. "I can't be concerned about who's going to think what. I try to make as good a story as I can and let the chips fall where they may. I can't

---

55. Schaefer, "Whiteness and Civilization." This is an excellent study, based on affect theory, for understanding the role that shame plays in the response that evangelicals, the former masters of shame, make to being shamed by a progressive pedagogy.

56. Hauerwas, *Unleashing the Scripture*, 100.

57. Brown, "Interview," 136.

58. Brown, "Interview," 130.

59. Brown, "Interview," 130.

write to please others; I must please me. I must trust my own judgment, and above all, I must be honest. Your art must evolve from your honesty, your experience."[60]

Novelist Sheila Bosworth adds pearls of wisdom to enrich those who preach. "We were," she says of her childhood family, "quiet followers of the Catholic faith, steadfast, without any question. They didn't talk about it anymore than you talked about the fact that you breathed or said, 'Look we're breathing. Let's all breathe together.'"[61] One of her off-the-cuff remarks grabbed my attention: "My father was educated at a Jesuit high school in New Orleans. I don't know what it is about a Jesuit education; it seems to 'take' for life."[62] Stanley Hauerwas has ventured an answer to that question: "The Jesuits, of course, thought smart Catholics ought to know something about philosophy. So Catholic laity got taught Plato to make them Catholic. What a world!"[63]

Bosworth speaks with an authentic concern when she says, "I've never met a fundamentalist who seemed to feel that his own soul was in any trouble; it was other people's souls who were in trouble."[64] The fearmongering has moved from fundamentalist visions of hell to apocalyptic versions of how the nation is going to hell because of liberals. David Brooks says, "We shouldn't be scaremongering."[65] Preachers should pay attention because the temptation to maximize the scope of our problems can lead to excess hyperbole and lead the preacher far from the primary concerns of the gospel. How preachers who know the teaching of Jesus—"Don't be afraid"—can spend pulpit time scaring people is a mystery.

When the allure of a false reading of apocalyptic texts calls to the preacher, there are words from Rowan Williams to keep us focused: "Because of Jesus we can now see that what God has always meant to happen is—to pick up two centrally important words in the Letter to the Ephesians—peace and praise. This and this alone is God's 'agenda': the world he has made is designed to become a reconciled world, a world in which diverse human communities come to share a life together because they share the conviction that God has acted to set them free from fear and guilt."[66]

---

60. Brown, "Interview," 133.
61. Bosworth, "Interview," 148.
62. Bosworth, "Interview," 148.
63. Hauerwas, *In Good Company*, 84.
64. Quoted in Ketchin, ed., *Christ-Haunted Landscape*, 152.
65. Brooks, "Problem with Wokeness."
66. Williams, *Tokens of Trust*, 8–9.

When Bosworth deals with sorrow, a constant theme and experience of the preacher, she walks on sacred ground where words fail all who attempt to speak. She says, "If anything makes sorrow go away, then the chances are it wasn't true sorrow to begin with. Sorrow is something you learn to live with. The grief is lifelong."[67] Preachers could learn here not to trample on holy ground with too many words—wasted, senseless, useless words.

Of all the basically pagan words I have heard uttered from Christian pulpits, they all pale from the tripe uttered at funerals. The preacher who says at the death of a child, "God needed another angel" is far removed from Paul's "O death where is your victory?"[68] Or the preacher who intones "He has gone to a better place." This preacher has wandered into Platonism, paganism, but not the language of the Christian faith. As Hauerwas concludes, "Moreover, such language can underwrite the pagan assumption that we possess a soul that is eternal and, thus, fail to gesture our conviction as Christians that our life with God on either side of death is a gift."[69] Perhaps preachers, desperate to be helpful, are determined not to feel helpless so they fill the atmosphere of helplessness with empty words. But it is not the language of faith.

When William Sloane Coffin Jr.'s son, Alex, died in a car wreck, Coffin preached a sermon at Riverside Church, "Eulogy for Alex."[70] He noted that many of his fellow pastors knew all the right Scripture verses, but not the reality of grief. He mentioned the healing flood of letters. Some of the very best, and easily the worst, knew their Bibles better than the human condition. He said, "I know all the 'right' biblical passages, including 'Blessed are those who mourn,' and my faith is no house of rest . . . But the point is this. While the words of the Bible are true, grief renders them unreal. The reality of grief is the absence of God. The reality of grief is the solitude of pain, the feeling that your heart is in pieces, your mind's a blank, that 'there is no joy the world can give like that it takes away' (Lord Byron)."[71]

Harry Crews recalls a statement from Karl Wallenda, the great high wire athlete, who fell sixty feet to a concrete flood to his death: "Walking the wire is living. Everything else is just waiting." Crews felt deeply that we have to care more about what we write: "If you care about fiction, or poetry, or music [or preaching]—if you care about it enough, doing it is like walking

---

67. Bosworth, "Interview," 155. Bosworth is paraphrasing Ernest Hemingway from *Islands in the Stream*.

68. 1 Cor 15:55.

69. Hauerwas, *Working with Words*, 88.

70. Coffin Jr., "Eulogy for Alex."

71. Coffin Jr., "Eulogy for Alex," 4.

the wire. Doing it is dangerous in its own way. You either disappear into a bottle, or you stick your head in an oven or cut your wrists."[72] (I would add, "You walk without fainting"[73] to the list.) And never stray from 2 Timothy 4:2—"proclaim the message; be persistent whether the time is favorable or unfavorable; convince, rebuke, and encourage, with the utmost patience in teaching."

The preacher's best response to tragedy and suffering remains the offer of hope. The sermon has to move—have a direction that matters, something in it that goes from despair to some sort of hope. I'm not talking about fairy tale endings, but I am talking about the struggle between good and evil that happens in every great sermon. Doris Betts suggests, "I still prefer in fiction that something changes between the beginning and the end. It may not be a big plot twist, but something becomes either larger, or deeper, or altered, and altered in some significant way, or else why'd you bother to write it? That is one profound influence the Bible had on me."[74]

THE PREACHER'S PRACTICES

My strategy is to try to help us recover the everyday practices that historically constituted the preaching of the church. These practices are necessary prequel to the act of preaching. There exists the possibility that preachers have lost the cosmic nature of the sermon, the life-and-death struggle between good and evil that has to inform every sermon. Having preached all these thousands of years, we have found it almost necessary to look for new ways, interesting ways, intriguing ways, attention-grabbing ways to secure the ear of the audience. Thus, sermons fall into the trap of biblical minutiae that tingles the ears, excites the emotions, but tells us nothing about why we feel the world in which we live is falling apart at the seams.

A sermon begins in the most basic Christian practice: confession of the preacher's sin. Ever since Frederick Buechner suggested that an AA meeting is more church than most churches, I have the feeling that my opening sentence in the sermon should be, "My name is Rodney Kennedy, and I am a sinner." Without confession we can't be incarnational. I am interested in actual, material practices that constitute the creation of sermons.

There's a sense in which we have lost the agony and the ecstasy of preaching, the larger-than-life moment of the sermon, the radical experience that it is to speak for Jesus in his church. Preaching, however, has

72. Crews, "Interview," 341.
73. Isa 40:31.
74. Betts, "Interview," 252.

succumbed to the temptations of the world and redefined for an entire generation what it means to preach. Instead of writing stories where issues of life and death are involved, too much preaching now sounds like a romance novel. Such practices, based as they are on the fear that the church will die if the preachers are not entertaining, exciting, interesting, exotic, and part and parcel of the culture, are not in the best interests of preachers or churches. I am fully committed to the principle that great preaching will save us from the false practices of the world and teach us the practices that allow us to face the cosmic enemies of the church with courage, truthfulness, and faithfulness. What better way to face the false politics of the world than by the practice of preaching? I have joined Stanley Hauerwas and Romand Coles in the quest for the "radical ordinary" that saves us all from the politics of death. They explain, "By the radical ordinary we gesture to the ways in which the inexhaustible complexities of everyday life forever call forth new efforts of attention, nurture, and struggle that exceed the elements of blindness that accompany even our best words and deeds."[75]

The preacher participates in the politics of life when she helps her congregation overcome the fear-driven character of American culture. Scott Bader-Saye locates our fear as intensifying after September 11, 2001.[76] Of particular interest to me is how much fear drives even the people still attending churches. The fear of white males that they are losing their way of life, the fear of evangelicals that they are losing Christian America, and the fear that we are sliding into total wickedness as a nation all combine to make this the Age of Fear. Geiko Muller-Fahrenholz says, "People who want to be invulnerable must make themselves impenetrable. Their search for invincibility must be paid for with the lifeless shield of numbed emotions and intellectual inertia."[77] The preacher's response to fear is vulnerability and openness.

Reading and writing are necessary practices and partners for life among those who preach. O'Connor makes the case for writing habits: "I'm a full-time believer in writing habits . . . You may be able to do without them if you have genius but most of us only have talent and this is simply something that has to be assisted all the time by physical and mental habits or it dries up and blows away."[78] The same development of habits is required for our reading lives.

---

75. Hauerwas and Coles, *Christianity, Democracy, and the Radical Ordinary*, 4.
76. Bader-Saye, *Following Jesus in a Culture of Fear*.
77. Muller-Fahrenholz, *America's Battle for God*, 99.
78. O'Connor, *Habit of Being*, 242.

A reading strategy is more than the earlier advice to read as much as possible. James McClendon, an Anabaptist theologian; Will Campbell, a preacher and novelist; and Stanley Hauerwas have done more to inform my reading strategy than any others. I include McClendon among the novelists because his theology is spoken in story form, and Hauerwas because of his commitment to narrative and practices.

We approach all biblical narratives with gospel-influenced reading strategies. The reading strategy by which the first Christians interpreted Scripture is a method they learned from the Bible itself. We should employ the same strategy today so that our understanding of Christian community is framed and shaped by that original benchmark of understanding. Such a church is provisional, subject to correction arising from further Bible reading. The reading of the Bible is not for us to prove we are right, but for us to be made right by the power of God.

McClendon calls our reading strategy the "baptist vision"[79] or the prophetic vision. The small "b" for baptist underscores that this is not limited only to those who are Baptists. He says, "I mean the guiding pattern by which a people (or as here, a combination of peoples) shape their thought and practice as that people or that combination; I mean by it the continually emerging theme and tonic structure of their common life."[80] What I'm suggesting is that the reading strategy proposed by McClendon may be the most important skill baptists have bequeathed to the Christian faith. The role of Scripture is the clue to the baptist vision. Scripture forges a link between the church of the apostles and our own. McClendon expresses the baptist vision in this way: "Shared awareness of the present Christian community as the primitive community and the eschatological community."[81] This opens the door to the analogical imagination, and the dance with metaphors.

The reading strategy employed in Scripture presents a pattern by which Scripture reads Scripture. This lays present claim to biblical words who's setting plainly lies in the past. It doesn't discount the past, the history, or the reality of the event, but reinterprets it. For example, consider Deuteronomy 6:21 "We were Pharaoh's slaves in Egypt." This is not true of the generation making the claim unless the strategy is "this is that." The Exodus motif became the archetypal metaphor of the African American prophetic tradition. This is the metaphor that has given life and hope and courage to the African American church and the unending struggle for civil rights. We can still hear the cries of those Hebrew slaves in the voice of Fannie Lou

---

79. McClendon, *Ethics*, 11.
80. McClendon, *Ethics*, 27.
81. McClendon, *Ethics*, 30.

Hamer: "I am sick and tired of being sick and tired; Nobody's free until everybody's free; I feel sorry for anybody that could let hate wrap them up. Ain't no such thing as I can hate anybody and hope to see God's face."[82]

This is not a mere exercise in reading words. The words must be felt deep in our hearts. Mrs. Hamer and several of her fellow civil rights friends were arrested and placed in the Winona, Mississippi jail.

> Their reception in the Winona jail was brutal. Annell Ponder apparently was the first to be beaten. Mrs. Hamer later remembered: "And I could hear somebody when they say, 'Cain't you say yessir, nigger? Cain't you say yessir, bitch?' And I could understand Miss Ponder's voice. She said, 'Yes, I can say yessir.' He said, 'Well, say it.' She said, 'I don't know you well enough.' She never would say yessir and I could hear when she would hit the flo', and then I could hear them licks just soundin' . . . But anyway, she kept screamin' and they kept beatin' on her and finally she started prayin' for 'em, and she asked God to have mercy on 'em, because they didn't know what they were doing. And after then . . . I heard some real keen screams, and that's when they passed my cell with a girl, she was fifteen years old, Miss Johnson, June Johnson. They passed my cell and the blood was run-nin' down in her face."[83]

McClendon's reading strategy represents the Anabaptist that lives in my mind. The Anabaptist faith was radical, simple, straightforward. It was defiant as a disturber of the peace. The Anabaptists refused to bow the knee to the political/religious status quo. "Forced to meet in secret, they suffered persecution and imprisonment for their antiestablishment beliefs. Some were executed as political criminals, martyrs to the cause of religious freedom."[84]

In Will Campbell's *Cecelia's Sin*, Cecelia consigns to the flames the story they have written. As she reached the last page she says, "A finished story which has no ending. We have reached the beginning. There is no ending. That was the error of Rome and Wittenberg. Of Geneva and Zurich. And almost of us as well. To end the story. The end of the story can only be defended with violence. Nothing else is left."[85]

---

82. Hamer, "Testimony Before the Credentials Committee."
83. Payne, *I've Got the Light of Freedom*, 227–28.
84. Campbell, "Interview," 200.
85. Campbell, "Interview," 210.

For preachers what is left is the precarious peace[86] Jesus offers—the nonviolent kingdom of God as the mega-story that outlives all others. This is the song that preaching sings. As Cecelia puts it, "Until we came together we knew the words. Now we know the tune."[87]

A reading strategy frames how the sermon takes the shape of Scripture. Hauerwas notes, "The sermon is at the heart of our ability to speak as well as sustain speaking Christian. The sermon is not your reflections on how to negotiate life. The sermon rather is our fundamental speech act as Christians through which we learn the grammar of the faith."[88]

Allan Gurganus maintains, "There are those who believe that the sermon is the primary literary form of American life . . . we feel the sermon's lash and balm in every great American book."[89] Gurganus says, "And when the *New Republic* compared chapters of my novel to Christ's open-ended, life-soaked parables, some still small voice in me went, 'Me? Me, with my own tent and pulpit? Yeah! Now we're cooking!' My pulpit stands wedged between the covers of each book."[90]

Reynolds Price argues that preaching in America has been enriched by contact with the King James Bible translation and all its marvelous reverberations in our lives. In the South, this biblical memory was enhanced by Anglo-Saxon preachers born of long generations of people who had spoken the English language. "And our language has added to it, as a great leavening and enriching factor, something that British English never had—a profound involvement with African American language."[91]

The preacher, like an athlete showing up every day for the hard discipline of practice, shows up for the difficult work of reading, thinking, writing, and speaking. Practice will not make perfection, but it does have the power to create great preaching. This effort is uniquely captured in McClendon's primary reading strategy: "This is that." Using Acts 2:16 as the archetypal example, McClendon says that when Peter preaches, "'this is that which was spoken by the prophet Joel' he is claiming that the events of Pentecost are the events of the prophetic message. And this is the familiar biblical pattern: This is that."[92] In other words, the preacher's overarching reading strategy is metaphorical and analogical. As Bloom puts it, "Weaker talents idealize";

---

86. See Huebner, *Precarious Peace*.
87. Campbell, "Interview," 211.
88. Hauerwas, *Working with Words*, 93.
89. Gurganus, "Interview," 395.
90. Gurganus, "Interview," 395.
91. Price, "Interview," 85.
92. McClendon, *Ethics*, 32.

strong preachers imagine because they are "figures of capable imagination appropriate for themselves."[93] The adventure of preaching then may be called troping.

NOVELISTS HAVE ONLY WORDS

Novelists are wordsmiths. The analogical connection here with the word "blacksmith" suggests the amount of hard work, blood, sweat, and tears that go into forging a sermon from raw materials. And words are the raw materials of preaching. Words uttered by preachers have to be incarnational because the preacher's words are connected to "In the beginning was the word."[94]

Words are the deck of cards issued to preachers. Our love for, our allegiance to, our pursuit of the best possible words is a practice that can never leave us. With words we craft sentences, paragraphs, thoughts, truth claims, appeals, arguments, and love for the people of God. Without words we are out of business. As preachers we are slaves to words. No other word in our language will suffice to describe the suffering, agonizing, and difficult task of stringing together words into phrases, sentences, and making not only sense but enlivening the imagination, rebuking the slothful, encouraging the weary, and lifting up the downtrodden. We do business with metaphors and speech acts.

Pat Conroy sets the table for the sheer vitality of words:

> You may find the harmonics of the Common of the Mass in every book I've ever written. Because I was raised Roman Catholic, I never feared taking any unchaperoned walks through the fields of language. Words lifted me up and filled me with pleasure. I've never met a word I was afraid of, just ones that left me indifferent or that I knew I wouldn't ever put to use. When reading a book, I'll encounter words that please me, goad me into action, make me want to sing a song. I dislike pretentious words, those highfalutin' ones with a trust fund and an Ivy League education. Often they were stillborn in the minds of academics, critics, scientists. They have a tendency to flash their warning lights in the middle of a good sentence.[95]

---

93. Bloom, *Anxiety of Influence*, 5.
94. John 1:1.
95. Conroy, *My Reading Life*, 50.

From first grade to the twelfth, teachers, especially teachers of English, required me to learn vocabulary, practice pronouncing, spelling, and defining words. This practice continues for a lifetime for those of us who write and preach sermons. Preaching a sermon is like publishing a short story every Sunday year after year.

For better or worse, the novelists and preachers have only words to tell their stories. But, rest assured, they are not "mere" words. Many preachers are dismayed by words. The advertisers, the political pundits, the consultants, the politicians, the propaganda tribe—they have all gotten to us. These "fake" pundits of words have convinced us that slogans will save us. Advertisers have kidnapped religious words to sell cars. Words are a jumble of conflicting meanings. Pundits now claim there are alternative facts! "Truthful hyperbole"—an oxymoron—has entered the political lexicon. People invading the capitol of the United States are called "patriots"! Words are said to mean nothing or everything.

The advertisers have kidnapped the language of faith to sell more products. The sponsors will sell us all they can. For example, Subaru's advertising slogan is "Love—It's what makes a Subaru a Subaru." That's the slogan. You'll pardon me if I find that offensive. I don't want to love or believe in a car. I want it to run and not break down. Our secular culture is making a religion out of all things material, mechanical, technological. We make gods of our sports teams and stars, and I love baseball, and I know at the same time it is indefensible as we pay baseball players millions of dollars to play a game.

As early as 1981, Alvin Toffler illustrated the possibilities of science as a warning: "Should we breed people with cowlike stomachs so they can digest grass and hay—thereby alleviating the food problem? Should we biologically alter workers to fit job requirements? Should we attempt to 'eliminate' inferior people and have a 'super-race'? Should we clone soldiers to do our fighting? Should we grow reserve organs for ourselves—each of us having a 'savings bank' full of spare kidneys, livers, or lungs?"[96]

The preacher can bring into stunning contemporary language the warning of the prophet, "This is the word of the Lord to Zerubbabel: Not by might, nor by power, but by my spirit, says the Lord of hosts."[97] Here are possibilities for prophetic sermons: "This is the word of the Lord to the USA: 'Not by military might, nor by technological ingenuity, but by m spirit, says the Lord of hosts.'" Our capitulation to the scientific/technological paradigm has produced the widespread consumption ethic. It has loosed the terrifying power of one of the ugliest of the seven cardinal sins:

---

96. Toffler, *Third Wave*, 146–47.
97. Zech 4:6.

greed. We act as if we have the right to take over, destroy, or encroach upon the environment, whether this means putting all plants and animals, and even humans on the endangered species list or not. The waste products of our technology threaten to drown us in plastic, old computers, and smart phones, and a host of other kinds of techno-trash.

Remember that the primacy of technology and military might gave us the atomic age. In this world, atomic power becomes the ultimate protector of the nation and replaces divinity. Cornel West warns that an escalating aggressive militarism threatens the existence of democracy. West says, "This dogma posits military might as salvific in a world in which he who has the most and biggest weapons is the most moral and masculine, hence worthy of policing others. In practice, this dogma takes the form of unilateral intervention, colonial invasion, and armed occupation abroad."[98]

One of our most gifted preaching professors entitled his Lyman Beecher Lectures *The End of Words*.[99] Yet his message was one of hope even in our word-saturated culture. I am interested here in the power of words. Many preachers have lost confidence in the power of words, but I wish to resist this malaise. There is still a word from God and there is still a need for people who believe in the power of words and speak words that are truth, especially truth to power. After all, preachers are a product of the word of the Lord.

Our words are secondary, tertiary, even seventh-level speech, but they are still words from the original Word Master who said, "Let there be light" and there was light.[100] Richard Lischer put it best: "The preacher's job is to do nothing less than shape the language of the sermon to a living reality among the people of God. The sermon is Jesus trying to speak once again to his own community."[101]

Hunting and collecting words requires memory. As actors memorize their lines, preachers cultivate memory for words and ideas. For decades I practiced remembering what I read. Sitting at my desk writing a sermon, I would remember a sentence or a word from a book that I had often read. I would go to the bookshelves, pull out that book, and turn to the page where I had marked the now necessary material. This gift has receded lately, but I still try to call to mind what I have read so that when I need it, the words will appear. Conroy remarks, "I've amassed a stockpile of books in vaults and storage bins in attics and unfinished basements and tortoiseshell-colored

---

98. West, *Democracy Matters*, 5.
99. Lischer, *End of Words*.
100. Gen 1:3.
101. Lischer, *End of Words*, Kindle ed. loc. 66.

boxes that I raid with willful abandon when I try to fix a sentence on a page. Words call out my name when I need them to make something worthy out of language."[102]

I am going to tell you something that you probably will never be told by anyone else in the business of preaching. I am going to take you to the Illustration River, and I am going to give you a large scoop and give you scooping lessons so that in the dead of night you can steal all kinds of great stories, analogies, and illustrations. I am going to make you a thief that rivals the greatest bank robbers in American history. Look, if you are going to preach well, there has to be a bit of thievery in your repertoire.

I'm telling you that preaching is the art of theft: of knowing what to steal and from whom. The gift of knowing good material when you read it should not be wasted. Exchange what you read from others with your congregation in the pews. You can pretend the gifts are yours, but at least use footnotes and acknowledge your source. Otherwise, you will sit in front of your computer waiting for the first original thought you have ever had and you will wait in vain. The great rhetorical theorist Kenneth Burke said "Literature" is "equipment for living."[103]

It's not that hard to discover the preachers and writers who have the gift of illustration and example. I learned from detective novelist, James Lee Burke, the majesty and beauty and glory of descriptive language. The man could describe a muddy bayou in New Iberia, Louisiana, and I would be so enthralled I thought a road trip was a necessity. I found the sermons of John Buchanan, when he was senior pastor at Fourth Street Presbyterian in Chicago, to have more illustrations in one sermon than a preacher can use in a month of Sundays. Look for people who know their way around the language. Share with your congregation the benefits of your research. Enough with sentences beginning with, "Now, in the Greek text, this word means . . ." Unleash the writer from your body and put the words on a page. People do not show up on Sunday panting to hear you go on and on till doomsday about the history of Nazareth or the origin of Cain's wife, or whatever in hell happened to the Jebusites. You are not a game show host of a Bible trivia contest. You are a preacher.

And learn how to steal only great material. This can be understood as a matter of quantity. If you are well-read, you will have thirty or more potential metaphors, examples, images, and illustrations to choose from in writing the sermon. If you are not reading you will have maybe three pieces of information. Those three may not be, and probably will not be,

---

102. Conroy, *My Reading Life*, 50.
103. Burke, "Literature as equipment for living," 293.

the best available, but Sunday's coming and you have to use what you have. A preacher who steals bad material is like a band playing in Texas without a fiddle.

Great material? How do you know? Look, there's a huge difference between good and great. If you read the story and it shouts from the page, "This will preach," take it. Wrap it carefully. Carry it with you and use it in your next sermon. As a "fisher of men and women," you are not in a "catch and release" program. You are in the business of fishing for every possible word that persuades others to know Jesus and his wisdom.

In a culture that both uses words as weapons and at the same time demeans words as "mere" or as "just words," don't fall for the illusions. Words are meant to help, to heal, to persuade in the direction of truth, justice, and peace. The dance with metaphors requires the best tune. Somewhere in the preacher's mind there should be an ongoing song: "Comfort, comfort, my people . . . Speak tenderly."[104] Someone once quipped that we should use words if necessary. Well, words are not only necessary; they are essential.

THE NOVELIST WONDERS, IMAGINES, AND CREATES

Wondering is the business of novelists and preachers. Ellen F. Davis says, "Teaching the Bible confessionally means enabling people to wonder wisely and deeply."[105] This capacity resides chiefly in the imagination. I believe that imagination is as crucial to good Bible reading as inspiration. Imagination involves discerning the spiritual meaning of the text. Historically we have believed that the Bible has a plain meaning and a spiritual meaning. What it doesn't have is an original meaning. Both fundamentalists and liberals struggle with imagination when they both insist on an objective meaning to texts. This is in no way an excuse not to study biblical texts closely. To the contrary, it insists that we learn to read the Bible slowly. I am cautioning preachers against the illusion that what the Bible says to any one preacher, is the only possible rendering. As N. T. Wright observes, "There are some strange bedfellows in the world of literary criticism"[106] (and the world of preaching).

Imagination provides the wood for the fire that produces great novels as well as sermons. In the story of Abraham and Isaac, Abraham "cut the

---

104. Isa 40:1.
105. Davis and Hays, eds., *Art of Reading Scripture*, 11.
106. Wright, *New Testament and the People of God*, 61.

wood for the burnt offering."[107] If the preacher's sermon is to be more than a burnt offering, the preacher will have to cut the wood every day and stockpile it for the long winters that may yield little imagination. The preacher is a laborer in a word factory, not a prima donna. This is our humble place in the promised land: "hewers of wood and drawers of water for the congregation and for the altar of the Lord."[108]

The imagination powers invention—the first of the rhetorical canons—the creative ability to gather materials that become powerful sermons. Every preacher possesses huge creative imagination. The challenge is to develop this power. A culture of imagination must involve preachers and congregations.

Imagination suffers in a religious culture that is primarily literal. There's a reluctance to be imaginative or to read Scripture between the lines. Literalism inhibits imagination. Perhaps no discipline has such an overt dependence upon tradition as much as preaching. Other disciplines do not operate on the strategy of subservience to precursors to the extent that Christian preaching tends to do. Timothy Binkley insists there is no pure core of literal meaning. Therefore we are not required to measure the literal as the ideal. As Binkley puts it, "Although metaphors are not literally true, there is no reason to suppose that the truth has to be literal."[109]

For example, scientists attempt to discover new paradigms, new evidence, new views of life. Biologist Kenneth R. Miller says, "A genuinely new discovery changes our view of the world around us. Truly great science overturns our accepted ideas of nature, and therefore always presents a threat to the established order. To be effective in science a young investigator has to feel free to contradict and even to disrespect scientific authority. He or she has to be bold (or foolish) enough to do work that flies in the face of existing ideas, and then must be willing to set his or her career on the line to continue that research."[110]

If a preacher dares to make this scientific strategy her own, she will walk a lonely road when she feels compelled to contradict and even disrespect religious authority. If she is bold (or foolish) enough to do work that flies in the face of existing literalism (the authority of precursors), she will have to put her career on the line to continue her journey. What if the most important ingredient for preaching success is the willingness of its

---

107. Gen 22:3.
108. Josh 9:27.
109. Binkley, "On the Truth and Probity of Metaphor," 178.
110. Miller, *Only a Theory*, 10–11.

practitioners to break free of the pack and try out their own ideas—to think, act, pray, and preach as a true individual?

Literalism, in the context of the primordial Christian metaphor, "Life is a journey," eventually comes to a dark dead end. Literalism, like those ancient maps that depicted the edge of the earth, comes to a dead stop. The ancient maps warned, "Beyond here monsters!" The literalist road map, on the other hand, only asserts, "Beyond here nothing!"

Harold Bloom makes an observation about poets that I believe applies to preachers: "Poetic history . . . is held to be indistinguishable from poetic influence, since strong poets make that history by misreading one another, so as to clear imaginative space for themselves . . . Let us give up the failed enterprise of seeking to 'understand' any single poem as an entity in itself. Let us pursue the quest of learning to read any poem as its poet's deliberate misinterpretation, as a poet, of a precursor poem or of poetry in general."[111]

For Bloom any meaning occurs as part of an agon or struggle with previous meaning. The sermon is a poem. The preacher seeks to develop her or his own sense of meaning over against the contributions of their precursors. This imaginative and creative effort proves impossible in literalism.

On the positive side, Wendell Berry's comment on the communal nature of writing poetry is apt also to preaching: "Any poem worth the name is the product of a convocation. It exists, literally, by recalling past voices into presence. . . . Poetry can be written only because it has been written. As a new poem is made, not only with the art but within it, past voices are convoked—to be changed, little or much, by the addition of another voice."[112] The great preachers hear these ancient voices, break bread with them, commune with them, make real the communion of preachers.

Metaphors have the power to break the bonds of literalism. Tropes produce a new kind of knowledge as opposed to being mere ornaments. Tropes are a defense against literal meaning "just as psychic defense mechanisms are defenses against death."[113] Literal meaning and the anxiety produced by the influence of precursors are equivalent to death that prevent the impulse to communicate further. Tropes make new communication possible.

There is a sense in which the preacher will perceive precursors in theology, ethics, biblical studies, and homiletics as an enemy. Kenneth Burke teaches that irony "is based upon a sense of fundamental kinship with the enemy, as one needs him, is indebted to him, is not merely outside him

---

111. Bloom, *Anxiety of Influence*, 5, 43.
112. Berry, "Responsibility of the Poet," 89.
113. Aune, "Burke's Late Blooming," 331.

as an observer but contains him within, being consubstantial with him."[114] The precursor, in the beginning, exercises too much presence, too much influence. The preacher makes an initial move away from the presence into a liberating absence of influence. This is the necessary move that makes imaginative work possible. The strong preacher is able to overcome her/his influence anxiety, create original work, and reveal new truths. In order for this transition to occur, the precursor presence must be experienced as absence.

What is left to say about creation, justification, Jesus, the Synoptic Gospels, the resurrection, theories of the atonement? Here is where imagination and metaphor combine to aid the preacher. Classical rhetorical tropes provide the preacher with unconscious strategies for discovering new meanings. Bloom uses the term "clinamen" as one of those strategies. The term originates with Lucretius describing the "swerve" of atoms to make changes possible in the universe. Bloom says, "The poet swerves away from his precursor ... This appears as a corrective movement."[115] The preacher is acknowledging the precursor's reading as right but now suggests that he should have swerved, precisely in the direction the preacher's new reading moves.

The primary manifestation of clinamen is the trope of irony. Burke defines irony as "that arrangement of experience ... which permits the spectator an insight superior to that of the actor."[116] This use of irony is crucial for the preacher because the Bible is filled with cunning and prolific irony. Walter Brueggemann argues, "When we notice the irony, we notice that the text speaks, perforce, in a double dialect. On the one hand, its language may be taken at face value by the innocent reader; on the other hand, what lies beneath the text contradicts the apparent meaning of a face-value reading. But then, subversives in the face of totalism have always had to speak twice in the same utterance, once for the official record and once for the truth of bodily reality."[117]

Wayne Booth claims there is a "secret communion" between the author and the reader, a shared understanding that is not on the surface of the world.[118] The trope of irony allows the preacher to speak the hidden language of the weak, the language of truth that opposes power. In his study of the weak, James C. Scott argues that peasant truth is closer to lived reality

---

114. Burke, *Grammar of Motives*, 514.
115. Bloom, *Anxiety of Influence*, 14.
116. Burke, *Grammar of Motives*, 513–14.
117. Brueggemann, *Truth Speaks to Power*, 6–7.
118. Booth, *Rhetoric of Fiction*, 300.

but is kept hidden from the false prophets of official truth. Scott says, "The struggle between rich and poor in Sedaka is not merely a struggle over work, property rights, grain, and cash. It is also a struggle over the appropriation of symbols, a struggle over how the past and present shall be understood and labeled, a struggle to identify causes and assess blame, a contentious effort to give partisan meaning to local history."[119] A visual metaphor here is the ironic story of Moses being hidden in a basket, discovered by the daughter of Pharaoh, raised in Pharaoh's house, and yet becoming the liberator of Israel from the oppression of Pharaoh. The word "hidden" suggests the hidden scripts of Scott and the irony is that power was defeated by the least likely—Hebrew midwives, a baby in a reed basket, and the daughter of Pharaoh himself.

This is an example of true irony as it is "based on a sense of fundamental kinship with the enemy, as one needs him, is indebted to him, is not merely outside him as an observer but contains him within, being consubstantial with him."[120] The preacher-author of Hebrews writes, "By faith Moses, when he was grown up, refused to be called a son of Pharaoh's daughter, choosing rather to share ill-treatment with the people of God than to enjoy the fleeting pleasures of sin."[121]

Given the challenges we face now, the most profound paradigm shift has to be in how we perceive the truth of the gospel, and how we think about our own abilities to imagine a new world. My premise is that we are all born with imagination and creativity, but somehow this essential aspect is trained out of us. Ironically, one of the primary culprits in this process is the methodology of the seminary. Students are taught to think critically in seminary. They produce papers in the exegesis of biblical passages. They write papers in theology, ethics, and history. I am amazed at the breadth and depth of knowledge that seminary students acquire in pursuit of the master of divinity degree. If, however, this leads to sermons that read like the pages of a biblical commentary, we are lacking in imagination. "Current approaches to education and training are hobbled by assumptions about intelligence and creativity that have squandered the talents and stifled the creative confidence of untold numbers of people," argues Sir Ken Robinson.[122] There is a systemic waste of talent, not from a lack of commitment to education or a lack of great teaching, but because of deep-seated assumptions about thinking as only rational rather than rational and emotional.

---

119. Scott, *Weapons of the Weak*, Kindle ed. loc. 183.
120. Burke, *Grammar of Motives*, 514.
121. Heb 11:24.
122. Robinson and Lee, *Out of Our Minds*, 8.

Without imagination, creativity, metaphor, and rhetoric nothing unexpected or astonishing can emerge, nothing new. Rhetoric is the way of truth that lights up our world with meaningful relationships. This recovery of the sense of humanism and the humanities is central to a preachers' sense of the incarnation as theological truth. Rhetoric was the centerpiece of Western education from ancient Greece until the Enlightenment. And what is rhetoric without humanism—mere technique without content or memory, an endless trail of uninspiring handbooks, or a tool for deconstructive language games? A recovery of the humanity of preaching is foundational to my thought. Hauerwas puts it in perspective: "That God's salvation is so fleshly, so material, is why we are here to worship God in one another's presence. We know that we cannot hear the word as isolated spirits, but rather we hear God's word as God's body. Through the hearing of the word God creates a unity unknown anywhere else."[123]

Imagination is required because of the literary complexity of Scripture. The gospel is not simple. The language of the Bible is often symbolic, mythological, imaginative, analogical, metaphorical, and apocalyptic. The language of the Bible often exceeds ordinary "commonsense" discourse. The language of the Bible is rhetorical, imaginative, poetic, narrative. Reading the Bible attentively and imaginatively is the preacher's task. The Bible is tailor-made as text for the unending dance with metaphors in the pulpit.

For example, Genesis is not a book written by a modern cosmologists, but by the poets and historians of Israel. It doesn't describe exactly how the universe was created; but it tells us that we are made by the love and freedom of God alone. Cell biologist Kenneth R. Miller asserts, "Science assures us that we are indeed the products of evolution, but it certainly does not tell us that we are its 'casual and meaningless' products. The scientific insight that our very existence, through evolution, requires a universe of the very size, scale, and age that we see around us implies that the universe, in a certain sense, had us in mind from the very beginning."[124]

The book of Job is not a historical event, but a sustained argument that God is God, and we are not. Ellen Davis reminds, "The divine speeches in Job counter an anthropocentric reading of Genesis 1: So you think the P(riestly) creation account means that the whole world was created for human beings and their self-gratification? Wrong again."[125] Daniel is a highly stylized story about how God expects his people to act in a corrupt empire. Revelation is a book written in code and the key to the code has been lost

---

123. Hauerwas, *In Good Company*, 37.
124. Miller, *Only a Theory*, 161.
125. Davis and Hays, eds., *Art of Reading Scripture*, 16.

forever. The parables are not literal; they are extended metaphors. They start with a conventional, everyday world and then inject the kingdom of God: SURPRISE!

Preaching involves imagination that goes beyond reductive, detached rationality. In our preaching, we are (or should aspire to be) something like a novelist or a short story writer. There's no more powerful way to connect with a congregation than by telling a story. The beauty of the story is beauty itself. There are short stories that are sermons without attempting to be sermons. Allan Gurganus' "It Had Wings" and Doris Betts' "This Is the Only Time I'll Tell It" are two wonderful examples.

Imagination on the part of the novelist produces plot lines, characters, conversations, drama, events, and scenes. For the preacher imagination inspires effective interpretation as the preacher has a connection to the imaginative power of God, to which the Bible bears witness. The very act of creation is the beginning of imagination and God gifted an antecedent imaginative power to us. Imagination, after all, envisions the existence of something that does not yet exist. God's imagination leaps from every page of the Bible from creation to covenant to calling a people of priests from a band of slaves to the incarnation of God in human flesh to the triumph of life over death in the resurrection to the universal embrace of all peoples in Israel. These are imaginative acts that may be a slow evolutionary process or a exploding series of revolutionary acts. Something totally new and never before imagined keeps occurring when God is present.

Since creation serves as the paradigmatic event of imagination, I find it incredible that so many preachers insist on defending a literal six-day creation rather than celebrating the imaginative and persuasive power of God. A large chunk of their time is spent defending what they insist on calling the "biblical account" of creation. Miller points out, "Even today creationists lead boat trips down the Grand Canyon of the Colorado, dismissing the towering testimony of distinct geological ages that surround them as the illusory product of a single worldwide flood."[126]

The sheer wonder of the Grand Canyon, its shimmering beauty, and its ancient ruggedness bears testimony to the patient persuasion of God in creation. To ride through that canyon analyzing the fossil record and attempting to justify that what people are seeing with their eyes, they are not really seeing, seems absurd when the Grand Canyon offers such beauty for praise, awe, and celebration of God's creative imagination.

A creationist preacher, who with a wink and a nod at the Bible, in particular Genesis (where all the answers allegedly hide), seems a living

---

126. Miller, *Only a Theory*, 40.

contradiction. He rejects all of science—biology, physics, geology, and astronomy. This means that the creationist rejects truth. Such irony that a person called to speak the truth rejects truth in order to accommodate his "biblical" assumptions. This leads to preaching that is unbiblical, unchristian, untrue, and dangerous. Where the imagination is lacking, understanding of creation becomes impossible.

In his book *On the Literal Meaning of Genesis*, St. Augustine warned preachers against using Scripture to make statements about astronomy, biology, and geology. To his mind, the worst scenario he could imagine was preachers "presumably giving the meaning of Holy Scripture, talking nonsense on these [scientific] topics." Augustine advised that "we should take all means to prevent such an embarrassing situation in which people show up vast ignorance in a Christian and laugh it to scorn."[127]

The preacher can discover better preaching materials on creation from Augustine and Aquinas than from all the creationist preachers in the world. "The universe was brought into a less than fully formed state, but was gifted with the capacity to transform itself from unformed matter into a truly marvelous array of structure and life forms."[128] Thomas Aquinas said in the thirteenth century that we should never think of creation as an event, with a before and after, or as a change of circumstances. Rather creation is an action of God that sets up a relationship between God and what is not God.[129]

Creation is the preachers' primary story. It is exhilarating to tell a congregation that creation is now, that God's creative action is going on here and now, in this present moment. The outpouring of life from God is the heart of all our preaching.

As preachers faithfully read the stories (there are multiple creation stories in the Bible), we will discover our own imaginations expanded and fulfilled. Each sermon becomes a new creation. The novelist Harry Crews says of finishing a story, "When I get through writing something and it's done and I look at it and I think before me this was not, and because of me, this is. Nobody's got a piece of this. All mine."[130]

The stories of Scripture will mark us as God's rhapsodes, storytellers, fools, heralds, ambassadors, watchpersons, and make us into powerful preachers with enlightened imaginations. I am saying that we learn the

---

127. Augustine, *On the Literal Meaning of Genesis*, 1:19, quoted in Miller, *Only a Theory*, 222.
128. Augustine, quoted in Rees, *Just Six Numbers*, 115.
129. Williams, *Tokens of Trust*, 35.
130. Crews, "Interview," Kindle ed. loc. 4606–7.

practice of imagination through apprenticeship to novelists who are masters of imagination.

The preacher, like the novelist, needs literary skills. As Davis remarks, "In addition to imaginations fit for the reading of Scripture, students also need literary skills, and these are often of a different kind than their earlier studies have required of them."[131] This is an overlooked part of our teaching because we assume that we think we know what is there in the Bible, even if we haven't read it in years. Our first task is to overcome the illusion that we know what the Bible says. We often don't know what the Bible says, because the Bible speaks in multiple languages, multiple voices, and in multiple histories. We may know Romans 3:23 or John 3:16, but we may not know what the Bible says. Knowing verses of Scripture doesn't mean that we know the Bible.

Literary criticism helps us know the kind of texts we are reading. In the movie *Metropolitan*, a character defends his obtuseness by saying, "You don't have to read a book to have an opinion on it."[132] These are the people insisting on complete freedom, and loudly proclaiming they have a right to their own opinions. They will tend toward belligerence: "Who are you think you are to tell me what to believe about God? The environment? Racism? Sexism?"

In the midst of all this opinion-laced noise, the preacher has to find that quiet spot in her heart that like Mary will ponder everything carefully. This requires the patience of not being in a hurry, the confidence that God has given us all the time we need to understand, grasp, and then proclaim the truth. This will help the preacher read slowly. Most of us read too fast.

Historical criticism is our ally. It helps us understand that the Bible is not a modern book, and it was not written in America. This means we must develop the capacity to wonder deeply and wisely. Again, Ellen Davis guides preachers as an expert mountain guide enables hikers to make it to the highest peaks: "The capacity for fruitful theological wondering resides chiefly in the imagination. Theologian Garrett Green has argued persuasively that in many instances the biblical term 'heart' (lev, kardia) refers to what we call imagination. This notion wonderfully illuminates the use of that word in the eucharistic liturgy: 'Lift up your hearts'—lift up your imaginations, open them toward God."[133]

Interpreting symbols, analogies, metaphors, and a complex variety of rhetorical tropes is the preacher's most difficult and most consequential

---

131. Davis and Hays, eds., *Art of Reading Scripture*, 11.
132. Tom Townsend, a character in the movie *Metropolitan*.
133. Davis and Hays, eds., *Art of Reading Scripture*, 11.

business. What is at stake is whether Scripture can be reinterpreted and open to radical theological reinterpretation. David Tracy has argued that interpretation can never be static. Instead, interpretation must always be done and must go in unexpected directions.[134] And I say YES to all of it.

The Bible is not full of comfortable and reassuring things about the life of faith. There's sacrifice, suffering, cost, but not ease. Sacrifice has been taken off the table in most American religion today and this is even more the case in politics. One party wants the poor to sacrifice, and the other party wants the rich to sacrifice. The people wanting to dump the consequences of American greed on the poor, or the rich or the middle class. No one volunteers to sacrifice. Perhaps careful preachers hide too much and rarely tell us what they really think. In the novel *Revelation*, Rev. Swain Hammond fits the stereotype of many preachers: "The church was an excellent choice for the careful, self-controlled man that Swain has grown up to be."[135]

The preacher will benefit from reading the novelists, from entering the difficult but creative art of putting together words in sentences that encourage, empower, and transform people. The novelist leads the preacher into a world of wonder, a world filled with words. The novelist shows us a journey that includes massive amounts of reading, how to have deep empathy for the human condition, how to work with a moral imperative, how to tell the big story of Jesus and his cross and resurrection, how to develop practices that lead to good writing, now to engage in the strenuous effort of wondering, imagining, and creating every day. Hail to the novelists!

---

134. Tracy, *Analogical Imagination*, 24, 156–67.
135. Payne, *Revelation*, Kindle ed. loc. 52.

Chapter 2

What the Poets Teach Us about Preaching

"I have refused to live locked in the orderly house of reasons and proofs.
The world I live in and believe in is wider than that.
And anyway, what's wrong with Maybe?"[1]

—Mary Oliver, *Devotions*

Poetry is as natural to preaching as breathing. Any preacher determined to proclaim the message will write poetry. "For the time is coming when people will not put up with sound doctrine, but having itching ears, they will accumulate for themselves teachers to suit their own desires and will turn away from listening to the truth and wander away to myths. As for you, always be sober, endure suffering, do the work of an evangelist, carry out your ministry fully."[2] Writing poetry is basic training for writing sermons.

As the piano is to the pianist, so poetry is to the preacher. The language of the church has always been rooted in poetry. Preachers turn naturally to poetry because the Psalms stand as the poetry volume in the biblical canon. Thus, the preacher does well to live with the Psalms and consider the possibilities for preaching the poems found there so full of humanity. Prophets, priests, and poets have been singing the songs of faith from the first descriptions of ancient creation to the coming of the new Jerusalem to earth in Revelation. Poetry is the preacher's language. From the poets the preacher

---

1. Oliver, *Devotions*, 5.
2. 2 Tim 4:3–5.

learns to sing the words of faith. The preacher does well if she matriculates in the school of the poets.

Scripture is like a musical score that must be played or sung to be understood; therefore, the church interprets Scripture by forming communities of prayer, service, and faithful witness. The Psalms, for example, are "scores" awaiting performance by the community of faith. They school us in prayer and form in us the capacities for praise, penitence, reflection, patient endurance, and resistance to evil.[3] "So Luther's dictum that in the Psalms we find the prayer of Christ and all the saints is not the imposition on these texts of an alien 'Christian' interpretation. If the gospel is true, it is simply the fact of the matter."[4]

Poetry, like preaching, has broken the bonds of previous generations and ponderous rules to produce free style. Poetry now rebels against structure and is an excellent dance partner for the sermon. Charles Taylor surmises, "Poetry is in search of 'subtler languages,' built without reference to a publicly accepted vision of things."[5] "[M]odern poetry doesn't rely," claims Taylor, "on already recognized structures. It opens new paths, 'sets free' new realities, but only for those for whom it resonates."[6]

The usual, traditional sermon structure feels foreign to the sermon. Dissecting the text makes the preacher more pathologist than poet. Three points and a poem sound ordinary, dull, boring, old. Plato's ironic depiction of rhetoric as cookery has been disinterred in preaching manuals to offer preachers recipes for sermons: take three points, add three stories, throw in an appeal and a dash of theology, and there's a sermon. What if texts don't lend themselves to this kind of division? What if texts already have a natural structure waiting to be discovered? What if texts are more of a freestyle dance rather than a distillation into lessons, objects, or points?

Walter Brueggemann suggests, "God in the covenantal traditions of the Old Testament is a free partner, not locatable or predictable by place or posture. I find the metaphor of dance helpful for our reflections."[7] In this "dance," the two partners take each other seriously and stay on the dance floor with each other. But that commitment is the only factor that is constant, mutual, and serious. Beyond that, everything is open for both partners and yet to be decided. The partners dance in many postures, many locations, many varied relationships, in which nothing can be counted on

---

3. Davis and Hays, eds., *Art of Reading Scripture*, 3–4.
4. Davis and Hays, eds., *Art of Reading Scripture*, 35.
5. Taylor, *Secular Age*, 718.
6. Taylor, *Secular Age*, 758.
7. Brueggemann, *Psalms*, Kindle ed. loc. 1546.

from the other one, except that each takes the partner seriously on the dance floor.

Gerard Manley Hopkins captures the playfulness of the dance in these lines: "What would the world be, once bereft / Of wet and wilderness? / Let them be left, / O let them be left, wildness and wet; / Long live the weeds and wilderness yet."[8] Taylor, reflecting on poetry, says, "Of the tasks for all of us to be sure, but especially poets, is to use language as an event with a performative force, words which open up contact, make something manifest for the first time."[9] Hopkins, a profoundly liturgical human being—as priest and as poet—produced a body politics that made possible the resonances between poet and reader, between preacher and congregation. Hopkins here speaks to the preacher whose poetic sensibilities gravitate between a closeness and a distance to God. In the shadows, Hopkins cries out, "Mine, O thou Lord of life, send my roots rain."[10]

POETRY AS FREE VERSE

The poet teaches the preacher the value of free verse. The teacher of poetry I have selected as our guide is Mary Oliver. The textbook is *A Poetry Handbook*.[11] While the label "free verse" sounds like writing a sermon in a disorganized way, that's not right. Design remains necessary. No external pattern, no prefabricated structure exists, but that opens the door for more creativity. A sermon in free verse is a cathedral rising to the sky with its gleaming steeples; a sermon in traditional structure is a prefabricated Kentucky Fried Chicken building thrown up on State Street in Schenectady, New York. Oliver writes, "Sometimes I want to sum and give thanks, putting things in order, but it starts dancing around the room on its four furry legs, and calling me outrageous."[12]

Poetry in free verse helps free us from attempting to communicate our message in the twenty-first century using eighteenth-century methods. As we shall see, the same holds true for the sermon. Neither late-eighteenth-century theology—fundamentalism or eighteenth-century poems that rhyme—is the path before us.

Poems, like sermons, have a design, but it is not always the easiest to see. The name—free verse—suggests a free-flowing, disorganized array of

8. Hopkins, *Poems and Prose*, 51.
9. Taylor, *Secular Age*, 758.
10. Hopkins, *Poems and Prose*, 67.
11. Oliver, *Poetry Handbook*.
12. Oliver, *Devotions*, 10.

ideas as if the preacher races across the biblical terrain in a runaway four-wheeler spinning the tires, splashing through mudholes, and teetering on the edge of a collision. The implication is that this kind of poetry rose out of a rebellion from the restraints of meter, the rules of poetry. Free verse suggests a bunch of hippies at Woodstock stomping on the grave of Shakespeare.

Free verse "is free from formal metrical design, but it isn't free from some kind of design."[13] It is poetry that expresses the emotions but is also a "composed, considered, appropriate, and effective creation."[14] It is the apex of creativity, where each design matches each new sermon perfectly and no two designs are the same. Free-verse sermon design is snowflake design.

Sermons have been written in predetermined patterns for centuries. This parallels the development of poetry. Mary Oliver points out that free verse is so new in poetry, in the sense of history, that it is hard to say exactly what free verse is. "Partly because it is so different from one poem to another. Partly because we are so close to the beginnings of it. Metrical verse has been written for centuries, and before that, poetry depended on strict application of alliteration or some pattern of light and heavy stresses."[15]

Gardner Taylor reaches for the heights of the poetic in his Lyman Beecher Lectures: "Altogether too much preaching . . . is too flat, too horizontal, too colorless, too unimaginative."[16] Walter Brueggemann sings the same theme: "The gospel is thus a truth widely held, but a truth greatly reduced. It is a truth that has been flattened, trivialized, and rendered inane. Partly, the gospel is simply an old habit among us, neither valued nor questioned. But more than that, our technical way of thinking reduces mystery to problem, transforms assurance into certitude, revises quality into quantity, and so takes the categories of biblical faith and represents them in manageable shapes."[17]

The free-verse sermon sets up a premise or an expectation or a promise, and then, before the sermon finishes, it makes a powerful response to the original thought: premise, expectation, or promise. "What it sets up in the beginning it sings back to, all the way, attaining a felt integrity"[18]—a wholeness like a solid piece of wood.

The premise arises from the text, directly from the text. There are emphatic uses of stresses in the premise, a musicality if you will. J. Barrie

---

13. Oliver, *Poetry Handbook*, 67.
14. Oliver, *Poetry Handbook*, 67.
15. Oliver, *Poetry Handbook*, 68.
16. Taylor, *How Shall They Preach?*, 60.
17. Brueggemann, *Finally Comes the Poet*, Kindle ed. loc. 38–41.
18. Oliver, *Poetry Handbook*, 68.

Shepherd laments the "dearth of delight"[19] and encourages the joy of the dance. He quotes from the poem "Mayflies" by Richard Wilbur, "Watching those lifelong dancers of a day . . . I had been called to be not fly nor star but one whose task is joyfully to see how fair the fiats of the caller are."

When the free-verse sermon is finished it must "feel" like a poem—"it must be an intended and an effective presentation. It need not be in chronological order. It certainly doesn't require a verse-by-verse plodding through a text as if the preacher is teaching Sunday school. It need not follow any of the old rules, necessarily. Neither does it have to avoid all of them necessarily."[20] The preacher has much more to pick from instead of three points and a poem of an earlier time.

Oliver suggests that with the growing idea of a democratic and classless society, the proliferation of privately owned books, and as more people moved to small towns in the West, the distance from tradition increased. The poet became not a lecturer as much as an invited guest in a private home. The poet needed to be more friendly—less teacherly. A new tone developed that reflected a relationship between poet and reader.[21]

In other words, "speech entered the poem. The poem was no longer a lecture, it was time spent with a friend. Its music was the music of conversation."[22] The sermon, at its best, is words set to music. Nowhere is this connection as clear as in the African American preaching tradition. James Cone says, "Only the song, dance, and the shout—voices raised to high heavens and bodies swaying from side to side—can express both the wretchedness and the transcendent spirit of empowerment that kept blacks from going under, as they struggled, against great odds, to acknowledge humanity denied."[23] Eddie Glaude Jr. adds, "The places where we danced, played cards, told jokes, and enjoyed the beauty of living a life together—not only helped black Americans to survive this racist country. They also gave us the courage to fight back."[24]

In his Lyman Beecher Lectures, Otis Moss III lifts up the dance of the sermon: "The Blue Note of interpretation pushes aside a Sunday-school faith and calls the preacher/prophet to dance to the rhythm of the Blues."[25] He adds: "You can't give up hope, because once you have a prophetic word

---

19. Shepherd, *Whatever Happened to Delight?*, 18.
20. Oliver, *Poetry Handbook*, 68–69.
21. Oliver, *Poetry Handbook*, 69.
22. Oliver, *Poetry Handbook*, 70.
23. Cone, *Cross and the Lynching Tree*, 174–75.
24. Glaude Jr., *Democracy in Black*, 126.
25. Moss III, *Blue Note Preaching*, 29.

in you, you know that God will eventually exalt every valley, that God will eventually bring every mountain low, that eventually the lion and the lamb will dance together, that eventually God will shift everything; but you've got to operate as if it's already happened."[26]

There's no better illustration for the preacher than Moss telling the story of his daughter dancing in the dark. He relates,

> I looked downstairs, and then I heard the noise again, and I made my way back upstairs and peeked in my daughter's room. There was a six-year-old girl dancing in the darkness . . . just spinning around, saying, "Look at me, Daddy." I said, "Makayla, you need to go to bed. It is 3:00 a.m. You need to go to bed." But she said, "No, look at me, Daddy. Look at me." And she was spinning; barrettes going back and forth, pigtails going back and forth. I was getting huffy and puffy wanting her to go to bed, but then God spoke to me at that moment and said, "Look at your daughter! She's dancing in the dark. The darkness is around her but not in her. But she's dancing in the dark." If you dance long enough, weeping may endure for a night, but joy will come in the morning. It is the job of every preacher to teach the congregation to dance in the dark. Do not let the darkness find its way in you, but dance in the dark. May God bless you. May God keep you. But dance. Dance! Dance![27]

Examples fill my mind because this is the primal metaphor of my preaching: Preaching is a dance. In the words of Eugene Lowry, we are "dancing the edge of mystery."[28] Leonora Tubbs-Tisdale of Yale Divinity School claims we are "rekindling the fire within."[29] Wendell Berry exults, "What can turn us from this deserted future, back into the sphere of our being, the great dance that joins us to our home, to each other and to other creatures, to the dead and the unborn? I think it is love."[30]

This is delicious biographical celebration for me. The preachers in my childhood considered dancing a dark sin, one of the dark arts of the Dark Overlord. Nothing good came from dancing. Now, I can't stop dancing with the words in my head. The words dance as fireflies in the hot summer night, twinkling in concert with the shaking stars and the rising tides. Don't tell the preacher but I'm dancing the dance of creation with all God's creatures.

---

26. Moss, *Blue Note Preaching*, 124–25.
27. Moss, *Blue-Note Preaching*, 20–21.
28. Lowry, *Sermon*, Preface.
29. Tubbs-Tisdale, *Prophetic Preaching*, 21.
30. Berry, *Standing by Words*, 67.

With Walt Whitman I scream the primal, "I am a dance . . . Play up there! the fit is whirling me fast."[31]

The dance between preacher and congregation becomes livelier when the sermon is a conversation, a dialogue. Stephen E. Lucas, author of a basic college textbook on public speaking, gestures in the same direction by pointing out the similarities between public speaking and conversation. These similar skills include organizing your thoughts logically, tailoring your message to the audience, telling a story for maximum impact, and adapting to listener feedback.[32] In his Lyman Beecher lectures, John Claypool argued that the sermon is an ongoing conversation with a congregation.[33]

I have preaching students keep a notebook of words and conversation phrases that can later be used in the writing of sermons. For example, we read David Bentley Hart's *The Doors of the Sea* and made a list of the words that this erudite scholar uses. We put those words into sentences and discussed growing our vocabulary. My favorite word in the book: *chimera*—"for the sake of argument, let us grant this chimera a moment's life."[34] The best preachers can traverse the great gulf fixed between these two "word realms" with amazing agility.

Preaching classes also kept a notebook of conversational phrases that are copied and distributed to all the students. The list begins each week with the phrases Buttrick includes in his sample sermons in Homiletic: "Guess what?" "Well." "But look!" "Of course!" "Now do you get it?" "So, what does God say to us?" "Then, dimly, we do begin to understand." "So what happened?" "Then, of all things." "Now, do you see?"[35] Students are encouraged to note and record the conversational bits and pieces that pop in their everyday lives.

Perhaps the first American poet to write in free verse was Walt Whitman. I recommend preachers to not only read Whitman, but to immerse themselves in his poetic genius. Pick up John Marsh's *In Walt We Trust* to revel in Whitman's greatness: "Whitman's sense of the divinity of all human beings (what allows him to celebrate himself); his interest in science (every atom); his tendency to speak directly to his reader (you); his urge to study what everyone takes for granted (the spear of summer grass, in which he

---

31. Whitman, *Leaves of Grass*, 132.
32. Lucas, *Art of Public Speaking*, 5–7.
33. Claypool, *Preaching Event*.
34. Hart, *Doors of the Sea*, Kindle ed. loc. 232.
35. Buttrick, *Homiletic*.

discovers all of life and creation."³⁶ Finally read all the way to the end, as Marsh makes clear how "a queer socialist poet can save America from itself."³⁷

Whitman's tone is also rhetorical. Historian David Blight, singing Whitman's praises, exudes, "And oh! how we love Walt Whitman's fabulously open, infinite democratic spirit. We inhale Whitman's verses and are captured by the hypnotic power of democracy.³⁸ 'O Democracy, for you, for you I am trilling these songs,'"³⁹ wrote our most exuberant democrat. Blight argues that we live in an age of disinformation where the truth-tellers must scream, sing, and fight. He recommends that among our many options we simply pick up Whitman's *Song of Myself* from the opening line, "I celebrate myself, and sing myself," to his musings on the luck of merely being alive.⁴⁰

Free-verse preaching unleashes imagination and imagery to give us a new way of seeing. Or as Hauerwas puts it, "To stress the importance of vision does not imply we need a 'total vision of life,' but that the moral life is much more a matter of learning the skill to see accurately what Aristotle called 'ultimate particulars'—e.g., red wheelbarrows, kestrels, suicide, murder, lying, and so on."⁴¹ Preachers, having eyes, have to be trained to see something since we cannot simply see by looking.⁴² Furthermore, the skill required to see involves the virtues, since our vision is dependent on our character; for without the virtues, practical reason is little more than what Aristotle characterized as "cleverness."⁴³

The preacher can adopt vision, along with refractive diseases and disorders, as a metaphorical framework. Rhetorical scholars Michelle A. Holling and Dreama G. Moon "assert that the nation's vision can be sharpened in ways perhaps not seen since the Civil Rights movement." They stress that "the U.S. is experiencing the consequences of vision loss. Systemic racism, social-economic-health inequities, and anti-Blackness bear similarities to the public health problem of vision loss. When one's physical vision is lacking acuity, it can be corrected; can the same be said for the nation's vision?"⁴⁴

"Could there be," Ludwig Wittgenstein queried, "human beings lacking in the capacity to see something as something—and what would that

---

36. Marsh, *In Walt We Trust*, 18.
37. Marsh, subtitle of *In Walt We Trust*.
38. Blight, "Trump Has Birthed."
39. Whitman, "For You O Democracy," *Leaves of Grass*, 99.
40. Blight, "Trump Has Birthed."
41. Hauerwas, *Working with Words*, 289.
42. Hauerwas, *Working with Words*, 289–90.
43. Hauerwas, *Working with Words*, 290.
44. Holling and Moon, "20/20 in 2020?," 435.

be like? What sort of consequences would it have?—Would this defect be comparable to color-blindness or to not having absolute pitch?—We will call it "aspect-blindness."[45] "Enabling human populations, their potentialities and pathologies alike, to be managed with unprecedented efficiency—and, when deemed unmanageable, to be efficiently discarded—aspect-blindness turns out to encompass more than a debased ethical disposition; it turns out to name an indispensable modality of effective governance."[46]

The sheer richness of the metaphorical construct of seeing and blindness correlates with the expansive existence of blindness in the Bible. The time of Jesus was populated by more blind people it seems than the sands of the sea. Jesus even encountered blind persons in groups. Forty times "blindness" appears in the Gospels. The Gospel writers referenced blindness both as a physical disease and as a metaphor for spiritual blindness. "The man born blind"[47] serves both as physical blindness and as a sign (metaphor) for blindness. Jesus accuses the Pharisees of being "blind"[48] five times. Jesus uses sight as a metaphor: "The eye is the lamp of the body. So if your eye is healthy, your whole body will be full of light."[49] The preaching possibilities are endless. If we have eyes that see, and see clearly, we will live into a new future. Amanda Gorman's popular inaugural poem, "The Hill We Climb," beckons individual and collective cognizance that "American is more than a pride we inherit. It's the past we step into and how we repair it."[50]

POETRY AS IMITATION

Preaching begins in imitation. This imitating practice, like Benjamin Button's odd life, must gradually decrease until the preacher has her own style. *The Curious Life of Benjamin Button*, based on a short story by F. Scott Fitzgerald, tells the tale of a man who ages in reverse.[51] This is the method of imitation that preaching requires. You start by imitating the old ones and bit by bit, the imitation decreases until there is a unique style belonging to the preacher. John said of Jesus, "He must increase, but I must decrease."[52] For the preacher, this is both true and false. It is true that for the preacher

---

45. Wittgenstein, *Philosophical Investigations*, 213e.
46. Hauerwas, *Working with Words*, 36.
47. John 9.
48. Matt 23:16, 17, 19, 24, and 26.
49. Matt 6:22.
50. Gorman, "Hill We Climb." See Liu, "Read the full text."
51. Fitzgerald, *Curious Case of Benjamin Button*.
52. John 3:30.

to grow in wisdom and power, Jesus must increase as the presence in the preacher's life. It is false in the sense that the imitation of others must decrease in the preacher until it remains only as a shadow, an influence.

The preacher matriculates in the school of imitation before graduating to a personal, unique preaching experience. As a young preacher I was enthralled by the evangelist preaching at my home church. He was from Scotland. For weeks after this, I unconsciously tried to imitate the Scottish accent until my father gently told me that Southern country boy and Scottish accents don't mix and to remember that I was Irish.

A preacher also faces the task of increasing in her/his own voice while decreasing the voice of one's precursors. As James Arnt Aune puts it, "Writing and life become an intricate kind of evasion, a search for imaginative space even though everything appears to have been said before."[53] Aune, reviewing Harold Bloom's *The Anxiety of Influence*, argues that all "poets" must seek to "develop their own sense of meaning over against the contributions of their precursors."[54] In reverse of the biblical order, the precursor must decrease and the poet must increase. The precursor, at some point, must be experienced as an absence.

Bloom, in images that will warm any preacher's heart, maintains that a major trope of the poet will be kenosis (borrowed from Philippians 2:5–11, one of the first Christian poems). The poem describes Jesus as being emptied out, accepting human status. For the preacher, this emptying is a move towards discontinuity with the precursor. In each case, the precursor will, at times, become the enemy but maintain a connection with the poet. The preacher as Jacob will wrestle with the precursor until he blesses him and lets him go. Then and only then will the preacher have matured into her authentic voice, now prepared to be the precursor that trains the next generation of poet/preachers. A cinematic analogy suggests that the precursor and poet are represented by the Jedi and the foundling. The training is intense. The tasks are hard.

Imitation glows with intense brightness at first but must fade into oblivion. Imitation is like the morning glory flower—beautiful and radiant early in the morning and gone by noon. All study begins with imitation. That's how we learn. This is how children learn to speak. In a sense the learning of the language recurs in every stage of life. Preachers learn a native tongue and then must learn to speak Christian. Hauerwas says, "To

---

53. Aune, "Burke's Late Blooming," 328.
54. Aune, "Burke's Late Blooming," 329.

learn to be a Christian, to learn the discipline of the faith, is not just similar to learning another language. It is learning another language."[55]

How would one write a sermon as poetry? "The poet/prophet is a voice that shatters settled reality and evokes new possibility in the listening assembly."[56] The repetition of lines, or the use of a refrain line, is a source of enjoyment. Both evoke the old pleasure of things occurring and reoccurring—rhythm, in fact.

Consider the closing paragraph in Gardner Taylor's sermon, "The Answer to a Riddle": "We have a friend in court; Christ is gone unto his Father and has sat down on the right hand of God. He ever makes intercession. We may call on him, for he says, 'Whatsoever ye shall ask in my name, that I will do.' He can do: he sits at the right hand of God. He can help in our needy hour, for he sits at God's right hand. We have but to ask him, to call him, to talk to him, and to plead with him, for he is at the right hand of the Father."[57]

We preach by reaching for the best words, the words that explode in mid-sentence, the words that carry the freight from coast to coast, the words that lead to life. The preacher doesn't shop for words at some Walmart Word Discount store. He works in words as the sculptor works in stone. This is the way.

THE PSALMS: ORIGINATING POETRY FOR PREACHERS

Poetry may feel like more of a natural partner to the preacher than philosophy or rhetoric because there's an abundance of poetry in the Bible. From muses, priests, prophets, singers, and poets, there is a wealth of material filled with the natural symbolic language of poetry. The preacher desiring to drink deep from the living waters of the River of Poetry will be a devoted reader of the Psalms. Here we find all the twists and turns of humanity, the need for blunt honesty, and the revealing of humanity. The people who wrote and sung the psalms were a people deeply embedded in the symbolic language of the Bible. A preacher whose life has been formed by the psalms will, among many other benefits, gain a rich deposit of metaphors for preaching the truth about God, for preaching humanely, and for preaching the stark realities of good and evil in the world.

The Psalms fit the preacher like a fine leather glove. Psalms and preachers were made for each other. The liturgy of the church has a psalm

---

55. Hauerwas, *Working with Words*, 87.
56. Brueggemann, *Finally Comes the Poet*, 4.
57. Taylor, *Words of Gardner Taylor*, 16.

for every Sunday. Reading the psalms connects Christians to our Jewish roots. Our salvation's poem is written in the book of Psalms. Jessica Wilson describes her first visit to an Anglican church: "The first time I attended an Anglican church, the most surprising part of the service was when they lifted the physical book of the Bible into the air and carried it down the aisle. People turned and bowed their heads as it moved past them. Their reverence for Scripture captivated my imagination." She says she was struck that "the people of God . . . .. stood for the reading of the Word. I felt as though I had been pulled back in time to when Ezra read the law to the returning Israelites, and they all stood to hear it. Going back to Christianity's Jewish roots, the Torah was carried with worshipers all around it. The word of God was central to their worship, their culture, their very identity."[58]

When the preacher turns from the other disciplines that inform and undergird the sermon, the preacher will find inspiration from the Psalter in the tears of confession and the sacrifice God will never disdain—a broken spirit, a heart that is humble and contrite.[59] Rowan Williams says, "What is distinctive about any hermeneutic of the Psalms is that singing them is quite simply and literally an appropriation of Christ's life in history and eternity."[60]

The humanity of the psalms connects the preacher to real life. The metaphors for good and evil pour out of the psalms. The metaphors for God and the Evil One are everywhere on the pages of the psalms. Poetry and the poetic imagination, for the preacher, means immersion in the psalms. The Psalms, for Jew and Christian, is the text for reflection on good and evil. For example, consider these words of the great Jewish theologian Andre Chouraqui, in his "Introduction to the Psalms": "It is not long before we meet the Prince of Darkness on the path of wickedness. The Psalter provides him with a frightful identity card that includes no less than a hundred and twelve names, surnames, titles, and qualities. He is essentially the Racha', the one who is unable to face God's judgment, the Reprobate. He is not a single or particular individual, but the very entity of evil under all its various visages."[61]

The psalms provide a literature of dissent against evil. One of the ways the preacher can articulate the feelings of a secular culture is turning to the psalms rather than secular politics. Evangelicals would have been better served in the last decade to turn to the psalms of dissent and lament to give expression to the emotions of their people rather than the power of secular politics.

58. Wilson, *Reading for the Love of God*, 12–13.
59. Ps 50:19.
60. Williams, *On Augustine*, 20.
61. Chouraqui, "Introduction to the Psalms," 119–20.

Chouraqui's descriptive list of the Psalter's names for the innocent is likewise powerful. "At times they are also quite unexpected: [T]here are also nearly a hundred names in the Psalter to designate the hero of light: the oppressed, the afflicted, the despoiled, the tramp; the humble, the poor man, the broken hearted; the faithful, the wise; the one who trembles, the upright; the stranger, the alien to the world, the beggar; God's devotee."[62]

There exists a primal connection between God and all creation. In *Reason for Hope*, the primatologist Jane Goodall describes a scene she witnessed many times in the forests of Gombe. Goodall's subjects, the chimpanzees of the Kakombe Valley community, arrive at a particularly lush and magnificent waterfall—an eighty-foot tower of rushing water. They stop walking and begin to, in Goodall's account, "dance." This dance involves a sequence of "displays" in the direction of the waterfall. "The animals swing through the spray on hanging vines, lift up and hurl heavy rocks and branches, and rhythmically stamp their feet in the water—sometimes for more than ten minutes—though they usually prefer not to get wet."[63]

A mistrustful skepticism exists across our history in the evolution of creation. Disraeli, poking fun of evolution, remarked, "The question is this—Is man an ape or an angel? . . . My lord, I am on the side of the angels . . ."[64] Kenneth R. Miller opens his book *Only a Theory* with this quote on the lips of William F. Buckley Jr. Buckley was also attacking evolution and so have generations of conservatives and evangelicals—often with sarcasm, humor, and scoffing. Siding with the apes doesn't seem to register with these critics—humor is not usually the best form for argument to take.

We read, sing, pray, and preach the psalms of lament because the lives of those who have been destroyed by injustice can't be forgotten or silenced. Closure—meaning a finally satisfactory resolution of the problem of God's goodness in the world—is found in trust and hope, not in some explanation of the world that makes sense of evil, and still less in the claim of human power to eradicate the evil that human reason has understood.[65] The Psalter doesn't offer us a vague theodicy. Terrence Tilley argues that theodicy is a project of the status quo of power.

Tilley offers the most thorough critique of the Christian appropriations of theodicies in his *Evils of Theodicy*. He argues that theodicies often assume a utopian view of the world in which all evils would be effaced. "The reason," according to Tilley, "that a monstrous generalization, or a

---

62. Goodall and Berman, *Reason for Hope*, 188–89.
63. Schaefer, *Religious Affects*, 1.
64. Miller, *Only a Theory*, 1.
65. Bauckham, "Reading Scripture as a Coherent Story," 51.

staggering lie, can pass where a more restricted claim would be challenged is not only that it stabilizes an inherently unstable world by declaring it stable, but that it displays a world which we wished existed, a world in which evil was manageable, if not by us, at least by God. This is why the vast assertion, the mighty lie, overwhelms our faculties and puts our art of criticism out of action: it holds out the boon of stability and fulfills our wishes. Jesus's words from the cross, 'My God, my God, why have you forsaken me?' should be sufficient to render all attempts at theodicy jejune."[66] The reference to Psalm 22 insists that the psalms will have nothing to do with huge lies, political pragmatism, and expediency.

The preacher gravitates toward the Psalms because its pull has existed for centuries, first in the Hebrew poets, prophets, and priests, and then in the liturgy of the church. For the early church, the book of Psalms was clearly one of the most important and familiar books of the Bible. The Psalms have a long and honored tradition of being used every week in public worship as well as in private devotions daily. With the advent of monasticism and the piety of the ascetics, the psalms became a constant in Christian daily prayer. The desert monks memorized large portions of the Psalter (in some cases, all 150 psalms) and practiced praying the Psalms constantly as they worked. Basil of Caesarea prefaced his homily on Psalm 1 with these words: "When, indeed, the Holy Spirit saw that the human race was guided only with difficulty toward virtue, and that, because of our inclination toward pleasure, we were neglectful of an upright life, what did he do? The delight of melody he mingled with the doctrines, so that by the pleasantness and softness of the sound heard we might receive without perceiving it the benefit of the words, just as wise physicians who, when giving the fastidious rather bitter drugs to drink, frequently smear the cup with honey."[67]

Rowan Williams observes, "The very first sentence of Augustine's *Confessions* is a quotation from the Psalms, and for the rest of the work hardly a page goes by without at least one such reference. It would not be an exaggeration to say that the narrative autobiographical voice of the *Confessions* is systematically blended with the voice of the psalmist."[68]

The preacher formed by the language skills of the Psalter will sound like a pastiche of the psalms. St. Augustine calls the psalms "songs of faith, sounds of devotion that banished the heaviness of spirit."[69] In addition, he

---

66. Tilley, *Evils of Theodicy*, 248–249. Quoted in Hauerwas, *Working with Words*, 32.

67. Basil of Caesarea, Homily on Psalm 1.1, quoted in Davis and Hays, eds., *Art of Reading Scripture*, 80–82.

68. Williams, *On Augustine*, 25.

69. Augustine, *Confessions*, 9.4.8.

believed the psalms could heal the "swelling tumor of pride."[70] "I had been moved by . . . . a poem and . . . . urged toward some better attitude or apprehension of the ethical possibilities."[71]

The point of portraying the whole range of human emotions, Athanasius explains, is not simply poetic imitation, mimesis, but therapy; the person who recognizes his own inner state in the Psalms "can possess from this, once again, the image contained in the words, so that he does not simply hear them and move on, but learns what one must say and do to heal one's disordered feelings."[72] Rowan Williams says that for Augustine, "The Psalms is a meaningful narrative structure, a history of the soul. And souls only have a history in conversation with God, Augustine argues. Without the divine interlocutor, the self is broken and scattered."[73]

The psalms are deeply personal. Reading these poems will result in what rhetorical theorists call "total identification"[74] of preacher with psalmist. The psalm and its reader become one. It is as if the reader is speaking her own words and is affected by the words as if they were her own. The Psalms become

> like a mirror to the person singing them, so that he might perceive himself and the emotions of his soul, and thus affected, he might recite them. For in fact, he who hears the one reading receives the song that is recited as being about him . . . And these words, as his own, he chants to the Lord. And so, on the whole, each psalm is both spoken and composed by the Spirit so that in these same words, as was said earlier, the stirrings of our souls might be grasped, and all of them be said as concerning us, and the same issue from us as our own words, for a remembrance of the emotions in us, and a chastening of our life.[75]

The psalms are not mere devotional readings; they are sermons of the "third heaven"[76] order.

---

70. Daley, "Is Patristic Exegesis Still Usable?," *Art of Reading Scripture*, 84.
71. Smith, *Poets Beyond the Barricades*, ix.
72. Athanasius, *Epistula ad Marcellinum [Letter to Marcellinus]*, 10, 27.20–21.
73. Williams, *On Augustine*, 25.
74. Skinnell, ed., *Faking the News*, Kindle ed. loc. 281.
75. Athanasius, *Letter to Marcellinus*, 111.
76. 2 Cor 12:2.

THE PSALMS AND AFFECT THEORY

The psalms are a gushing waterfall of emotions. Mapping the affect dimensions of the psalms offers the preacher insights that might otherwise go unnoticed. What better place to turn for sermons than the poems of the psalms when we live in an age of affects (emotions). Here the preacher can interface rhetorical studies on affect theory with the psalms. Affect theory is a field of conversations emerging from queer theory, poststructuralism, feminism, and antiracist theory. Following a loose typology developed by thinkers like Sara Ahmed, Ann Cvetkovich, Mel Chen, Elspeth Probyn, and Donovan O. Schaefer, affect theory can be divided into two branches.[77] In the one stream, thinkers inspired by the philosopher Gilles Deleuze, like Patricia Ticineto Clough, Erin Manning, and Brian Massumi, identify affect as a radically precognitive, preconscious, and nonconceptual force that shapes subjectivity upstream of self-awareness.[78] I follow Lauren Berlant in affirming that political communication is *always* affectively organized: "All the messages are emotional."[79] Mapping the landscape of feeling, emotion, experience, and communication in the psalms will produce a rich tapestry of all the emotions that are possible in humanity.

Bodies, in affect theory, are coalitions of affective drivers pulling us in different directions, but loosely affiliated into a single social organism. Spinoza, one of the key background figures of affect theory, wrote that the "human body is composed of a great many individuals of different natures, each of which is highly composite."[80] Lawrence Grossberg writes that affect "encompasses a variety of ways in which we 'feel' the world in our experience, including moods, emotions, maps of what matters and of what one cares about, pleasures and desires, passions, sentiments, etc."[81] "Affect theory focuses on the messy felt composites of experience that sediment to become macrolevel political subjectivities."[82]

Affect theory gives the preacher a vocabulary for fleshing out deep emotions written large in the Psalms. The messages in the Psalms are loaded with affects. All of them are emotional. The preacher, accustomed to a method of thinking rationally, will benefit from experiencing the Psalms

---

77. Ahmed, *Promise of Happiness*; Chen, *Animacies*; Cvetkovich, *Depression*; Probyn, "A-ffect"; Schaefer, *Religious Affects*.

78. Clough, "Introduction"; Manning, *Always More than One*; Massumi, *Parables for the Virtual*. See also Deleuze, *Spinoza*.

79. Berlant, "Trump, or Political Emotions."

80. Spinoza, *Ethics*, 44.

81. Grossberg, *Under the Cover of Chaos*, 11.

82. Schaefer, "Whiteness and Civilization," 3.

emotionally. For example, "My God, my God, why have you forsaken me?" You have to feel the psalms to preach Psalms.

Without damaging the historical meanings of the Psalms for Israel, Christians read the texts metaphorically and this opens the door to the Psalms as presenting a unity between God and humanity that culminates in Jesus. Williams asserts,

> Jesus speaks in the voice of the suffering Christian. This principle is of particular significance where texts in the Psalter express spiritual desolation and struggle: the Psalms are the words of Jesus, the Word who speaks in all scripture. But how can we understand words that imply alienation from God when they occur on the lips of Jesus? Only by reading them as spoken by the whole Christ, that is Christ with all the members of his Body. He speaks for us, makes his own the protesting or troubled cry of the human being, so that his own proper and perfect prayer to the Father may become ours.[83]

This means that Psalms are the words of preachers from the pulpit every Sunday morning.

There's this deep identification of the preacher with Christ. As Williams puts it, "Singing the Psalms, in this perspective, becomes a means of learning what it is to inhabit the Body of Christ and to be caught up in Christ's prayer."[84] "The meaning of our salvation is that we are included in his life, given the right to speak with his divine voice, reassured that what our human voices say out of darkness and suffering has been owned by him as his voice, so that it may in some way be opened to the life of God for healing or forgiveness."[85]

The gamut of human emotions inhabits the Psalms as if they were the beating heart of every person to ever face the trials of life. All the usual pretense falls away as brutal honesty between the psalmists and God erupts in Psalms. Chouraqui says, God's people "had carried this book with them when they went into exile; they experienced each and every one of its verses in their own flesh, in their own blood. This book was something written down; but they lived it even as they read it, and it was no less necessary to live this book than to read it. This book was their own drama, their own hope; it caught them up even as it crucified them: for it held the key to their own mystery."[86]

---

83. Williams, *On Augustine*, 27.
84. Ps 85:1.
85. Williams, *On Augustine*, 28.
86. Chouraqui, "Introduction to the Psalms," 4.

The pain and sorrow of Israel can be felt in the Psalms. Wittgenstein argued that if we showed no outward signs of pain, we could not even learn the meaning of words. If we are not of one piece with the language of pain, suffering, and sorrow, naming our pain would make no sense.[87]

The Psalms are the scars of the body of God—the people of Israel. These are both emotional and physical scars. The psalmists never attempt to hide the scars as if all Israel ever needed was a gifted plastic surgeon. The scars that are the Psalms are meant to stick out to indicate the sign of the injury. The body of Israel has been shaped by their injuries, reminding us that scars shape the body. The Psalms might be considered good scars because they expose the effects of injustice; "signs of an unjust contact between our bodies and others."[88] The scars never become invisible; they are seen, remembered, and made part of the life of God's people.

Israel's life was lived in the presence of God with nothing held back. They celebrated God and they blamed God. Samuel D. Proctor tells the story of a fellow student who had experienced more physical maladies than any group of forty other persons. On his appointed day to preach, the student asked the class to sing a hymn with him. It was the student's hymn—"On Jordan's Stormy Banks I Stand." Proctor remembers that after the hymn the student "did not need to give a sermon . . . He had convinced us all that from the worst of circumstances, from his pit of agony, it is possible to discover that God is alive, alive, aware, and able to sustain us in the total range of human situations [and emotions]."[89]

Preachers often face congregants and a culture riddled with rage, anger, resentment, disgust, and even shame. The Psalms have the power to change us and act as a corrective to affects that are out of kilter. The Psalms are a prescription for the treatment of these emotional maladies. The deep emotional messages of the Psalms offer us a form of therapy for what ails our culture, bodies mobilized by the unruly matrix of dense affects working their way through us.

The Psalter contains the hand-wringing collection of the basic question, "Why?" "Why do the nations conspire and the peoples plot in vain?" (2:1). "Why, O Lord, do you stand far off? Why do you hide yourself in times of trouble?" (10:1). "My God, my God, why have you forsaken me? Why are you so far from helping me, from the words of my groaning?" (22:1). "Why are you cast down, O my soul, and why are you disquieted within me? Hope in God, for I shall again praise him, my help" (42:5; 42:11; 43:5). "I

---

87. Wittgenstein, *Philosophical Investigations*, sec. 257, 92.
88. Ahmed, *Cultural Politics of Emotion*, Kindle ed. loc. 4653.
89. Proctor, *"How Shall They Hear?"*, 32.

say to God, my rock, 'Why have you forgotten me? Why must I walk about mournfully because the enemy oppresses me?'" (42:9). "For you are the God in whom I take refuge; why have you cast me off? Why must I walk about mournfully because of the oppression of the enemy?" (43:2). "Why do you sleep, O Lord? Awake, do not cast us off forever!" (44:23). "Why do you hide your face? Why do you forget our affliction and oppression?" (44:24). "Why should I fear in times of trouble, when the iniquity of my persecutors surrounds me?" (49:5). "O God, why do you cast us off forever? Why does your anger smoke against the sheep of your pasture?" (74:1). "Why do you hold back your hand; why do you keep your hand in your bosom?" (74:11). "O Lord, why do you cast me off? Why do you hide your face from me?"(88:14). "Why should the nations say, 'Where is their God?'" (115:2).

Here the preacher can make use of the spiritual depth of the Psalms to deal with the feelings of the congregation. This means the sermon will not be a group therapy lesson in pop psychology or the best-selling book of the positive thinking guru du jour. Let's face it. The preacher can't get by with only "common sense and a subscription to *Psychology Today*."[90]

The Psalms do not land on a flat plain. They actively seek out the feelings, desires, and affects of the audience. These desires are ultimately a configuration of affects. As Brian L. Ott and Greg Dickinson write, "[A]ffective aesthetics links the sensual, immediate, and prediscursive responses of bodies to specific environmental energies with historically situated discursive processes and practices."[91]

When national leaders deliberately use rhetorical tropes of demolition, destruction, despair, and demonization, the preacher can respond with the poetry of the Psalms. For example, the repudiation of anchor institutions that have become garden variety fodder for demagogues finds repudiation in the Psalms. Jerusalem, in the Bible, represents all the institutions of God and nation and people. The psalmists praise and defend Jerusalem. Psalm 51:18 exhorts, "Do good to Zion in your good pleasure; rebuild the walls of Jerusalem." Psalm 122:1–6 reads, "I was glad when they said to me, 'Let us go to the house of the Lord!'"

When the anchor institutions of the nation are under attack from the rhetoric of demagogues, the preacher has ample resources for rebuttal from the Psalms. The Psalms provide us with our rudimentary language training in speaking the words of God. Our spiritual vocabulary can be shaped by the Psalms. When a people have more experiences of an element, they acquire more words for describing it. For example, the Sami people, who

---

90. Buttrick, *Homiletic*, Kindle ed. loc. 5305.
91. Ott and Dickinson, *Twitter Presidency*, 31.

live in the northern tips of Scandinavia and Russia, have as many as a thousand words for "reindeer."[92] The Psalms, similarly, have almost one hundred words for God.

The Psalms are a dialogue between God and the poet, the poet and the people, God and the poet and the communion of saints across the ages. Like the parables of Jesus, the Psalms relate the impossible wonders of God's acts that upend conventional ways of thinking and acting. The Psalms repeat the sounding joy of God's steadfast love and faithfulness in the midst of adversity, awful enemies, and death. Praise rises to the heavens and descends to Sheol to break the dullness, anger, and fear of the daily grind. Such praise is an act of basic trust in Almighty God. Issues of justice and injustice rise to the surface in the dialogue of the Psalms. Since the exodus has left its tracks all over the Psalms, the primal cry of the Hebrew slaves is heard throughout the Psalms and so is God's response.

The humanity of the Psalms shows up most concretely in the psalms of lament. The lament is a liturgical act, set in the temple where the innocent seek justice and plead for acquittal.[93] Imagine the different outcome if those who feel ignored, left out, and persecuted adjudicated their feelings of unjust treatment in the Temple—the house of God—in the church. Rather than turning to the political arena, God's people would turn to God's house.

Preachers have an alternative resource for the vast range of negative emotions that are impacting them at every level. Instead of turning to secular political rhetoric and power, I believe that the resource that best meets the emotional needs of evangelicals can be found in the book of Psalms. I argue the psalms of lament are contained in one of the last seven words of Jesus from the cross, "My God, my God why have you forsaken me?"[94] The voice of the exiles in Psalm 137—"How can we sing the Lord's song in a foreign land?"—are now contained in the cry of Jesus. Singing the Lord's song requires going through death to resurrection. The one who previously felt forsaken is now the one crowned Lord and King.

I am interested in how our sermons work as they aim at the affects (emotions) of our congregations. We can learn how to convert lament into praise rather than converting shame into a fake dignity. The most appropriate response to shame is for the preacher to make the huge affirmation of St. Paul, "I am not ashamed of the gospel." The moving words of David Bartlett in his opening Lyman Beecher Lectures ring true now as then: "The first time I came to Yale Divinity School was to hear my father deliver the

---

92. Recio, "One Thousand Words for Reindeer."
93. Brueggemann, *Psalms*, Kindle ed. loc. 167–69.
94. Matt 27:46; Mark 15:34.

Beecher Lectures from the high pulpit in Marquand Chapel. When I discovered this year we have the lectures at this splendid setting at Bethesda, I was only slightly disappointed that I would not be able to stand where my father stood. But in the more important sense, I hope I stand exactly where he stood: for I am not ashamed of the gospel."[95] And to that I say "Amen."

Emotional forces, many of them operating at the subconscious level, dominate our decisions. "The forces run through us, we are made by them, and our decisions reflect the priorities of those forces rather than an abstract assessment of the world around us according to a standard of detached calculation. This resonates with the fundamental insight of rhetorical studies, namely, that communication is not (necessarily) effective because it appeals to the machinery of rational persuasion. Instead, rhetoric works on listeners through a range of devices that are not necessarily thoughtful—nor even necessarily discursive."[96]

Christians often struggle with the material, fleshly, bodily aspect of being human. Gnosticism has made more inroads into our Christian experience than we might realize. I grew up in a faith tradition that mistrusted all things of the "flesh." In a reminder of how important words are to our faith, we constructed an entirely misleading moral edifice around our misreading of the word "flesh." Having been told in Scripture that we are not to live according to the flesh, we abhorred all things fleshly, and this made us gnostics. Our efforts to not live in the flesh caused us to make everything "spiritual." Our preachers affected a particular tone or accent that was more than Southern; it was supposed to be what "holy" sounds like.

The Gnosticism in the Baptist DNA makes for discomfort. After all, it is hard to get fleshlier than, "This is my body," and "This is my blood." Hauerwas makes the daunting suggestion that "if Christianity is really about the spiritual then we are pretty much left alone to do what we want with the stuff that really matters—that is the body, sex, and money."[97] We have a fleshly, material, bodily faith that is also a bundle of emotions. This is especially relevant to the collection of a series of negative emotions like rage, anger, fear, shame, and resentment. In Sara Ahmed's language, these emotions possess "stickiness"[98]—they stick together, and they stick to people who are demeaned.

Issues as complex and potentially harmful as stickiness require a sort of interlude as a specific example of how preachers are to preach about

---

95. Bartlett, *What's Good about This News?*, 6.
96. Schaefer, "Whiteness and Civilization," 3–4.
97. Hauerwas, *In Good Company*, 35.
98. Ahmed, *Cultural Politics of Emotion*.

human emotions. As preachers, our attempts at "emotional proof" must expand from touchy-feely "Praise the Lord" to the more complex feelings that animate so many American churches. Emotions accumulate over time, as a form of affective value. This is why social transformation is so difficult to achieve. The emotions of previous generations are cast in stone, and the origin of the emotion is erased—its history of production and circulation denied or obliterated. Ironically, this is the very method that evangelicals are using in the attempt to deny systemic racism. This is behind an excessive devotion to patriotism.

The primary affect of the evangelical history is that of "disgust." Disgust works to produce the disgusting. In what passes for righteous indignation, "disgust" becomes the weapon deployed to eject the "disgusting" ones from the community. Disgust is a major form that stickiness takes. It sticks objects together. The words "That's disgusting" reveals an entire ancient history of revulsion, rejection, and resentment. "Horrifying things stick, like glue, like slime." Jean-Paul Sartre, reflecting on slime, says, "It clings to me like a leech."[99]

Stickiness relates to fear. Fear is bound up with the loss of the object. For Freud, fear is indeed part of the story of loss in that one also fears the loss of the object of love. In the evangelical world, there is a powerful fear that their object of love—a Christian nation—is in danger of being lost.

Repetition has a binding effect. Say the word "fag" often enough and it has particular effects on others. The use of the word also blocks the word from acquiring a new value. Evangelicals actively attempt to block the acquisition of new values for the word by screaming "political correctness." This is an attempt to salvage the stickiness of the word that has a long history as an affect of articulation. This is how Fred Phelps was able to have a banner headline on his church website: "GOD HATES FAGS!"

Gays, women, and minorities have suffered through the centuries. Histories of colonialism, slavery, abuse, and violence shape their lives in the present. Their scars are evidence of past injuries. When evangelicals insist that they were not alive in that past and should not be held responsible, they are denying that "stickiness" and emotions have kept those awful histories alive, even when they are not consciously admitted, remembered, or repented of. Isn't it time for mercy to make a new appearance in the preaching of evangelicals?

The time of emotion is not always in the past. Emotions also open up futures. Things that are stuck together can become unstuck. The objects of emotions slide and stick and they join the intimate histories of bodies. With

---

99. Sartre, *Sketch for a Theory of the Emotions*, 609.

a different orientation, we can passionately work to create stickiness between justice, love, hospitality, forgiveness, diversity, acceptance, inclusion, and empathy. We can be part of an entire new vocabulary of "sticky" words—words that create a new world where the "disgusting" no longer exists.

Preachers not only speak to the specific context of the local community. We also speak to all those who have ever lived, especially those buried under centuries of dark soil. We address the "communion of all humanity"—past, present, and future.

The other preliminary consideration has to do with the subconscious mind that hosts our jangle of emotions. George Lakoff, in *The Political Mind*, insists that most of our decisions are made subconsciously in our emotions. According to Lakoff, progressives are still stuck in an eighteenth-century understanding of the mind. The tendency is to believe that people are universally rational, unemotional, and interest based. And in every case progressives are wrong.[100]

When we, as preachers, are unconscious of the impact of the unconscious mind, "we will think that we do not have any need to appeal to emotion—indeed, to do so would be wrong! We will not have to speak of values; facts and figures will suffice. We will not have to change people's brains; their reason should be enough. We will not have to frame the facts; they will speak for themselves."[101] And we will be wrong! Lakoff takes no prisoners here: "You will be ignoring the cognitive unconscious, not stating your deepest values, suppressing legitimate emotions, accepting the other side's frames as if they were neutral, cowering with fear at what you might be called, and refusing to frame the facts so that they can be appreciated. You will be ineffective. In a word, wimpy."[102]

The lament, in its raw humanness, offers authentic expression of real life and the deepest emotions. The lament can be a way forward for churches pushing the limits of secular political power. Brueggemann notes, "The lament makes clear that faith and worship deal with and are shaped by life as it comes to us."[103]

"Israel unflinchingly saw and affirmed that life as it comes, along with joys, is beset by hurt, betrayal, loneliness, disease, threat, anxiety, bewilderment, anger, hatred, and anguish. The study of the lament may suggest a corrective to the euphoric, celebrative notions of faith that romantically

---

100. Lakoff, *Political Mind*.
101. Lakoff, *Political Mind*, Kindle ed. loc. 251.
102. Lakoff, *Political Mind*, Kindle ed. loc. 251.
103. Brueggemann, *Psalms and the Life of Faith*, Kindle ed. loc. 839.

pretend that life is sweetness and joy, even delight."[104] I am struck by the irony of euphoric, celebrative, charismatic worship in evangelical churches on Sunday mixed with emotions of hurt, anger, betrayal, persecution, threat, anxiety, precarity, bewilderment, hatred, anguish, resentment, and outrage. Where do these two oceans of emotions meet? Watching the evangelical dance is watching cold air from the Arctic meeting a warm front from the Gulf and spawning vicious weather and killer tornados.

Israel viewed the hurts and pains of life as crises of faith; evangelicals now meet hurts and pains as political crises. John Claypool, in his grief after the death of his eight-year-old daughter Laura Lou, preached a series of sermons that are a lament in modern language. Claypool said, "We do not first get all the answers and then live in the light of our understanding. We must rather plunge into life meeting what we have to meet and experiencing what we have to experience and in the light of living try to understand. If insight comes at all, it will not before, but only through and after experience."[105]

The Psalms show us people feeling conflicted, feeling ignored, feeling trapped, feeling besieged, feeling tired, feeling persecuted, feeling muted—with no voice. Roderick P. Hart, in *Trump and Us: What He Says and Why People Listen*, traces the same emotions in evangelicals.[106] American historian John Fea chronicles evangelicals in the USA as riddled with fear, lusting for political power, and soaked in the melancholy of nostalgia. These dense affects have led evangelicals to embrace "a highly problematic interpretation of the relationship between Christianity and the American founding. It is playbook that too often gravitates toward nativism, xenophobia, racism, intolerance, and an unbiblical view of American exceptionalism. It is a playbook that divides rather than unites."[107]

Evangelicals are clinging to a world that has passed away. They refuse to let it go in peace and see it as a loss that is unbearable. They have trouble seeing a new world being formed and given by the grace of God. The postmodern, post-truth world has created a brokenness among evangelicals. They are seeking to heal this rupture with secular, political power in the name of Jesus. What they experience as loss is actually lack. Thus, they are melancholic and in a sense without hope. They wish to return to an enchanted world that has been destroyed. It never was as they thought it was. It is a lack.[108]

104. Brueggemann, *Psalms and the Life of Faith*, Kindle ed. loc. 839–42.
105. Claypool, *Tracks of a Fellow Struggler*, 12.
106. Hart, *Trump and Us*.
107. Fea, *Believe Me*, 10.
108. Biesecker, "No Time for Mourning."

The times of disorientation are those when persons are driven to the extremities of emotion, of integrating capacity, and of language. In the company of Isaiah, we are "undone."[109] There is no speech, and there is no safe reality about which to speak. "The loss of an orderly life is linked to a loss of language, or at least to a discovery of the inadequacy of conventional language."[110] Human persons are not meant for situations of disorientation. They will struggle against such situations with all their energies. Insofar as people are hopeful and healthy, they may grow and work through to a new orientation. But as Freud has seen, human people are mostly inclined to look back, to grasp old equilibria, to wish for them, and to deny that they are gone. Periods of disorientation evoke the dangerous language of extremity, which may express hope but more likely resistance, destruction, and demolition.[111]

Preachers in our highly politicized culture face an unrelenting nostalgia for a return to a time when America was Christian, great, and white people ruled. This is an illusion, but it is a powerful affect. Preachers and politicians appeal to their followers' "memories of a bygone era in which enjoyed the unearned assets of [white, male] privilege."[112] Historian John Fea says, "For too long, white evangelical Christians have engaged in public life through a strategy defined by the politics of fear, the pursuit of worldly power, and a nostalgic longing for a national past that may have never existed in the first place. Fear. Power. Nostalgia."[113]

These feelings are prominent in the Psalms. But the Psalms often move to a new way of life. While the temptation is to believe that the old time of orientation can be recovered, that is rejected as illusion. The replacement is a mood of hope. "This mood leaves the impression that the speaker believes that the loss of orientation is reversible, and the old orientation is retrievable."[114]

Psalm 88, for example, speaks to our nation. It is a situation of unrelieved lament and disorientation. It ends in hopelessness. While it may seem strange to think of evangelical pushback against a liberal culture as a kind of melancholy, that is precisely what I believe has happened. "More precisely,

---

109. Isa 6:5.

110. Brueggemann, *Psalms*, Kindle ed. loc. 200. See also Lischer, *End of Words*; Taylor, *When God Is Silent*; Grassi, *Rhetoric as Philosophy*; and Funk, *Language, Hermeneutic, and the Word of God.*.

111. Brueggemann, *Psalms*, Kindle ed. loc. 199–204.

112. Ott and Dickinson, *Twitter Presidency*, 41.

113. Fea, *Believe Me*, 11.

114. Brueggemann, *Psalms and the Life of Faith*, Kindle ed. loc. 226–29.

it is one of a melancholic rhetoric's primary effects."[115] Following Biesecker's analysis of melancholy, I find the evangelical commitment to secular politics to be the material upshot of a carefully crafted and meticulously managed melancholic rhetoric whose distinct features are: one, the discursive transfiguration of a historical and political fiction, namely that America was born as a Christian nation, into a ubiquitous trope now deployed to position all liberals as unpatriotic Americans; and two, a verbal and visual rhetoric of repetition. The specific aim of this melancholic rhetoric is the formation of a public/"Christian" "political will" that, with considerable irony, cede the power of the citizenry to the remilitarized, religious state for the sake of protecting what will have been lost: namely, the democratic way of life. To preach this melancholic message is to preach death.

In the language of the Psalms, the evangelicals are preaching lament, not as outrage against injustice, but as a melancholic message of fear, anger, and resentment. Such preaching is not worthy of the label "gospel." The confusion of legitimate emotion raging against injustice with fear, anger, and resentment borders on blasphemy. In the same way, white males now attempt to claim they are persecuted and inhabit a land of precarity rather than the poor who are actually living and breathing physical, material precarity.

Evangelicals have a lament with only one part: it raises the oldest fears, the censured question, the deepest hates, the venom, and a yearning for a recovery of the past. They have cut off the praise part of the lament that anticipates the future as gift, that looks ahead, consents to receive and intends to respond in gratitude.

THE PSALMS—A GOLD MINE OF METAPHORS

The Psalms swim in an ocean of powerful metaphors. Poetry always provides us with more metaphorical expressions than the preacher can use. Metaphor is our hope. This language has a creative function. It does not simply follow reality and reflect it, but it leads reality to become what it is not. Metaphor possesses epistemic power to produce a new reality in the face of an oppressive old reality. The preacher hunts for these metaphors day and night, for they possess the light and hope and courage that the people require.

Thus, the openness to the universal and the passion for the concrete come together in these poems.[116] The "language event" of the lament thus permits movement beyond naivete and acceptance of one's actual situation

---

115. Biesecker, "No Time for Mourning," 147.
116. Brueggemann, *Psalms and the Life of Faith*, Kindle ed. loc. 392–94.

critically.[117] Metaphors possess an epistemic power to make a new way of being—a new reality.

The Psalms evoke and form new realities that did not exist until, or apart from, the actual singing of the song. Thus, the speech of the new song does not just recognize what is given, but evokes it, calls it into being, forms it. Israel's hymnic assertion "Yahweh is king" is not just a description of Yahweh the king but evokes Yahweh to kingship. It calls Yahweh to the throne.[118] The function of the Psalms is to bring forth new realities.

The Psalms are metaphors writ large. Psalms are strategies for dealing with situations, as Burke suggests of proverbs.[119] Another way of thinking of the Psalms might be attitudes. A person who life has been formed by the Psalms develops attitudes about God that are strong and hopeful, attitudes about evil that are realistic, and attitudes about life that transcend tragedy, suffering, and pain. The attitude of the psalmist that is human reality can attain the state of celebration not in returning to the good old days, or an old, safe religious world where God was what we said God was, but instead is a new way of living. The desire to return to the old primal symbols must be treated with suspicion because it is the wrong direction to go for people who are being set free from oppression. The redescription of reality in terms of positive celebration has a lament behind it that decisively cuts it off from the primal. There is no return. The second creation is a new one and not a return to the first one. Thus, the hymn of celebration is not regressive, but anticipatory. The preacher can preach the doxologies of the Psalms with confidence because there are times when theology enters the third heaven in those doxological expressions.

There is no return to the "good old days." There is no longer a naïve, enchanted world. This is not about going back to the old. It is about progressing to the new. The people of God are not called to live around the foot of the mountain, but to climb it, as Robert Frost insists: "I've always meant to go / And look myself, but you know how it is: / It doesn't seem so much to climb a mountain / You've worked around the foot of all your life."[120] There can be no return to an old, safe religious world where God was on the throne and all was well. The second creation is a new one and not simply a repeat of the first one.

---

117. Brueggemann, *Psalms and the Life of Faith*, Kindle ed. loc. 398–405. In *A Secular Age* Charles Taylor writes on the enchanted world and the disenchanted world, making the same points.

118. Brueggemann, *Psalms and the Life of Faith*, Kindle ed. loc. 408–10.

119. Burke, "Literature as equipment for living," 293–94.

120. Frost, "Mountain," in *Poetry of Robert Frost*, 43.

THE POETRY OF JUBILEE

The Psalms also have a deeply economic poetry—the poetry of Jubilee. The poet expresses God's intention of returning all property to previous owners. Jubilee is the great equalizing of the disparities of a hyper-capitalistic system. According to Leviticus, "Every fifty years you must give back to the people the land and property that is inalienably theirs that they have lost in the rough and tumble of the economy. You must give it back, even if you own it legally and it is properly yours . . . So, imagine, when the yabal sounds, when the signal is given, everybody returns property, everybody cancels debts, everybody breaks off the mad scramble of accumulation and acquisition."[121]

The road to Jubilee is paved with failure, repeated failure as poets/preachers lose their nerve and words lack power. A different language, a new language, with more powerful words is required for Jubilee to have a ghost of a chance in our greed-infested culture. Poetry has always had a love affair with words. There's no waste or superficiality or flat prose in poetry. Such words would be thrown out with the trash. Poetry has no patience with diminished speech because diminished speech leads to diminished lives.

Good word hunters will naturally go to the house of poetry. The disciples of Jesus once fished all night and caught nothing. Turns out they were fishing on the wrong side of the boat. Jesus says to the disciples, "'Cast the net to the right side of the boat, and you will find some.' So they cast it, and now they were not able to haul it in because there were so many fish."[122] Catching the right words, like catching fish, depends upon fishing in the right spot. A preacher, in the company of Jesus, learns to fish for the right words, the best words, for the sermon.

As a country preacher, I live in a world of country images. When I went fishing with my father as a young boy, he would catch four of five fish in a row while I didn't even get a nibble. I would then put my fishing line right next to his and still no bites. He would smile and tell me, "You aren't holding your mouth right." I think that happens to us as preachers at times. We are not saying our words as well as we should. Something is off-key and it's in the words.

We are tempted to think, "Any old words will do." Such a thought is a death sentence to great preaching. If we think that any old stick can preach and any old words are enough, we will get what we have invested, any old kind of response. All preachers string words together to stitch out a sermon

---

121. Brueggemann, *Collected Sermons* 2:140–41.
122. John 21:6.

in a pattern, but not all strings are equal. Some are merely a ball of string. Other strings are wimpy like half-cooked spaghetti falling on the floor from the boiling pot of water. Then there are strings full of brightly colored lights that show the way in the darkness. These are the true words of the great preacher.

The discovery of the best words is a crucial part of the preaching task. "I don't want to diminish the art, the imagination that's involved."[123] Doris Betts reflecting on the right word to use, says, "It's that soul-searching, that sensitivity. And it doesn't have anything to do with how educated they were, just with how vividly they lived. How much they paid attention. Religion makes you pay attention." Check out Madeline L'Engle's essay where she's looking after her grandmother, and she says, "And now I will go on loving her as long as this dwindling may last."

"Dwindling, Betts thought, that's the best word, and the loving that can cope with that is the best, too. But 'dwindling'; when I read it, I just shook. Some words are so right, they do feel sacred. See, that's one place where I find a link between scripture and other kinds of writing: that sacredness of words in works that are ostensibly secular, when I think, yes, there it is!"[124]

Brueggemann says that the paucity of truth in our culture requires the preacher "to be poets that speak against a prose world."[125] He adds, "Those whom the ancient Israelites called prophets, the equally ancient Greeks called poets. The poet/prophet is a voice that shatters settled reality and evokes new possibility in the listening assembly."[126]

Cornel West, in a similar vein, argues that the prophetic voice and the Socratic dialogue are two of our most essential weapons against the dogmas of authoritarianism, aggressive militarism, and free-market fundamentalism. West says, "Three crucial traditions fuel deep democratic energies. The first is the Greek creation of the Socratic commitment to questioning, also Jewish invention of the prophetic commitment to justice—for all peoples. And indispensable is the mighty shield and inner strength provided by the tragicomic commitment to hope."[127]

West may have been reading Brueggemann, who explains: "that public power is everywhere wielded and administered by those with concentrations of wealth, who thereby control the supply of money, who control the legislation that governs credit and debt, and who fund (or refuse to fund) military

---

123. Ketchin, ed., *Christ-Haunted Landscape*, Kindle ed. loc. 3951–52.
124. Ketchin, ed., *Christ-Haunted Landscape*, Kindle ed. loc. 3502–7.
125. Brueggemann, *Finally Comes the Poet*, Kindle ed. loc. 56.
126. Brueggemann. *Finally Comes the Poet*, Kindle ed. loc. 70–71.
127. West, *Democracy Matters*, 16.

adventurism and technological advances that are often in the service of the military."[128] As Alasdair MacIntyre puts it, "The modern nation-state, in whatever guise, is a dangerous and unmanageable institution, presenting itself on the one hand as a bureaucratic supplier of goods and services, which is always about to, but never actually does, give its clients value for money, and on the other as a repository of sacred values, which from time to time invites one to lay down one's life on its behalf. As I have remarked elsewhere it is like being asked to die for the telephone company."[129]

The powers and principalities want no poetry in the realm. Poetry dismantles power. As Brueggemann puts it, "The newly claimed territory becomes a new home of freedom, justice, peace, and abiding joy. This happens when the poet comes, when the poet speaks, when the preacher comes as poet."[130] Poetry opens the possibility for Jubilee, but the ruler of this present arrangement on behalf of the rich will not yield willingly.

Perhaps the greatest example of the power of poetry to fuel a new reality arose when Vaclav Havel, poet, threw off the shackles of communism in Czechoslovakia. His poetic dissent took out the power of the state military. Havel asked, for example, why Solzhenitsyn was thrown out of Russia. His response: "Solzhenitsyn's expulsion was something else: a desperate attempt to plug up the dreadful wellspring of truth, a truth which might cause incalculable transformations in social consciousness, which in turn might one day produce political debacles unpredictable in their consequences."[131] If you take an imaginary trip down the corridors of history you will hear kingdoms, empires, dictatorships, and beast-kings sounding like clods of dirt falling on ancient coffins. Isaiah voiced the reality for all tyrants: "How you are fallen from heaven, O Day Star, son of Dawn!" In place of Day Star, or Lucifer (if you follow Blake) place the name of any old tyrant because if you have seen one tyrant you have seen them all. David Livingston Smith unveils the multiple reasons that humans demean, enslave, and exterminate one another.[132] Short answer: because they can. Longer answer: They can because they have the name of a god to use in carrying out the monstrosities of their imagination. Preaching stands against all of this horror. Smith ventures a powerful answer: "Subhumans, it was believed, are beings that lack that special something that makes us human. Because of this deficit, they don't command the respect that we, the truly human beings,

---

128. Brueggemann, *Truth Speaks to Power*, 2.
129. Quoted in Hauerwas, *In Good Company*, 26.
130. Brueggemann, *Finally Comes the Poet*, Kindle ed. loc. 155–56.
131. Havel, *Power of the Powerless*, 42.
132. Smith, *Less Than Human*.

are obliged to grant one another. They can be enslaved, tortured, or even exterminated—treated in ways in which we could not bring ourselves to treat those whom we regard as members of our own kind. This phenomenon is called dehumanization."[133]

Poetry is counter-truth to the dehumanizing of the established truth of the world of political power. In the Old Testament, truth is carried by song, oracle, and narrative that continually subvert official truth. "In the New Testament, that counter-truth is carried by Jesus and his followers, a community that regularly and with great risk subverts and bewilders the establishment and so turns the 'world upside down' (Acts 17:6). The occupants of power are, of necessity, always seeking out versions of truth that are compatible with present power arrangements."[134] That means no Jubilee. God's poets propose a counter-truth that brings Jubilee. The preacher, as poet/prophet, proclaims the counter-truth. This makes the current marriage of evangelical faith with political power idolatrous.

To speak of, about, or for God, poetry is required. No other language suffices. When God brought the Israelites to Mount Sinai, the poetic description of how that happened takes the breath away. God says, "I bore you on eagle's wings and brought you to myself." There on Mount Sinai, where the voice of God resides, is also the house of poetry. To speak of poetry is not to speak of nursery rhymes or soft words. Poetry is frightening. There was thunder and lightning, as well as a thick cloud on the mountain, and a blast of a trumpet so loud that all the people who were in the camp trembled. "Moses brought the people out of the camp to meet God. They took their stand at the foot of the mountain. Now Mount Sinai was wrapped in smoke, because the Lord had descended upon it in fire; the smoke went up like the smoke of a kiln, while the whole mountain shook violently. As the blast of the trumpet grew louder and louder, Moses would speak, and God would answer him in thunder."[135]

And the people were afraid. I do not blame them in the slightest. God is frightening. Hauerwas says, "Indeed, I sometimes think the reason that Protestants, and in particular Methodists, are more likely to believe in the 'real absence' rather than the 'real presence' is that God just scares the hell out of us—and for good reason if God is just this God of Abraham, Isaac, Jacob, and Jesus."[136]

---

133. Smith, *Less Than Human*, 2.
134. Brueggemann, *Truth Speaks to Power*, 3–4.
135. Exod 19:17–19.
136. Hauerwas, *In Good Company*, 37–38.

Barbara Brown Taylor, one of our most gifted poet/preachers, demonstrates the use of the right words: "According to the book of Exodus, all the people were there. Not one of them missed it: God's own voice, with thunder in it and lightning cracking all around; the sound of a trumpet none of them knew how to play, with notes that made their scalps crawl; the mountain itself, smoking like a kiln, shaking so violently that the ground slid beneath their feet."[137] Do not dare miss the reality that the poet of all poets, the mother of all poets, is God.

God's poetry begins in the cry of the Israelites. The necessity of Jubilee begins here. Pharaoh, the symbol of all anti-Jubilee movements, can only be defeated by God's Words—poetic words of Jubilee. "Then the Lord said, 'I have observed the misery of my people who are in Egypt; I have heard their cry on account of their taskmasters. Indeed, I know their sufferings, and I have come down to deliver them from the Egyptians, and to bring them up out of that land to a good and broad land, a land flowing with milk and honey."[138] This is where poetry begins and belongs—as voice for the voiceless, as liberator of the oppressed. Moses was God's poet facing off with Pharaoh. "Thus you shall say to the Israelites, 'I am has sent me to you.' God also said to Moses, 'Thus you shall say to the Israelites, "The Lord, the God of your ancestors, the God of Abraham, the God of Isaac, and the God of Jacob, has sent me to you": This is my name for ever, and this my title for all generations.'"[139]

This has always been God's poetry. Jesus, reading from the poet Isaiah, who was channeling the primal poet—God—announces: "The Spirit of the Lord is upon me, because he has anointed me to bring good news to the poor. He has sent me to proclaim release to the captives and recovery of sight to the blind, to let the oppressed go free, to proclaim the year of the Lord's favor."[140] Poetry begins at the throne of grace with the Spirit of the Lord. The poet is the one of whom it is said, "The Spirit of the Lord is upon me." The poem is good news for all people—the poor, the captives, the blind, the oppressed. The poem's creative words produce God's purpose: Jubilee. The poem of Jubilee is the poem the world has been waiting for since God heard the cries of his oppressed people way back there in Egypt. Jubilee is not good news for the rich and the mighty. As Mary's poem proclaimed, "He

---

137. Taylor, *When God is Silent*, 58.
138. Exod 3: 7–8.
139. Exod 3:13–15.
140. Luke 4:18–19.

has brought down the powerful from their thrones and lifted up the lowly; he has filled the hungry with good things and sent the rich away empty."[141]

At the heart of God's poetry there is always Jubilee—the concrete, material, economic act that gives back to the poor all they have lost. Guess what? The poetry rises from the most unexpected of the books of Torah—Leviticus. "God wants the little ones, who always lose in the market game, to have their stuff."[142] Reparations are a drop in the bucket compared to Jubilee. God put the Jubilee poem on the lips of Moses. Brueggemann explains, "Moses observed the working of the market, the practice of accumulation and acquisitiveness and greed and monopoly. He observed, as anyone can see, that in the long run the operations of accumulation and acquisitiveness tend to monopoly, so that some end up with a lot and some end up with a little or with none, have and have-nots, wealth and poverty. And what Moses figured out is that such a process is an impossible way to run a community."[143]

Jubilee is divestment signaling the end of free-market fundamentalism. In Jubilee the very, very, very rich will no longer get very, very, very richer. The poor will no longer be poor. This is not an easy poem to enact. After all, there's never been a Jubilee. Too much resistance. Brueggemann notes, "You see, what Moses understood, what we all understand in our society, is that you cannot have a viable, peaceable, safe urban community when deep poverty must live alongside huge wealth, when high privilege is visible alongside endless disadvantage in health and housing and education."[144]

American historian Robert McElvaine reminds us that there are always false poets who show up in each generation to resist, refute, and refuse Jubilee. McElvaine says,

> In a book titled *The Forgotten Man: A New History of the Great Depression*, Amity Shlaes came out whole hog in support of the hogs. This "new history of the Great Depression" is grounded in very old economics. Not content to resurrect her Lord and Savior, the Market God, Shlaes endeavored also to disinter another, far more discredited creed: the one that is known by the misnomer "Social Darwinism." In truth, few if any doctrines have ever been further from being "social," and the application of a brutal

---

141. Luke 1:52–53.
142. Brueggemann, *Collected Sermons* 2:141.
143. Brueggemann, *Collected Sermons*, 2:141.
144. Brueggemann, *Collected Sermons* 2:143.

survival-of-the-fittest doctrine to society would more accurately be termed antisocial Darwinism.[145]

When Dr. Otis Moss Jr. applies the poetic genius of the African American preaching tradition to the poetry of Isaiah and Jesus, here's the end result:

> So, if you are preaching a gospel that has nothing about politics, nothing about economics, nothing about sociology, it's empty gospel with a cap and some shoes and no body to it. It might be popular, but it's not powerful. It might be expedient, but it's not saving. Let me put it another way: it might be safe, but it's not saving. God told me to tell you that we need prophets in this age where prophets are not liked. We need prophets of peace—I didn't say peaceful prophets.[146]

The poet/preacher proclaims Jubilee against all the gathered forces of the powers and the principalities. This, of course, means that the preacher has an inexhaustible supply of sermon ideas in using words to attack the rulers of this current culture. Proclaim the Jubilee in poetic language.

In exiting the poetry room, I leave you with three poems that refuse to leave me. Mona Van Duyn's "Letters to a Father" branded me for life as if I was one of the ex-convicts with the Yellowstone imprinted on the chest as a sign of eternal loyalty. Nothing says sermon to me like this story of an old man, thinking he is finished, at the edge of the grave, being brought to life again by the gift of a bird feeder. Then there's the poem "Otherwise," by Jane Kenyon. The poem celebrates the joys of an ordinary day but lives in the shadow that "But one day I know it will be otherwise."[147] No Easter is complete without a reading of "Seven Stanzas at Easter," by John Updike. "Make no mistake: if He rose at all it was as His body; if the cells' dissolution did not reverse, the molecules reknit, the amino acids rekindle, the Church will fall."[148]

Never leave the poets behind in your ministry. The poems we read, and love will stay with us forever and accompany us to the great transition from life to death to life again. Poets long dead and consigned to the grave live in me as ghosts that are alive. I can summon them to slay dragons, disperse the fog of doubt, and defeat the demons of my spirit. Poetry is a hint

---

145. McElvaine, *Great Depression*, Kindle ed. loc. 320.
146. Moss Jr., quoted in Gilbert, *Pursued Justice*, Kindle ed. loc. 3203.
147. Kenyon, *Otherwise*.
148. Updike, "Seven Stanzas at Easter," 110.

of eternal life as it can't be silenced by the grave. "Where, O death, is your victory? Where, O death, is your sting?"[149]

PRAYER
May I never not be frisky,
May I never not be risqué.
May my ashes, when you have them,
friend, and give them to the ocean,
leap in the froth of the waves, still loving movement, still ready,
beyond all else, to dance for the world.[150]

---

149. 1 Cor 15:55.
150. Oliver, *Devotions*, 84.

Chapter 3

What the Philosophers Teach Us about Preaching

THE TWO MOST IMPORTANT ancient philosophers to Christian preachers were Plato and Aristotle. A preview of the philosophers that preceded Plato will give us a better sense of the revolutionary impact Plato and then Aristotle made in Christian faith. David Lindberg notes that the scientific mentality first developed in the sixth century BC in Greece. According to Lindberg, the world of Homer and Hesiod was "a capricious world, in which nothing could be safely predicted because of the boundless possibilities of divine intervention."[1] At some point in the sixth century BC, a philosophy arose that depicted the world as a "cosmos," an ordered world. The philosophers of this concept included Thales, Heraclitus, Anaximander, and Anaximenes. They were thoroughgoing materialists because they excluded the gods. Within this circle of thinkers, Lindberg says, "A distinction between the natural and the supernatural was emerging; and there was wide agreement that causes . . . are to be sought only in the nature of things," rather than in the "personal whim or the arbitrary fancies of the gods."[2]

Into this godless cosmos, Plato restored divinity to account for the cosmos. Plato emphasized the reality of ethical forms. He taught that all objects—animate and inanimate—possessed eternal forms. Each object could say "yes" or "no" to the perfect form of itself. His cosmology included divinities, including a creator and a world soul. In opposition to the materialists, Plato insisted that a god was necessary to account for order in universe.

---

1. Lindberg, *Beginnings of Western Science*, 24.
2. Lindberg, *Beginnings of Western Science*, 26–27.

As Lindberg points out, "Plato's deities never interrupt the course of nature. Quite the contrary, the function of the divinity for Plato was to undergird and account for the order and rationality of the cosmos."[3] Plato's doctrines of eternal forms, the human soul, and the divine creator have influenced Christian theology across the centuries and may be seen now in the principles of process theology. Among Plato's contributions is his account of the good. This suggests that there is a mystery about how someone may actually be good that suggests something like the Christian understanding of grace.

Socrates's address to the jury in the *Apology* suggests a contribution of Plato that has been largely overlooked: "You too gentlemen of the jury, must look forward to death with confidence and fix your minds on this one truth—that nothing can harm a good man either in life or after death."[4] Socrates did not mean that people who live virtuously could not suffer, but that even in their suffering, people who see their life in the light of a certain kind of love, a love of philosophy, which could not be harmed. Given Christian reluctance to embrace the suffering servant and his cross in our positive-thinking world, Plato's insight into goodness deserves more than a casual glance from preachers.

As Hauerwas explains,

> There can be no question of the significance of the Platonists for Augustine, but this passage in praise of God's creation indicates that for Augustine Platonism was a way station on the way for Augustine to become a Christian. Augustine never left his Platonism behind though I think the assumption that he remained more Platonist than Christian is clearly wrong. He understood that he could not remain a Platonist because to be a Christian requires that you believe that all that is as it is because it has been created. Augustine tells us that "by reading these books of the Platonists I had been prompted to look for truth as something incorporeal, and I caught sight of your invisible nature, as it is known through your creatures," but what he could not find in the Platonist books was "the mien of the true love of God."[5]

Aristotle, Plato's most famous student, is the second great philosophical influence on Christian theology. According to Aristotle, the world was not created at all, but is eternal. Thomas Aquinas, one of the greatest minds in Christian history, and a thoroughgoing Aristotelian, said "in the thirteenth century that we should never think of creation as an event, with a

---

3. Lindberg, *Beginnings of Western Science*, 43.
4. Plato, *Apology*, Kindle ed. loc. 1634.
5. Hauerwas, *Working with Words*, 32.

before and after, or as a change in circumstances—as if first there was a chaotic mess, then God came along and organized it, which was a popular view in the ancient world. Creation is an action of God that sets up a relationship between God and what is not God."[6]

Aquinas thought so highly of Aristotle that he referred to him simply as "the philosopher"[7]—the one who had shown what reason would come to on its own, without the aid of supernatural revelation. Aquinas ventured beyond Aristotle to proclaim, "According to our faith, nothing has always existed except God alone."[8]

Perhaps the most salient contribution of Plato, especially considering the degradation of ethos (character) as a political virtue, was his insistence on the moral character of a person. Hauerwas says, "The moral agent's character, the structure of his desires and dispositions, became at best a peripheral rather than a central topic for moral philosophy, thus losing the place assigned to it by the vast majority of moral philosophers from Plato to Hume."[9] My point here is that the incubator of Christian thought was Plato and Aristotle.

The teachings of Aristotle came to be mandated in the church. In 1323, Aquinas was elevated to sainthood, and this helped his system of thought to become the dominant synthesis of biblical and Aristotelian thought. The modified version of Aristotle would prevail in the church until the seventeenth century.

In this stance, I am in the good company of the Jesuits. As Hauerwas points out, "The Jesuits, of course, thought that was not enough. They thought smart Catholics ought to know something about philosophy. So Catholic laity got taught Plato to make them Catholic. What a world!"[10] I think great preachers ought to know something about philosophy. So I would teach seminarians Plato, Aristotle, and the philosopher/preachers of the ages. After all, preachers have the challenge of out-thinking the secular world of intellectual atheists.

Preaching faces daunting challenges in a secular culture. Will D. Campbell asked decades ago, "Who in hell listens to a pulpit sermon anymore?"[11] Preachers often think if they merely report what the Bible says, mention certain doctrines, exegete each word of the text, or enunciate a

---

6. Aquinas, quoted in Williams, *Tokens of Trust*, 36.
7. Griffin, *Two Great Truths*, 9.
8. Quoted in Griffin, *Two Great Truths*, 9.
9. Hauerwas, *Working with Words*, 207.
10. Hauerwas, *In Good Company*, 84.
11. Cited in Connelly, *Will Campbell and the Soul of the South*, 42.

certain number of truths, this is enough to automatically arouse the interest of their congregations. This illusion that the Bible speaks for itself is rooted in the Enlightenment view of rationality—that facts speak for themselves and "make such an indelible imprint on any human mind that the latter is forced to give its adherence regardless of its inclination."[12]

Evangelicals have inherited a tradition rooted in the eighteenth-century Enlightenment, in Scottish Common Sense philosophy, and the rationalism of Francis Bacon. The Enlightenment mind thought that reason was logical. It assumed the Bible should make rational sense to anyone who reads it. In addition, it assumed that the rationality and morality that were characteristic of the American character were the result of the nation's status as Protestant nation.

The evangelical mind also assumed that reason was literal. Every truth fit an objective world precisely, with the logic of the mind able to fit with the logic of the world. "The fundamentalists were such rationalists that they assumed the higher critics [of the Bible] represented something of a conspiracy of intellectuals."[13] If this were right, Christianity in America would be universally rational.

Instead, we are flooded with a plethora of divisions and differences that in some cases qualify as outliers and irrational. If telling the people what the Bible plainly says is all it takes to make them Christian, people would naturally be converted and fill the churches. They would do what was in the best interest of others, especially the least of these. They would support policies and programs that had good news for the poor, release for the prisoners, and economic equity for all. But Christians in America are not behaving that way. They take social stances against the common good, against Others who are deemed unworthy. They allow self-interest, greed, bias, prejudice, and emotion to guide their decisions; they argue violently about values and goals. The Enlightenment view of reason, Scottish Common Sense and Francis Bacon, can't account for real human behavior in the church, because these views are false and misleading.

Preachers stuck in the eighteenth-century Enlightenment mind and the nineteenth-century fundamentalist strategy amble into the pulpit, staring glumly at the back of the sanctuary, and abruptly announce, to themselves or not, we never know, "It has been shown by the theological authorities that the earth was created in six literal days." These preachers never note how many people in the audience respond, "All right, sir! So what? Tell me first why I should care; then I will listen." Flannery O'Connor observed,

---

12. Perelman and Olbrechts-Tyteca, *New Rhetoric*, 17.

13. Hauerwas, *Unleashing the Scripture*, 32.

"Redemption is meaningless unless there is cause for it in the actual life we live, and for the last few centuries there has been operating in our culture the secular belief that there is no such cause."[14]

Again, O'Connor: "When you can assume that your audience holds the same beliefs you do, you can relax a little and use some more normal means of talking to it; when you have to assume that it does not then you have to make your vision apparent by shock—to the hard of hearing you shout, and for the almost-blind, you draw large and startling figures."[15]

Soren Kierkegaard said, "A little [biblical] knowledge has gradually percolated to the simplest classes so that no one any longer reads the Bible humanly."[16] People who still attend church likely feel their opinions about the Bible are as valid as those of the preacher. This means that the preacher faces a skeptical audience even among believers. They show up in church armed with the teachings of the "new atheists" or they have read Bishop Spong. Or they have latched onto the interest in Gnosticism that permeates the theological arena. Or they are reveling in the writing of the "happy agnostic"—Bart Ehrman. With the fearless individualism running amuck in the land, the person in the pews is of the opinion that his opinion is as good as the preachers' even if said congregant has never read the Bible. The illusion that everyone has a right to his own opinion is exactly that—an illusion. Perhaps Hauerwas wasn't off base when he opened his book *Unleashing the Scripture* with this audacious claim: "Most North American Christians assume that they have a right, if not an obligation, to the read the Bible. I challenge that assumption."[17]

Another segment of the audience attends church with no sense of connection to biblical texts or interest in "what the Bible says." They are distracted, distant, not sure why they bother to attend. Peggy Payne, in *Revelation*, shows the vast gulf between preachers and congregations. When the Rev. Swain Hammond tells his congregation that he has actually heard the voice of God, "Bill Bartholomew looks as if he just ate the bitter part of a pecan; sitting there in his gray suit and his shiny glasses, he could be made out of nothing but gray metal."[18] Bernie Morris rolls his bulletin into a tube and hits it against the pew ahead. "What is all this coming out of the blue? Did he come to me and say 'Bernie, old buddy, I got to tell you what happened to me. Bernie, what do you think, what do I do?' No, not Swain. No, he gets

---

14. O'Connor, *Mystery and Manners*, Kindle ed. loc. 312.
15. O'Connor, *Mystery and Manners*, Kindle ed. loc. 313.
16. Kierkegaard, *Journal of Kierkegaard*, 150.
17. Hauerwas, *Unleashing the Scripture*, 15.
18. Payne, *Revelation*, Kindle ed. loc. 377.

up there and mouths off and looks like an idiot doing it. Voice of God. What am I doing here anyway? Sitting an hour every Sunday, mainly because of him, I'm up to my eyebrows in this church and I've hardly gotten a nickel's worth of business out of the lot of them, and now he gets up and does this."[19]

Preachers may be unaware of the great gulf that now exists between the pulpit and the pew. Call it the Sea of Secularity. A vast chasm that has not been navigated even by those preachers who have dispensed with actual pulpits, who parade around on a huge stage, making sermons into Ted Talks and enthralling a huge audience with pop psychology, ancient Christian heresies in new clothes, and superficial positive thinking. If you detect here some jealousy, I'm getting therapy.

The words of Father Abraham to the rich man have come to full-orbed life in our culture: "'They have Moses and the prophets; they should listen to them.' He said, 'No, father Abraham, but if someone from the dead goes to them, they will repent.' He said to him, 'If they do not listen to Moses and the prophets, neither will they be convinced even if someone rises from the dead.'"[20] The preacher's challenge is that people now have neither miracles nor any interest in the Word—Moses and the prophets. Preaching in a secular world can give the preacher the feeling that no one is listening.

The more obvious reason for the preacher to study philosophy stares us right in the face: the definition of philosophy. The etymological definition of philosophy flashes its light in the preacher's face: "love of wisdom." This definition has the advantage of not discriminating against disciplines outside of Christian theology. As lovers of wisdom, preachers are thus open to finding wisdom wherever it is available. No higher praise of wisdom exists than that found in Proverbs, especially Proverbs 1. I read Proverbs as a rhetoric textbook.

After a long week of pastoral work, busy stuff, appointments, denominational gatherings, and general wandering around, the preacher desperate to find material for the weekly sermon can be visualized as tearing through the pages of *The Christian Century* or *The Christian Post* like soccer moms before book club night. This may be all the time the preacher had that week, but this is not mental struggle; this is mental anxiety.

Philosophy, in a broader sense, means mental struggle. More than that, it means facing challenges. There are as many philosophies as there are people. There are no unchallenged truths; all truth is contestable. Here the preacher comes face to face with the need to think, write, and preach philosophically. Believing without doubt, without questions can lead to accepting

---

19. Payne, *Revelation*, Kindle ed. loc. 386.
20. Luke 16:29.

falsehoods, heresies, and even conspiracy theories. Preaching is not the easy task that it appears to be on the surface. The journey of preaching is a journey of searching. "Hard truth is not available without hard struggles."[21]

WHY PREACHERS HAVE PAID LITTLE ATTENTION TO PHILOSOPHY

Since philosophy gave birth to science, there has been an aversion to philosophy and science by many preachers, especially of the evangelical variety. Disdain of science and fear of philosophy have led to neglect of philosophy as a natural ally of preaching. Philosophy means the love of wisdom. To do philosophy is to think out loud. As Clyde Edgerton's Raney insists, "'Think?' I said. 'Who don't think? Everybody thinks.'"[22]

Preachers may be turned off because many philosophers and scientists are atheists, and this has caused preachers to ignore the truths that these philosophers and scientists have to offer. Preachers have the tendency to discriminate against atheistic philosophers. I remind my preaching students to read the great scientists, not for their atheistic theology, but for their rigor in searching for the truth. No preacher should live in an intellectual straitjacket or in a house with only one room. The intersection of philosophy with preaching makes the preacher a more mature thinker. McClendon says, "In 'discovery' and 'understanding, or interpretation,'" the preacher shows "homage to what is handed to them."[23]

There should be no fear as the preacher enters the Great Hall of Philosophy. Grab the great pagan philosophers by the throat, squeeze from them all the ideas that can be employed in the proclamation of the gospel, and then baptize those ideas in the name of the Father (Mother), Son, and Holy Spirit. Whatever else you do, do not be afraid.

Preachers have the best example of relating to philosophers in St. Paul. As St. Chrysostom felt the presence of St. Paul looking over his shoulder as he prepared his sermons, we need to have the same sense that the great ones are there in the study with us. Imagine that you are sitting in ancient Athens observing Paul among the philosophers. "While Paul was waiting for them in Athens, he was deeply distressed to see that the city was full of idols."[24] Is this not the agony of the preacher's heart? Our distress, like that of the Hebrew prophets and St. Paul, is deep. Our cities are full of idolatry.

21. McClendon, *Ethics*, 17.
22. Edgerton, *Raney*, 69.
23. McClendon, *Witness*, 23.
24. Acts 17:16.

To make our plight even more complicated, the people are not even aware of the idolatry. They don't believe idolatry is a problem in our culture. Somehow, they missed the essential lesson that idolatry is anything that we love more than God. Like the Athenians we worship unknown gods that control our lives with fear and anger and violence. The preacher's life is one of facing the idols and the temples of idols.

As Charles Taylor notes, Hopkins's poetry was deeply infused with a sense of what he called "instress," "the inner tension by which a thing maintains its proper form"—its "inscape" or particular "thisness." Instress and inscape both are in a being's relation to God, as are we, and "this means that we discern the particularity that God has chosen for us, and ratify it, choose it in our turn."[25] Here lies the preacher's response to idolatry. We maintain our proper relationship with God. The word "justification" literally means to be in parallel perfection with one another. The preacher aligns her/his life in relation with God and chooses this particular "thisness" as a defense against the distress caused by living among idolators.

As you watch the arguments flying back and forth, listen to the debates, you notice that some Epicurean and Stoic philosophers debated with Paul. Here's what the philosophers said about the preacher of the gospel: "What does this pretentious babbler want to say?" "He seems to be a proclaimer of foreign divinities." (This was because he was telling the good news about Jesus and the resurrection.) So they took him and brought him to the Areopagus and asked him, "May we know what this new teaching is that you are presenting? It sounds rather strange to us, so we would like to know what it means."[26] In the paradigmatic symbol of Greek philosophy—the Areopagus—Paul tells the good news about Jesus and the resurrection. Preaching should never fear to speak the good news.

Paul enters the holy of holiness of ancient philosophy—the dragon's lair filled with the riches of the world's greatest thinkers. There is a key here to how shallow and superficial all this talk has become: "Now all the Athenians and the foreigners living there would spend their time in nothing but telling or hearing something new."[27] I wondered if the sermons of we preach were labored attempts to always say something new and novel. Did our contemporary heresies come to life in pulpits where preachers were reaching for the spectacular and the superficial and repeating it so often that it became doctrine? I decided to listen to the sermons of the pastors of the largest churches in America. Among the good preaching I encounter, I

---

25. Taylor, *Secular Age*, 763–64.
26. Acts 17:19–20.
27. Acts 17:21.

also noticed a trend: how much some of these preachers, like the Athenian philosophers and the large crowds that gathered at the Areopagus, spend their sermons in nothing but telling or hearing something new.

Here is Paul's big moment on the stage of thought. Here the epistemology of Jerusalem confronts the knowledge of Athens. All the great minds of ancient Greek reside here, the communion of thinkers comparable to the communion of saints: Thales, Pythagoras, Socrates, Plato, Aristotle, Epicurus, Diogenes, Democritus, and Heraclitus. They invite us to explore their rich insights and expressions of wisdom.

Most of all, the philosophers put the questions on full display. What Kitty Ferguson calls "the fire in the equations,"[28] the energy in the mathematical and physical structures of things, is here in the relationship with the philosophers because they are the keepers of the fire. The fire increases its intensity by being fed questions. The questions are piled onto the flames as sticks of wood to provide heat and light. Ferguson deals with questions ranging from the nature of time, the big bang, the "unreasonable effectiveness" of mathematics, laws of nature and their possible relation to God, chaos theory, black holes, Heisenberg's uncertainty principle, particle physics, Darwin's theory of evolution, and the role of God in all these equations. It even raises such questions as "how God might answer prayers" from the point of view of physics.

Here originates the coming merger of Athens and Jerusalem. The power and passion of the gospel joins with the profound knowledge of the philosophers. Paul praises the Athenians for "how extremely religious you are in every way."[29] Then he selects one of the idols of the Greek culture as a metaphor for his sermon. Paul addresses the hidden anxiety, the submerged, unconscious fears of the Athenians. The "unknown God" suggests an anxious, nervous people. Afraid they might exclude a god that might later have a fit of rage and punish them, the Athenians built a statue to a god they didn't know. Paul's homiletical genius is to tell the Athenians that he will proclaim to them the name of the unknown God. "Naming God," as David Buttrick claims, is what preachers do.

Whether any of the philosophers became Christians or not, we are given this amazing clip of Paul conversing with the philosophers. Notice that the philosophers scoffed at the resurrection of the dead. The "New Atheists" who are enjoying a bit of popularity in our culture are no different

---

28. Ferguson, *Fire in the Equations*. The book's title is derived from Stephen Hawking's pondering, "What is it that breathes fire into the equations and makes a universe for them to describe?"

29. Acts 17:22.

from these Athenian philosophers. Paul's courage shines like the stars in the Milky Way on a clear night.

As we face the powers and the principalities, the elite demagogues, manipulators, and masters of the lie, preachers need to draw on the philosophic tradition rooted in Socrates, Plato, and Aristotle. The relentless commitment to questioning can be irritating to the reader of Socrates, for example, but serious self-examination and honest critique of the anchor institutions are necessary tasks of the preacher. The search for intellectual integrity, ethical consistency, and powerful speech never ends for the preacher. The Greeks coined a word for this kind of speaker—parrhesia—the bold, risky truth-telling that disrupts the status quo, unnerves the rulers of earth, and startles people out of their illusory dreams. As Socrates says in Plato's *Apology*, "Plain speech [parrhesia] is the cause of my unpopularity."[30]

As students once engaged Socrates as teacher, preachers need to sit at his feet and learn some of his rock-hard courage against the seductive yet nihilistic sophists of his day. Recall that the bad Sophists were the ones who would take either side if the money was right and they engaged in superficial, clever, and misleading arguments to impress the crowds. Socrates disrupted, even turned upside down, those whose only purpose was the pursuit of power and wealth. For the most penetrating exposure of this so-human characteristic, one has only to read Plato's *Gorgias* for the dialogue between Socrates and Callicles.

David Bentley Hart takes what I consider a necessary Christian stance—an aggressive argumentative stance against the "New Atheists" in his *Atheist Delusions*. Hart, using his immense range of the English language says, "Never before have the presses or the press been so hospitable to journalists, biologists, minor philosophers, amateur moralists proudly brandishing their baccalaureates, novelists, and (most indispensable of all) film actors eager to denounce the savagery of faith, to sound frantic alarms against the imminence of a new 'theocracy,' and to commend the virtues of spiritual disenchantment to all who have the wisdom to take heed."[31]

Hart minces no words in arguing that the "New Atheists" have nothing of substance to offer. Of Richard Dawkins, he says "despite his embarrassing incapacity for philosophical reasoning—[he] never fails to entrance his eager readers with his rhetorical recklessness."[32] Hart argues the Christopher Hitchens had a "talent for intellectual caricature which exceeds his mastery

---

30. Plato, *Apology*, 24a.
31. Hart, *Atheist Delusions*, 3.
32. Hart, *Atheist Delusions*, 3–4.

of consecutive logic."[33] And Sam Harris, in Hart's words, has published an "extravagantly callow attack on all religious belief."[34] Hart is aghast at Dan Brown's *Da Vinci Code*, "surely the most lucrative novel ever written by a borderline illiterate."[35] Do not fear the philosophers. Read them. Use them. Adapt their practices to the service of the gospel of Jesus.

The sum of the "New Atheists" is to protest against reasonable truth that is featured by established power and to insist that there is another more elemental, more bodily truth that hovers beneath what is acceptable and that continues to haunt social reality, no matter how much we pretend and insist otherwise. To be sure, the exposé of modernist reason in these proponents of truthfulness is cast in a rhetoric that is remote from and strange to biblical faith.[36] Philosophy trains the preacher to have a legitimate skepticism about her own interpretations. The rigorous thinker will be able to sidestep the temptation of "prooftexting."

Rather than thinking that the Bible always says what the preacher has always thought the Bible says, rather than reading the Bible to maintain self-interest or protect cherished beliefs, the philosopher preacher will go deeper, struggle more, and think better.

The world, where the preacher lives most of the time, pushes back against the preacher's faith. The study of philosophy enables the preacher to know the world on the world's own terms. Not all secular philosophy is the enemy of the preacher. Putting aside the old prejudices of preachers about philosophy, as if God were saying to us as he did to Moses about the rod become a snake, "Put it down,"[37] we need to stop seeing philosophy as elitist and arrogant, as imperialistic, and as irrelevant. There is much to learn about the truth available to Christians who dare to seek, ask, and knock at the door of philosophy. This is especially important now that we now preach after Christendom. There's been a violent shaking and rearrangement of the power of the church. A postmodern culture imposes upon preachers a postmodern philosophy and a post-truth age. Now we preach from the margins rather than the center of power. In spite of the growth of megachurches we work as a minority, not the majority. Our privilege has been overwhelmed by diversity and plurality. Some preachers have not adjusted well and continue to push for the status of white males, for example. Perhaps the hardest adjustment is that preachers feel a loss of power and control and are having

33. Hart, *Atheist Delusions*, 4.
34. Hart, *Atheist Delusions*, 4.
35. Hart, *Atheist Delusions*, 4.
36. Brueggemann, *Truth Speaks to Power*, 5–6.
37. Exod 4:3.

difficulty shifting to witness instead of announcing what people must do. From being pastors of large and expensive facilities, many have to change from maintenance to mission. Instead of the comforts of institutional hierarchy, we now face the uncertainty of movements.

The passion for knowing, thinking, writing, and preaching—that's what I'm attempting to teach. The importance of the emotions for preaching can't be dismissed as "feelings" that we mistrust or that we have turned over to the Pentecostals, the shopping mall megachurches, and the televangelists. The most powerful depiction of how critical emotion is to the religious experience is found in Chaim Potok's *The Chosen*. The rabbi says, "The Master of the Universe blessed me with a brilliant son. And he cursed me with all the problems of raising him. What an anguish it is to have a Daniel, whose mind is like a pearl, like a sun. When my Daniel was four years old, I saw him reading a story from a book. And I was frightened. He did not read the story, he swallowed it, as one swallows food or water. There was no soul in my four-year-old Daniel, there was only his mind."[38] The rabbi then recounts telling Daniel a story of a man who suffered greatly. "And my Daniel enjoyed the story. He looked at me and told me back the story from memory, and I cried inside my heart. I went away to the Master of the Universe, 'What have you done to me? A mind like this I need for a son? A heart I need for a son, a soul I need for a son, compassion I want from my son, righteousness, mercy, strength to suffer and carry pain, that I want from my son, not a mind without a soul.'"[39]

The love of true knowledge equates to fear of the Lord. Here's a lesson where preachers need remedial instruction: "The danger they have been taught to fear is not error but intolerance. Relativism is necessary to openness, and this is the virtue, the only virtue, which all primary education for more than fifty years has dedicated itself to incubating. Openness—and the relativism that makes it the only plausible stance in the face of various claims to truth and various ways of life and kinds of human beings—is the great insight of our times. . . . The point is not to correct the mistakes and really be right, rather it is not to think you are right at all."[40]

Are we willing to allow faith to do her work? Do we have the strength and the wisdom to allow faith to discard the ideas that don't work, and to search for genuine truth? "As Wittgenstein famously remarked: the real difficulty in philosophy is one of the will, more even than of the intellect. What is hard is to will oneself to accept things that are true that one doesn't want

---

38. Potok, *Chosen*, 262–64.
39. Potok, *Chosen*, 262–64.
40. Miller, *Only a Theory*, 170.

to believe."[41] There's a sense in which it is absurd for preachers to see truth or reason as regrettable constraints upon their thinking, to see freedom as more important than truth; but, as Wittgenstein sought to teach us, x"it takes effort and courage, and not mere intellectual acuity, to demonstrate this in our actual lives together, i.e., to will to want to see reality, and to live accordingly."[42] As Flannery O'Connor is purported to have said, "You shall know the truth and it will make you odd." Sometimes I get the impression that we spend a lot of our time trying not to be odd. Some of our training for ministry seems determined to cure us of our oddness.

To be sure, being odd requires a certain degree of faith in faith, so to speak, a faith that there is an objective reality to nature, and the faith that such a reality is indeed worth knowing. There is risk in embracing faith, even faith in reality, even the faith of a preacher. As Griffin says, "But faith promises rewards as well, and in finding the strength to embrace what science [and philosophy] tell us about the nature of reality, we will find reward beyond measure. For it is such faith that will ultimately redeem our souls."[43] I again invite the preacher to explore the insights of cell biologist Kenneth Miller, and his powerful rhetorical work in defense of science, *Only a Theory*, and Francis Collin's personal Christian experience told in his *The Language of God*. From there you can move to a more challenging work, *The Beginnings of Western Science*, by David C. Lindberg, where you can revel in the discovery that the church was the incubator for the development of science. As Griffin points out, "The church gave great support, including remarkable freedom, to the universities that began emerging in the twelfth century, thereby providing natural philosophy [the precursor to science] with an institutional home. . . . Much of the credit for the emergence of modern science would have to go to the Christian tradition for its institutional support."[44]

I refuse the binary choice between a populist, evangelical ministry and a progressive ministry. I believe both evangelicals and progressives have much to learn from the secular disciplines, as the early preachers in the church so amply demonstrated. My preference lies with the rhetorical philosopher preacher, and this means that the preacher should be a student of philosophy.

---

41. Read, "What Is New in Our Time," 89.
42. Read "What Is New in Our Time," 93.
43. Griffin, *Two Great Truths*, 221.
44. Griffin, *Two Great Truths*, 7.

CHARLES TAYLOR: A SECULAR AGE

Of all the philosophers that I could have invited to share this chapter, the one that I choose is Charles Taylor and in particular his monumental book *A Secular Age*. The text that follows will show that Taylor dominates the conversation like the towering figure of Socrates. Taylor's *A Secular Age* matters to preachers because he makes clear the challenges preachers face in attempting to communicate the gospel to a secular population, a secular age where even the church is secular.

In order to help my understanding of Taylor I have also invited another philosopher to join in conversation with Taylor. He is James K. A. Smith. His ticket to this conversation is his own work, *How (Not) to Be Secular*. Smith asks one question of Taylor: "What does it look like to bear witness in a secular age?"[45] This is the question that preachers face now. We attempt to preach the "big" story, the metanarrative of the gospel in a postmodern age that believes all metanarrative are oppressive and misleading. In addition, we try to speak truth to power in what philosophers have dubbed the "post truth age." Smith says, "So I'm trying to distill and highlight this aspect of his argument precisely because I think it matters—and matters especially for those believers who are trying to not only remain faithful in a secular age but also bear witness to the divine for a secular age."[46]

Smith says, "Taylor not only explains unbelief in a secular age; he also emphasizes that even belief is changed in our secular age. There are still believers who believe the same things as their forebears 1,500 years ago; but how we believe has changed. Thus, faith communities need to ask: How does this change in the 'conditions' of belief impact the way we proclaim and teach the faith? How does this impact faith formation? How should this change the propagation of the faith for the next generation?"[47]

Can we recognize our mixed legacy and exercise more humility in offering the gospel to a secular age? If the Protestant Reformation opened a door to exclusive humanism, how do preachers find a way to live with and confidently express the gospel as counterclaims to exclusive humanism? The Reformers' rejection of sacramentalism is the beginning of naturalism. It is also the beginning of a certain evacuation of the sacred as a presence in the world. Perhaps we should rethink this. The Reformers' insistence on individual salvation opened the door to a runaway liberalism that puts freedom over truth, and it has now infected the evangelicals. The challenge of

---

45. Smith, *How (Not) to Be Secular*, Kindle ed. loc. 43.
46. Smith, *How (Not) to Be Secular*, Kindle ed. loc. 78.
47. Smith, *How (Not) to Be Secular*, Kindle ed. loc. 494.

postmodernism and post-truth give preachers reasons for nightmares. We need all the assistance we can garner.

I am convinced that preachers inhabit a world that has become more pagan and that it therefore has more in common with the first century and the Roman Empire than any other era. Preachers cannot afford to face twenty-first-century challenges with nineteenth-century understandings of church, witness, and God. Any philosopher who can help us navigate the turbulence of a secular age is welcome in this house of preaching. If Taylor can move us from flat, reduced prose, from thinking that people are still interested in what amounts to Bible trivia, then he will be well worth the time it takes to read *A Secular Age* multiple times.

Taylor makes a statement early in *A Secular Age* that has become my key text: "The shift to secularity in this sense consists, among other things, of a move from a society where belief in God is unchallenged and indeed, unproblematic, to one in which it is understood to be one option among others, and frequently not the easiest to embrace."[48]

Taylor's words throw down the gauntlet to preachers who still preach as if the default setting is belief in God. These preachers insist on continuing to preach as if we still inhabit a naïve age, an enchanted age, an age of belief. This is how we end up with creationism, the rapture, the imminent return of Jesus, America born as a Christian nation, and an array of sermons that border on being unbiblical, unchristian, and dangerous.

The refusal to accept the reality of a secular age has led to a charade of pretentious actions among preachers. For example, there's the church growth movement. What if the church growth movement encapsulates the pervasive of the secularization of our nation? The church growth movement has not proven conducive to the development of a robust philosophical, theological, intellectual life. The movement, concentrated as it is on the number of people attending church, hasn't paid much attention to developing a pedagogy for Christian understanding or for a Christian-centered philosophy of life. The movement has leaned heavily on pop psychology and what I call "pop philosophy." The pop psychology with its heavy emphasis on individualism and self-help (from God, of course) has been easily recognized and seriously critiqued. The pop philosophy, however, has been carving away the epistemological foundations of Christianity for decades. Preachers preach cultural slogans, offers ways of being that are more philosophically secular than Christian. The philosophy of a secular culture has been parasitical on Christian faith. In previous centuries we would have dispensed these philosophical excursions with ease. Irenaeus against the

---

48. Taylor, *Secular Age*, 3.

Gnostics is a key historical example. Now, the power of the secular has managed to make the church secular.

Whether the church has been inhabited by this secular age, or the secular age has simply overpowered the church, the reality is that the secular has emerged, and it has changed not only the world but also the church. The secular not only inspires unbelief; it also changes belief—it impinges on Christianity. The question for us to ask: "To what extent do we 'believe' like secular humanists?"[49] Hauerwas puts it bluntly: "Current 'church-growth' strategies seem intent on proving that you can get people to come to church whether or not God exists. No doubt they will be successful for a time, but the 'churches' that result from such strategies are nothing more than paganism in Christian disguise. Indeed, such a description may be far too complementary, since paganism in the past was more substantive than the 'religion' associated with the church growth movement."[50]

Preachers struggle to maintain confidence when asked to consider that their message is only one of numerous alternatives for hearers. No wonder some preachers need to be propped up by theories of inspiration, like inerrancy, plenary verbal inspiration, and notions of the authority of God's Word. "This is, of course, in keeping with the long-standing obsession to nail down with ultimate, unattainable and finally self-destructive precision the bases of final, unchallengeable, inerrant authority, be it in a certain form of Papal decision, or a literal reading of the Bible."[51] The thought of standing on equal ground with skeptics, atheists, and exclusive humanists may lead some preachers to something akin to a nervous breakdown. What it should lead to is a greater appreciation for all the disciplines involved in the search for wisdom. At times I am tempted to believe the seminary would be more at home as a department within the university.

We should teach preaching as evangelicals. I am encouraged by the words spoken by Kenneth Miller to biology graduate assistants at Brown University. Miller explains:

> When I meet with my teaching assistants in the large introductory biology course I teach each spring at Brown, I confess to them that I take an evangelical approach to the teaching of biology. The word "evangelical" shocks them, because in modern America they've learned to associate it with religious fundamentalism, but they shouldn't. The word actually means nothing more than speaking the truth and bringing that "good

---

49. Smith, *How (Not) to Be Secular*, Kindle ed. loc. 43.
50. Hauerwas, *In Good Company*, 4.
51. Taylor, *Secular Age*, 512.

> message" of truth to others—which is exactly how I ask my assistants to approach the course. One year I remember telling my staff something like this: "I teach at a university, so I do know there are other disciplines. I also know that some of our students will major in history or art or chemistry. But for the life of me, I cannot understand why any young person at this point in time would want to study anything other than biology—and that's exactly the attitude I want you to convey to our students."[52]

My "Amen" here rattles the test tubes in the biology lab.

Miller tops even this passionate speech with a humble appreciation for other disciplines:

> I hope you won't get the wrong impression from this confession. I do indeed appreciate the value of the humanities and social sciences, as well as the other natural sciences, and I feel fortunate to teach at a university where the scale of our campus is small enough to actually allow me to know scores of colleagues in these fields. I expect them to present their own disciplines to students with the same evangelical fervor that I try to apply to the science of life. Learning is nothing without passion, and I would hope that every person privileged to instruct college-age students would pass along the same passion that led them to select their chosen field.[53]

When I envision seminary students in cross-disciplinary courses with biology, zoology, philosophy, history, rhetoric, and creative writing I see a more informed, more trustful group of seminarians—less likely to spread the poison of mistrust of the intellect and anti-intellectualism that lies at the base of too much evangelical teaching. One of my most rewarding teaching experiences occurred at Wright State University where medical students, biblical studies students, and law students took a course in medical ethics together.

Taylor defines and traces how we have moved from a society "in which it was virtually impossible not to believe in God, to one in which faith, even for the staunchest believer, is one human possibility among others."[54] Our minds have to be challenged to reassess old convictions because "belief in God is no longer axiomatic. There are alternatives. And this will also likely mean that at least in certain milieux, it may be hard to sustain one's faith."[55] This puts preachers in a double bind: there are so many people who don't

---

52. Miller, *Only a Theory*, 165–66.
53. Miller, *Only a Theory*, 166.
54. Taylor, *Secular Age*, 3.
55. Taylor, *Secular Age*, 3.

believe in God and have no need for the church on the one hand, and then there are those who are in the church but are barely holding on to faith. This is why the question that Smith asks, the question that haunts all preachers, is so essential: How does one preach in a secular age?

The primal fear is that no one is listening or that the preacher has not clearly communicated why anyone should care about the gospel of Jesus. David Buttrick tells the story of a famous preacher who lost the ability to speak. "The condition was diagnosed as psychological, for as a friend explained, 'He looked up one day and nobody was listening!' Is that our problem?"[56]

Have preachers forgotten that we are witnesses of and for Jesus? "Just as Jesus sent the seventy to every place he intended to go, so he would have you and me go to where his name is not known, places like Durham and Chapel Hill, North Carolina, to be witnesses to his name."[57] Is that it? We are embarrassed, even in the pulpit, to say too much about Jesus. Perhaps we invite people to attend church, but when is the last time we ask someone to believe in Jesus as the Son of God? How to communicate the gospel in a secular age hangs heavy on the preacher's mind.[58]

In *When God Talks Back*, anthropologist Tanya Luhrmann asks: "If you could believe in God, why wouldn't you?" At the same time, she concedes: "It ought to be difficult to believe in God."[59] To live in a secular age is to inhabit just this space and tension. What are the implications of this for Christian witness in a secular age? How do we recognize and affirm the difficulty of belief?

There are other testimonies from honest atheists that shed light for the darkness the preacher encounters. For example, Steven Weinberg ends his essay, "Without God," explaining why he cannot believe in God with the confession, "Living without God isn't easy. But its very difficulty offers one other consolation—that there is a certain honor, or perhaps just a grim satisfaction, in facing up to our condition without despair and without wishful thinking—with good humor, but without God."[60] What about the difficulty that it is by no means easy to live with God? The positive thinking preachers with the perma-press smiles never allow even a sliver of darkness into the message even when it covers the lives of his listeners. "One of the great virtues of Taylor's book is how he helps us see that atheism may not

---

56. Buttrick, *Homiletic*, Kindle ed. loc. 2080.
57. Hauerwas, *Working with Words*, 167.
58. Craddock, *As One Without Authority*.
59. Luhrmann, *When God Talks Back*, Kindle ed. loc. 57.
60. Weinberg, "Without God."

be all that interesting."[61] The preacher lives and breathes the life of faith and resides in the land of unbelief, including her own at times. Like Isaiah, we too may scream, "Woe is me! I am lost, for I am a man of unclean lips, and I live among a people of unclean lips."[62] Flannery O'Connor, reflecting on the struggle with believe and unbelief, put it this way: "I don't think you should write something as long as a novel around anything that is not of the gravest concern to you and everybody else, and for me this is always the conflict between an attraction for the Holy and the disbelief in it that we breathe in with the air of our times. It's hard to believe always but more so in the world we live in now. There are some of us who have to pay for our faith every step of the way and who have to work out dramatically what it would be like without it and if being without it would be ultimately possible or not."[63]

Smith locates all of us in the same place:

> Even a faith that wants to testify and evangelize—as certainly O'Connor did—has to do so from this place. Indeed, consider the dramatis personae of religiously attuned literature over the past fifty years, from Graham Greene's whisky priest to Walker Percy's Dr. Thomas More to Evelyn Waugh's Charles Ryder, even Marilynne Robinson's Protestant pastor in Gilead: not a one matches the caricature of either the new atheists' straw men or fundamentalist confidence. Their worlds seem as fraught as our own—and more honestly fraught than the areligious, de-transcendentalized universes created by Ian McEwan or Jonathan Franzen.[64]

Here, if we put our ear to the sounds of sacred writ, we will hear Moses: "Who am I that I should go to Pharaoh, and bring the Israelites out of Egypt?"[65] Or we will hear the pleading of Elijah in utter fear of Jezebel: "I have been very zealous for the Lord, the God of hosts, for the Israelites have forsaken your covenant, thrown down your altars, and killed your prophets with the sword. I alone am left, and they are seeking my life, to take it away."[66] And the most wretched words uttered in the New Testament about the struggle, apart from Jesus' cry of forsakenness, are these words from

---

61. Hauerwas, *Working with Words*, 188.
62. Isa 6:5.
63. O'Connor, *Habit of Being*, 349.
64. Smith, *How (Not) to Be Secular*, Kindle ed. loc. 311.
65. Exod 3:11.
66. 1 Kgs 19:10.

St. Paul: "Wretched man that I am! Who will rescue me from this body of death?"[67]

In our pursuit of honesty, of honest admission of faith and doubt always being mixed, perhaps the preacher arrives at the place where he or she knows that the end of Christendom is a good that secularism has provided. Walker Percy, for example, welcomed the disestablishment of Christendom. Writing to his lifelong friend Shelby Foote, Percy mused that "Christendom no longer can or even should call the tune. If Christians believe in the kingdom, that's their business, but they should realize that the world has by and large turned away. There is no longer such a thing as Christendom, and as Kierkegaard said, maybe it's just as well."[68] "In the old Christendom, everyone was a Christian and hardly anyone thought twice about it. But in the present age the survivor of theory and consumption becomes a wayfarer in the desert, like St. Anthony, which is to say, open to signs."[69] I believe it is right to disavow Christendom as Taylor does.[70] The preacher, in an age that needs great affirmations, should acknowledge his or her Christian convictions. There's much to admire in Taylor's unapologetic acknowledgment of his Christian convictions[71]

I think evangelicals have created an insulated panic room in which their faith remains solidly secure. What often happens in these cases is some fundamental accession to some aspect of a competing narrative—for example, the individualism of the American republic—that is then assimilated to a mutated version of faith. Hauerwas argues that "America" has become our church and "war" our main liturgical act.[72] This suggests a reason for the rise of Christian nationalism. This may be the attraction of megachurches—large groups of people gather to reassure one another that what they believe is the truth and that everyone else is dead wrong. The preacher thus lives in a secular society where belief in God is only one of many options and is a contested option. This, according to Taylor, has happened because there has been a shift in "the conditions of belief."[73] As Taylor notes, the shift to secularity "in this sense" indicates "a move from a society where belief in God is

---

67. Rom 7:24.
68. Quoted in Smith, *How (Not) to Be Secular*.
69. Percy, "Why Are You a Catholic?," 314
70. Taylor, *Secular Age*, 514.
71. Taylor, *Secular Age*, 637.
72. See Tooley, "Stanley Hauerwas's America."
73. Taylor, *Secular Age*, 36.

unchallenged and indeed, unproblematic, to one in which it is understood to be one option among others, and frequently not the easiest to embrace."[74]

This brings us to the full-blown arrival of an exclusive humanism, spreading across the land like those alien ships in the movie *Independence Day*. It is the emergence of "the secular" in this sense that makes possible the emergence of an "exclusive humanism"—a radically new option in the marketplace of beliefs, a vision of life in which anything beyond the immanent is eclipsed. As Taylor maintains, "For the first time in history a purely self-sufficient humanism came to be a widely available option. I mean by this a humanism accepting no final goals beyond human flourishing, nor any allegiance to anything else beyond this flourishing. Of no previous society was this true."[75]

The preacher no longer has the authority of what now sounds like glib assurances and reassurances based on "Thus saith the Lord." The old message that unbelievers are sad, depressed, lonely, and unable to flourish loses validity as humans appear to be fine without God. David Buttrick relates a scene from an off-Broadway play. There's a couple sitting in a big-city apartment, when all of a sudden, a Salvation Army band paraded by the window blaring a Jesus song. The young man gets up, and slams the window, saying, "I really don't see what Jesus can do for us?"[76] The preacher can riff on the story: Can Jesus fill our tanks with cheap gas, or stop inflation or curb the national debt? Can Jesus cure our mind-numbing loneliness, anxiety, exhaustion? Can Jesus get us a high paying, more exciting job? Can Jesus stop politicians from lying? Look, Jesus can't reduce the price of gas or eggs.

No matter if we claim that secular people are "rich, free, and miserable" as some argue, the freedom and the affluence seem to fill the hole left by the lack of faith in God. How many people would agree with Lee Trevino saying, "I've been poor and I've been rich. Rich is better." How deep into the secular power of affluence have we descended when we don't even recognize greed as a vice but as a necessary virtue in society? How many preachers even bother to preach sermons about greed? Hauerwas wonders, "Scripture is clear. If you are a Christian who is wealthy or desires to have wealth, you have a problem. Yet in our day greed is seldom identified as a major problem for Christians."[77] Sermons that once thundered that the love of money was the root of all evil have dissolved into the prosperity gospel of "name it and claim it."

---

74. Taylor, *Secular Age*, 3.
75. Taylor, *Secular Age*, 18.
76. Buttrick, *Homiletic*, Kindle ed. loc. 2076.
77. Hauerwas, *Working with Words*, 128.

A rhetorical/philosophical preacher would struggle mightily with these questions. Buttrick insists that a "homiletician ought to be a competent theological dilettante concerned with the church's poetics."[78] One doesn't have to be a card-carrying member of the theological union of scholars to be a theologian, but the best preachers lean in that direction. Much that passes for popular preaching today has more in common with a Ted Talk than with Christian theology.

Taylor argues that this state of affairs has happened because we moved from an "enchanted world"[79] to a "disenchanted" one as descriptor of our postmodern condition. Evangelicals still inhabit the enchanted world of 1500. The fantastical world of evangelicals is an isolated alternate universe. The enchanted world is the world of spirits, demons, and moral forces that our ancestors lived in.[80]

One option for the preacher is to hold on for dear life to the old world—the "enchanted" world, or, as rhetorical scholars dub it, the fantastical world. This option has been chosen by many evangelicals. They are convinced they can convert a secular culture in the twenty-first century using eighteenth-century methods. American historian of the Great Depression Robert S. McElvaine says, "I argue in these pages that a major part of the problem in the 1920s was that eighteenth-century theories were being used to deal with twentieth-century realities."[81]

The evangelicals have inhabited a fantastical world since the dust-up over evolution in the late nineteenth and early twentieth centuries. A look at the fantastical world of evangelicals is a necessary one for evangelicals and as well as for Christians of a more progressive bent.

THE FANTASTICAL WORLD OF EVANGELICALS

Conservative evangelicals have always inhabited a fantastical world different from the world of the rest of humanity. In this fantastical land, a charismatic, powerful preacher with no theological education will be granted more authority on global warming, COVID, immigration, and abortion than a room full of Yale and Harvard PhDs, scientists, historians, and philosophers. The notion of the fantastic used here originated with my fascination with the genre of fantasy in cinema and television. Mainstream fantasy violent movies and television programs garner huge ratings because they

---

78. Buttrick, *Homiletic*, Kindle ed. loc. 64.
79. Taylor, *Secular Age*, 25.
80. Taylor, *Secular Age*, 26.
81. McElvaine, *Great Depression*, Kindle ed. loc. 405.

encourage identification with violent antiheroes. As I watched season 1 of *The Old Man*, I gasped at the main character's proficiency in killing people. Yet I found myself pulling for the ex-CIA killing machine, played by Jeff Bridges. The New Zealots support violent antiheroes in order to win at any cost. Now, the only principle that matters is "Might makes right." The evangelicals have morphed into an army of Plato's Callicles—the definition of pure evil masquerading as a good person.[82]

When we encounter an extraordinary event, for a moment that we cannot decide whether we are hallucinating or witnessing a miracle, and we are participants in the fantastic. In fantasy, truth has no role to play. Beliefs about truth and reality are arbitrary. The fantastical world of conservative evangelicals is an imaginary world that they believe they once inhabited, and they believe it is being taken away from them. In the fantastical world, there is a war against fellow Christians who accept abortion, gay rights, feminism, and climate change.

Rhetorical scholars suggest that the holding of fantasies in common transforms collections of individuals into cohesive groups. Through what has been labeled as symbolic convergence theory, individuals can build a group consciousness that grows stronger as they share a cluster of fantasy themes. In the case of the New Zealots, this cluster of fantasy themes includes white male precarity, melancholy, and victimization; notions of freedom from a libertarian background; commitment to a gun culture; climate denial; history denial including attacks on wokeness, political correctness, and critical race theory; and an insistence that America was founded as a Christian nation. These issues bounce around our culture like the metallic balls in an old-fashioned pinball machine—creating noise and flashing lights, but no substance. The unifying trope of this cluster: Fantasy.

In the process of creating this fantastic world, a certain ethos was created, an ethos that ultimately overshadowed and conquered its creators. "I believe it because it is unbelievable," the church father Tertullian allegedly said. When a version of the Christian faith that depends upon believing twelve or more unbelievable ideas before breakfast dominates our politics, we live in a fantasy world. The same people who brought us a literal Bible, a real Adam and Eve, an actual flood, rocks that float, a sun made to stand still by the word of a prophet, a preacher swallowed by a large fish and then spat out on dry ground (indigestion?) now bring their fantastical, naïve, enchanted world to politics.

What I am trying to describe here is not a theory. Rather my target is our contemporary lived understanding; that is, the way we naïvely take

---

82. Plato, *Gorgias*.

things to be. We might say: the construal we just live in, without ever being aware of it as a construal, or—for most of us—without ever even formulating it.[83] Even people who don't live in the "enchanted world" often accept the evangelical view as if it is the only religious response available. They live as if they are still in the world of demons and spirits, but they don't believe in either.

The evangelicals attempt to reconstruct this prior world of enchantment. They bemoan what they experience as the loss of a way of life. African American rights, women's rights, gay rights—evangelicals feel they have lost their culture. What they experience as loss is really a lack. Therefore, they are melancholy. There's a sense that they are living out an apocalyptic death wish. Casey Ryan Kelly's *Apocalypse Man: The Death Drive and the Rhetoric of White Masculine Victimhood* examines white masculine victimhood and its compulsion toward death and self-destruction as an "apocalyptic turn." White males, especially of the evangelical tribe, see their movement as threatened by a feminized society. As a result, white males experience the melancholy for better days when men could be men. They believe that their world is being taken from them. To hear men's rights advocates tell it, they have been disenfranchised by a social order that strips economic and political power from white men in order to empower women and minorities. Kelly insightfully explains that "[w]hen one lives a life of entitlement, even the most modest demands for equality can be perceived as an assault."[84] As fallacious as these perceptions may be, there is an enormous investment in the notion that white men have been left behind by social justice movements. Kelly argues that white men, cast as virtuous and long-suffering, engage in a melodramatic portrayal of themselves not as weaklings or simpletons, but as unjustly persecuted and unsung heroes of the modern world. This investment in the identity of being wounded but proud, Kelly suggests, animates a melancholia where men grieve the loss of their status and "wholeness." Kelly connects this misplaced sense of victimhood among white masculine discourse to the death drive through the concept of melancholia. Reacting to demographic and societal shifts that compel white men to relinquish even a fraction of their hegemonic power incites a desire to return to a prior state where white men supposedly possessed a coherent subjectivity. The problem is that this moment never existed. Kelly suggests that melancholia captures what white masculinity perceives as a loss of power and purpose but is truly a *lack or absence*. This lack leads to ambivalence and frustration, characterized by a need to express a victimized status—to be wounded—but

---

83 Taylor, *Secular Age*, 30.

84. Kelly, *Apocalypse Man*, 7. See also Groundwater, "Review of *Apocalypse Man*."

also to exercise control over this "trauma" through repetition. In turn, this melancholia compels white masculinity to eradicate the libido and Eros (the instincts toward survival, sex, and other libidinal releases). Men's rights groups, Kelly tells us, mobilize the death drive to "extinguish those ideas and attachments that align themselves with Eros."[85] In doing so, they identify "feminist and queer movements as the culprits responsible for their suffering."[86] This apocalyptic vision of white masculinity sees no future beyond violence toward the Other and its own self-destruction. Therefore, it lashes out at the perceived abominations of a secular world.

In the enchanted world, meanings are not in the mind in this sense, certainly not in the human mind. If we look at the lives of ordinary people—and even to a large degree of elites—five hundred years ago, we can see in a myriad of ways how this was so. First, they lived in a world of spirits, both good and bad. The bad ones include Satan, of course, but beside him, the world was full of a host of demons, threatening from all sides: demons and spirits of the forest, and wilderness, but also those which can threaten us in our everyday lives. Spirit agents were also numerous on the good side. Not just God, but also his saints, to whom one prayed, and whose shrines one visited in certain cases, in hopes of a cure, or in thanks for a cure already prayed for and granted, or for rescue from extreme danger, e.g., at sea.[87]

Your preaching can imbibe and then proclaim this fantastical world that no longer exists in the secular age. But it is a dangerous road for the preacher to travel. Such preaching may be satisfying. It may even draw large crowds. As John Howard Yoder says, "But all this is not the gospel."[88]

This is the greatest fear of evangelicals; the malevolent mind or spirit of liberals will rob the nation of its glory, destroy its Christian foundations, and allow diversity to weaken us. In the enchanted world, the meaning exists already outside of us, prior to contact; it can take us over, we can fall into its field of force.[89]

If we preach to a universal audience that we imagine is still a premodern, porous self of spirits and demons rather than a buffered self—complete in its glorious individualism—our sermon misses the target. And to miss the target is a "homiletical sin." So, the modern self, in contrast to this premodern, porous self, is a buffered self, insulated and isolated in its interiority,

---

85. Kelly, *Apocalypse Man*, 19.
86. Kelly, *Apocalypse Man*, 19.
87. Taylor, *Secular Age*, 32.
88. Yoder, *Original Revolution*, 32.
89. Taylor, *Secular Age*, 34.

"giving its own autonomous order to its life."[90] Philosopher Rupert Read claims that this excessive individualism has led to a choice of freedom over truth.

> We live at a point in history at which the demand for individual freedom has never been stronger—or more potentially dangerous. For this demand—the product of good things, such as the refusal to submit to arbitrary tyranny characteristic of "the Enlightenment," and of bad things, such as the rise of consumerism at the expense of solidarity and sociability—threatens to make it impossible to organize a sane, collective democratic response to the immense challenges now facing us as peoples and as a species. How dare you interfere with my "right" to burn coal / to drive / to fly; how dare you interfere with my business's 'right' to pollute?[91]

The preacher has to find ways to respond to this desire for total freedom and individualism.

Preachers traffic in truth. Read says, "As a philosopher, one wants to say: this must surely be roughly right. One surely can't be indifferent to truth. This is a conceptual point. The only question can be of which truths one cares about."[92] We preach against the currents of a mighty river of secularism: "Dogmatic, boringly contrarian hyper-'individualists' with a fixed set of beliefs impervious to rational discussion. Adherents of an 'ism', in the worst sense."[93]

What we face, from a philosophical perspective, is that evangelicals are libertarians, and "above all though: libertarians can't stand to be told that they don't have as much epistemic right as anyone else on any topic that they like to think they understand or have some 'rights' in relation to: 'Who are you to tell me that I have to defer to some scientist?'"[94] As Wittgenstein famously remarked: the real difficulty in philosophy is one of the will, more even than of the intellect. It takes strength, fiber, it takes a truly philosophical sensibility—it takes a willingness to understand that intellectual autonomy in its true sense essentially requires "submission" to reality—to be able to acknowledge the truth, rather than to deny it.[95]

---

90. Taylor, *Secular Age*, 37–39.
91. Read, "What Is New in Our Time," 84.
92. Read, "What Is New in Our Time," 82.
93. Read, "What Is New in Our Time," 85.
94. Read, "What Is New in Our Time," 88.
95. Quoted in Read, "What Is New in Our Time," 89.

THE CHALLENGE OF INDIVIDUALISM TO THE PREACHER

Let's face reality: Many people are disengaged. Not interested. Not present in church. Stephen Bullivent has coined the term "nonverts" in his work *Nonverts: The Making of Ex-Christian America*. Earlier terms have made it into our English lexicon, such as the Nones (no religious affiliation) and the Dones (finished with religion). At the same time, Taylor's account should also serve as a wake-up call for the church, functioning as a mirror to help us see how we have come to inhabit our secular age. Taylor is not only interested in understanding how "the secular" emerged; he is also an acute observer of how we're all secular now. The secular touches everything. It not only makes unbelief possible, it also changes belief—it impinges upon Christianity (and all religious communities). Taylor's account also diagnoses the roots and extent of Christianity's assimilation—and hints at how we might cultivate resistance.

"So if there is going to be room to not believe (or believe in exclusive humanism), then this very sociality or communitarianism has to be removed as yet another obstacle. The emergence of the buffered self already lays the groundwork for this since this understanding lends itself to individuality, even atomism. . . . The buffered self is essentially the self which is aware of the possibility of disengagement."[96] We seem unaware of what we were forsaking when we fell for the allure of individual freedom. "Living in the enchanted, porous world of our ancestors was inherently living socially."[97] The common good is a collective good, dependent upon the social rituals of the community. "We are all in this together" is more than an advertising jingle. It is a social reality that is now challenged by an excessive individualism.

This attitude of individualism has now invaded the arena of truth. What we have are people dealing with truth as individuals and as consumers. Truth becomes a commodity like toothpaste, with just as many varieties available on the epistemic shelves of the mind. My hunch is that this runaway individualism has evolved as a bastard child of political liberalism with a major proponent being John Rawls and his concept of the "good."

In a prior time, a premium was placed on consensus, and "turning 'heretic'" was "not just a personal matter." That is, there was no room for these matters to be ones of "private" preference. "This is something we constantly tend to forget," Taylor notes, "when we look back condescendingly

---

96. Smith, *How (Not) to Be Secular*, 41–42.
97. Smith, *How (Not) to Be Secular*, 42.

on the intolerance of earlier ages. As long as the common weal is bound up in collectives rites, devotions, allegiances, it couldn't be seen just as an individual's own business that he break ranks, even less that he blaspheme or try to desecrate the rite. There was immense common motivation to bring him back into line."[98]

There's a level where the hyper-individualism of the secular mind can confuse a preacher trained to preach an individual salvation. At first glance, an age of individualism seems exactly right for a preaching of individual salvation. Hauerwas doesn't hide his disdain for individual salvation ideologies: "I have little use for the current fascination with individual salvation in either its conservative or liberal guises. Such accounts of salvation assume that God has done something for each person which may find expression in the church. I do not assume that salvation is first and foremost about my life having 'meaning' or insuring 'my' eternal destiny. Rather, salvation is being engrafted into practices that save us from those powers that would rule our lives making it impossible for us to truly worship God."[99]

Truth is prior to any claim of rights and freedom. At some point, the complete-freedom individual will hit the wall: the limits imposed on thought and action by adhering to the truth. The Christian moral life cannot be an individual achievement but requires a community of friends we call the church to challenge our endemic drift toward self-deception. Faced with the ethos of our culture, we need a more powerful presentation of the church's most archetypal metaphor: the body. The very idea of inalienable rights is the product of individuals who no longer trust their lives to the hands of those they live with and who thus seek to protect themselves through having "trumps" against the actions of their neighbors.[100] Is it possible for the preacher to find a proclamation that unifies a divided people? Pope Pius XI suggests, "For a nation is happy when its citizens are happy. What else is a nation but a number of men living in concord?"[101] Conceptually, this is a most remarkable assertion, for the pope is dissolving several of the leading antinomies of modern social theory—individual/society, individual/state, and individual/family antinomies—much in the way that Augustine dissolved the antinomies that shaped antique political theory.[102]

Pius XI thus arrayed himself and the church against the tendency in secular social theory to create spheres whereby Christ's kingship is confined

---

98. Taylor, *Secular Age*, 42.
99. Hauerwas, *In Good Company*, 8.
100. Hauerwas, *In Good Company*, 188.
101. Quoted in Hauerwas, *In Good Company*, 212.
102. See Milbank, *Theology and Social Theory*, 403–6.

to "the soul," "the individual," or at best "the family," and is thereby prevented from directly shaping "the political," "the social," and "the economic." Pope Pius XI spares no judgment:

> The rebellion of individuals and of nations against the authority of Christ has produced deplorable consequences. We lamented them in the *Encyclical Ubi Arcano*; we lament them today. They are the seeds of discords sown far and wide; those bitter enmities and rivalries between nations which hinder so much the cause of peace; that insatiable greed which is so often hidden under a pretense of public spirit and patriotism, and gives rise to so many private quarrels; a blind and immoderate selfishness, making men seek nothing but their own comfort and advantage, and measure everything by these.[103]

Here we have powerful notes that have previously been sung and shouted by Walter Rauschenbusch, Washington Gladden, and John Howard Yoder. We also detect similar resonances with Cornel West's critique of our culture. West identifies three dominating, antidemocratic dogmas that threaten our world: free market fundamentalism, aggressive militarism, and escalating authoritarianism.[104] I would add a fourth dogma: American fundamentalism wrapped in Christian nationalism. I repeat these threats now because repetition underscores the seriousness with which preachers must take the threats.

Reinhard Hütter, in "The Church as Public: Dogma, Practice, and the Holy Spirit," argues that the church needs to provide a "defining and constitution set of binding conviction, rules, and key practices"[105] that differ from such attempts by fundamentalists to offer a religion that is private individual and depends on motivation, positive thinking, emotion, and choices.

Once individuals become the locus of meaning, the social atomism that results means that disbelief no longer has social consequences. Taylor defines this as the "buffered self."[106] "The buffered self is essentially the self which is aware of the possibility of disengagement."[107] "We" are not a seamless cloth, a tight-knit social body; instead, "we" are just a collection of individuals—like individual molecules in a social "gas."[108] Even people who attend church may do so in what feels like a bubble. The irony is that

103. Quoted in Hauerwas, *In Good Company*, 213.
104. West, *Democracy Matters*, 4–6.
105. Hütter, "Church as Public," 349.
106. Taylor, *Secular Age*,
107. Smith, *How (Not) to Be Secular*, Kindle ed. loc. 795.
108. Smith, *How (Not) to Be Secular*, Kindle ed. loc. 795.

this commitment to individualism turns out to be an illusion. As Rupert Read notes, such individualism "involves a fantasy of atomism; and an unhealthy dogmatic contrarianism. Too often, ironically, it involves precisely the dreary conformism so wonderfully satirized at the key moment in the Monty Python film *Life of Brian*, when the crowd repeats, altogether, like automata, the refrain 'We are all individuals.'"[109] Too often, evangelicals to a man (and, tellingly, the vast majority of evangelical leaders are males) think that they are being radical and different: "by all being exactly the same as each other. Dogmatic, boringly contrarian hyper-'individualists' with a fixed set of beliefs impervious to rational discussion. Adherents of an 'ism', in the worst sense."[110] You are now free to be a heretic, and this frees you to be an unbeliever, an atheist. Hauerwas suggests that we are practical atheists. In *In Good Company*, Hauerwas states that

> we associate Christianity with this sense of the spiritual is not surprising, given the world in which we live. If we did not put God in something like the "spiritual realm," we would not know where else God might be. We know that no matter how much our belief in God might matter to us—and I know that it matters a great deal to most of you—most of us live our lives as practical atheists. We think that we need God to give "meaning" to our lives, but if in fact it turns out that God just is not God, most of us, surprisingly, would not have to change how we live. We could go on doing pretty much what we are doing.[111]

Taylor identifies the crucial elements in creating a climate for unbelief: The buffering of the self protects us from the danger of not believing in the gods; the privatized, individual self protects us from the social stigma of not being part of the community; the lowering of the bar for what it means to flourish. The individual faces an option that didn't exist previously: "You can drop the expectations of eternity that place the weight of virtue on our domestic lives—that is, you can stop being burdened by what eternity/salvation demands and simply frame ultimate flourishing within this world."[112]

Taylor's account celebrates the Reformation's "sanctification of ordinary life" while also suggesting that this was the camel's nose in the tent of disenchantment—that somehow the Protestant Reformation opened the door to what would become, by a winding, contingent path, exclusive

---

109. See https://www.youtube.com/watch?v=khbzSif78qQ.
110. Read, "What Is New in Our Time," 85.
111. Hauerwas, *In Good Company*, 35.
112. Smith, *How (Not) to Be Secular*, Kindle ed. loc. 841.

humanism. "Are there ways that Protestants can recognize this mixed legacy of the Reformation and yet also affirm it as a renewal movement within the church catholic? If the Protestant Reformation opened a door to exclusive humanism, did it not also open the door that led to Vatican II?"[113]

In other words, the Reformers' rejection of sacramentalism is the beginning of naturalism, or it at least opens the door to its possibility. It is also the beginning of a certain evacuation of the sacred as a presence in the world. So, Taylor summarizes the point: "A way of putting our present condition [our secular age] is to say that many people are happy living for goals which are purely immanent; they live in a way that takes no account of the transcendent."[114]

Preaching to such flourishing humanists puts us squarely in the Areopagus where the philosophers called Paul a "scoffer" and said of his sermon that he was "babbling." This is where we are as we try to discover how to preach to flourishing humanists.

Taylor suggests that those who convert to unbelief "because of science" are less convinced by data and more moved by the form of the story that science tells and the self-image that comes with it (rationality = maturity). Moreover, the faith that they left was often worth leaving. If Taylor is right, it seems to suggest that the Christian response to such converts to unbelief is not to have an argument about the data or "evidences" but rather to offer an alternative story that offers a more robust, complex understanding of the Christian faith. "The goal of such witness would not be the minimal establishment of some vague theism but the invitation to historic, sacramental Christianity."[115] Rather than a vague humanistic approach to Christianity, the preacher moves in the opposite direction and offers gigantic affirmations. Like St. Paul, we preach again the resurrection. Instead of arguing facts and evidence or thinking we have proof, we return to the rhetorical principle of pathos. We speak to the intelligent emotions of values and goals.

Perhaps we can follow the guidance of Rowan Williams, who suggests that we talk about how people can trust God in the sense of having confidence that God is working for us as our friend and not out to get us as the enemy.[116] We help people find an anchorage for life within the context of Christian faith.

---

113. Smith, *How (Not) to Be Secular*, Kindle ed. loc. 946.
114. Taylor, *A Secular Age*, 143.
115. Smith, *How (Not) to Be Secular*, Kindle ed. loc. 1688.
116. See Williams, *Tokens of Trust*, 11.

Taylor insists that, while he believes a Christian "take" can account for aspects of our experience that an exclusively humanist "take" cannot, he is not primarily interested in winning an argument. This seems exactly right. St. Ambrose said many centuries ago, "It did not suit God to save his people by arguments."[117]

Taylor's concern is to foster a "badly needed" conversation. How might evangelism and outreach in a secular age be considered a form of just such a "conversation"? Could unapologetic "witnessing" also involve attentive "listening"? Taylor might not wish to win arguments, but I do. How might preaching in a secular age be considered a form of argument? Could unapologetic witnessing also involve a different take on the secular world?

Lakoff argues that "we will need to embrace a deep rationality that can take account of, and advantage of a mind, that is largely unconscious, embodied, emotional, empathetic, and metaphorical."[118] In addition, "we will need a new philosophy—a new understanding of what it means to be a human being; of what morality is and where it comes from."[119] Most of all, we will need a "full" gospel—embracing the economic, political, ethical, philosophical, rhetorical, social, science, psychology, and humanity itself. Carlyle Marney always believed that we had more to offer humanly than all the other options of the secular culture.[120] I stand by that belief now.

My conviction is that as preachers we make the case for our take on the world. Arguing doesn't mean that disagreement must create division. The very strategy is worth noting. The goal isn't demonstration or proof; the point isn't to offer a syllogism that secures analytic truth.

For example, in a long testimony from Václav Havel, we get a sense of how to witness to a secular age:

> Again, I call to mind that distant moment in [the prison at] Hermanice when on a hot, cloudless summer day, I sat on a pile of rusty iron and gazed into the crown of an enormous tree that stretched, with dignified repose, up and over all the fences, wires, bars and watchtowers that separated me from it. As I watched the imperceptible trembling of its leaves against an endless sky, I was overcome by a sensation that is difficult to describe: all at once, I seemed to rise above all the coordinates of my momentary existence in the world into a kind of state outside time in which all the beautiful things I have ever seen and experienced

---

117. Ambrose, *De Fide (On Belief)*, 1:42.
118. Lakoff, *Political Mind*, Kindle ed. loc. 277.
119. Lakoff, *Political Mind*, Kindle ed. loc. 277.
120. Marney, unpublished paper.

existed in a total "co-present"; I felt a sense of reconciliation, indeed of an almost gentle assent to the inevitable course of events as revealed to me now, and this combined with a carefree determination to face what had to be faced. A profound amazement at the sovereignty of Being became a dizzy sensation of tumbling endlessly into the abyss of its mystery; an unbounded joy at being alive, at having been given the chance to live through all I have lived through, and at the fact that everything has a deep and obvious meaning—this joy formed a strange alliance in me with a vague horror at the inapprehensibility and unattainability of everything I was so close to in that moment, standing at the very "edge of the infinite"; I was flooded with a sense of ultimate happiness and harmony with the world and with myself, with that moment, with all the moments I could call up, and with everything invisible that lies behind it and has meaning. I would even say that I was somehow "struck by love," though I don't know precisely for whom or what.[121]

Havel's appeal is to a "sense," a feel for things. The operative terms are affective: "sensation," "I felt a sense . . . ," "I was somehow 'struck by love,' though I don't know precisely for whom or what."[122] These are emotions and yet they are intertwined with a deep intelligence. Taylor gravitates to those whose conversion was on the order of "sense." And the "story" of *A Secular Age* is intended to work in the same way, appealing to something like a "gut feeling," a "vibe."

Taylor does this work by regularly pointing to exemplars. Would a Protestant proceed this way? While Smith says that this is not likely, I would offer the work of Anabaptist theologian James William McClendon. His three-volume systematic theology offers a variety of exemplars as he models his conviction that theology should be done biographically. Among McClendon's exemplars are Sarah and Jonathan Edwards, Dietrich Bonhoeffer, and Dorothy Day in *Ethics, Volume I*. McClendon's central claim throughout his *Biography as Theology* is that "'The truth of faith is made good in the living of it or not at all; that living is a necessary condition of the justification of Christian faith.' The lives of Christians not only reflect the faith of particular people, they also make present the true faith to which all Christians are commonly called."[123]

His methodology, applied in interesting ways in the first volume of his systematic theology, is to consider beliefs not as propositions but as living

---

121. Quoted by Taylor, *Secular Age*, 728.
122. Taylor, *Secular Age*, 729.
123. Quoted in Isaac, "*Biography as Theology*."

convictions embodied in actual communities. Such theology requires that we speak of exemplars, heroes, saints. "In or near the community there appear from time to time singular or striking lives, the lives of persons who embody the convictions of the community, but in a new way; who share the vision of the community, but with new scope or power; who exhibit the style of the community, but with significant differences. It is plain that the example of these lives may serve to disclose and perhaps to correct or enlarge the community's moral vision, at the same time arousing impotent wills within the community to a better fulfillment of the vision already acquired."[124] I plead the case for McClendon to be read as primal text in all Baptist seminaries. Protestants need a calendar of saints because the world we inhabit is filled with the "beast kings" of Daniel, the "man of sin," "the beast from the sea," and the entire panoply of the apocalyptic enemies of God. These metaphors speak of how difficult it is for the church and how much we need saints strong enough to stand up to the secular.

An added advantage of biography in preaching will be the attention preachers pay to the Old Testament. There are more developed characters in the Old Testament than the New Testament, more examples that are fleshly, material, humans like us. Within the canon of the Old Testament itself there is warning that the Old Testament may one day die. "The time is surely coming, says the Lord God, when I will send a famine on the land; not a famine of bread, or a thirst for water, but of hearing the words of the Lord."[125] Brent A. Strawn argues that the Old Testament is disappearing from the sermon in *The Old Testament Is Dying*. With all the attention given in the last two decades to the fear that the church is dying, who has noticed that the canon has been greatly reduced as preachers concentrate on the Gospel texts of the lectionary? Is there a hidden anti-Semitism in our midst? Do we no longer know that our salvation is from the Jews? Strawn tells the story of teaching a Sunday school class on biblical poetry and asking the group of senior citizens what Jesus was quoting in the cry of derelicition—"My God, my God why have you forsaken me?"—and no one knew this was a direct quote from Psalm 22. Strawn says, "That's when I realized, in a way that I had never realized before, that the Old Testament was dying."[126]

Ellen Davis, in her Lyman Beecher Lectures on Preaching, *Wondrous Depth*, makes the case for preaching the Old Testament. She asks, "Can we really believe that these ancient texts, which reflect a world—even, in many respects, a religion—so different from our own, provide reliable guidance for

---

124. James Howell, "Christ Was Like St. Francis," 102.
125. Amos 8:11.
126. Strawn, *Old Testament Is Dying*, Kindle ed. loc. 407.

contemporary Christian life? Can preachers draw upon the work of critical biblical and theological study so as to meet the pastoral needs and the urgent questions of their hearers?"[127] She answers with a gigantic affirmation.

Our preaching could bear stories of saints—and not of the whitewashed, pastel-colored variety. Here we open the door in the house of faith where the historians live. Biography. McClendon says to teach theology biographically. I say preach biography. The gospel is incarnational, even messy, and we learn as much from the foibles of saints as from their luminous moments of genuine imitation of Christ. Stanley Hauerwas and Romand Coles also lift up exemplars as a way of life—life that transcends death.

> We believe that the people at the center of the book—Ella Baker, Bob Moses, Will Campbell, Jean Vanier, Ernesto Cortes; as well as the movements, organizing efforts, and communities such as SNCC (in its early days), the IAF, and L'Arche—represent a politics of life. They do so because they refuse the seduction of a politics that attempts to defeat death by promising 'results.' Even as the more frequently recognized ends for which they struggle (e.g., education, wages, jobs, health care, infrastructure) are of great importance, we find these people most exemplary for how, with patient intensity, they cultivate modes of attention and political engagement that perform a redemption that is otherwise than immortality.[128]

In *The Art of Reading Scripture*, James C. Howell offers an intriguing essay, "Christ was like St. Francis." Howell takes up the case for preaching the lives of the saints: "The disciplines of biblical interpretation should incorporate biography in order to illuminate ways in which texts have invited, and continue to invite, transformed lives . . . We are well-served by stories that expose how our own kin, real flesh and blood, have both embodied the faith and misshapen it as well. No nostalgia here: the tradition of the saints excites in us creative and risky engagement to embody the text just as they did, in a manner that is faithful today."[129]

G. K. Chesterton, noting how Francis of Assisi sought to fashion himself after Christ, how Francis was "a most sublime approximation to his Master," "a splendid and yet a merciful Mirror of Christ," shrewdly suggested that if St. Francis was like Christ, Christ was to that extent like St. Francis. "Now in truth while it has always seemed natural to explain St. Francis in the light of Christ, it has not occurred to many people to explain

---

127. Davis, *Wondrous Depth*, Kindle ed. loc. 83–85.
128. Hauerwas and Coles, *Christianity, Democracy, and the Radical Ordinary*, 2.
129. Howell, "Christ Was Like St. Francis," 103.

Christ in the light of St. Francis.... St. Francis is the mirror of Christ rather as the moon is the mirror of the sun. The moon is much smaller than the sun, but it is also much nearer to us; and being less vivid it is more visible. Exactly in the same sense St. Francis is nearer to us, and being a mere man like ourselves is in that sense more imaginable."[130]

As Athanasius insisted, "Anyone who wishes to understand the mind of the sacred writers must ... approach the saints by copying their deeds."[131] I have added that it is also necessary to preach biographically, preach the saints, the heroes, and the exemplars of the faith. This is the way to the life that opens to faithfulness in the midst of secular storms.

The incarnate, fleshly, material, emotional exemplars bring us back to Aristotle, to pathos, emotional proof. Taylor asks, "Don't you feel it?" That alternative account is what Taylor has been trying to make room for all along. In our religious lives we are responding to a transcendent reality. We all have some sense of something called fullness and seeking to attain it. So, the structural characteristic of the religious (re)conversions described above involves one feeling oneself breaking out of a narrower frame into a broader field, which makes sense of things in a different way, and corresponds to reality. "This is an unapologetic claim. It is not demonstrable except insofar as it offers a better account of our experience."[132] And the "better-ness" of that account is something that has to be felt.

Then what does the future look like? Smith expositing Taylor hazards two interesting predictions: "In societies where the general equilibrium point is firmly within immanence, where many people even have trouble understanding how a sane person could believe in God, the dominant secularization narrative, which tends to blame our religious past for many of the woes of our world, will become less plausible over time." This is in part because we'll see that "other societies are not following suit." However, there will be internal pressures as well, which leads to his second prediction. "At the same time, this heavy concentration of the atmosphere of immanence will intensify a sense of living in a 'waste land' for subsequent generations, and many young people will begin again to explore beyond the boundaries."[133] This is the philosophical challenge for preachers, but it is also the suffering servant challenge of Jesus. As Smith puts it, "And in ways that they never could have anticipated, some will begin to wonder if 'renunciation' isn't the way to wholeness, and that freedom might be found in the

---

130. Chesterton, *St. Francis of Assisi*, 117–18.
131. Athanasius, *On the Incarnation*, 96.
132. Smith, *How (Not) to Be Secular*, Kindle ed. loc. 2994.
133. Smith, *How (Not) to Be Secular*, Kindle ed. loc. 3003.

gift of constraint, and that the strange rituals of Christian worship are the answer to their most human aspirations, as if, for their whole lives, they've been waiting for Saint Francis."[134]

Go find your own stories. This is not intended as one of those awful books of illustrations that once haunted the preacher's library offering him slim pickings of hagiography, fictional, husks of stories that tempted the preacher to tell then autobiographically. Go find your own stories. Read biography.

As preachers we need clarity on the project of the philosophy attempting to establish an uncontested hegemony of the secular. These philosophies consider all Christian efforts to push back as weakness, immaturity, lack of courage, being out of touch, superstitious, and ignorance. We repeatedly face "the perorations and tirades of secular moralists, gravely and condescendingly informing us that the last slender supports ports for our irrational religious allegiances have been ripped away and exhorting us to repent at last of our savage age credulity."[135]

Taylor's *A Secular Age* provides a map that not only registers the hazards faced by preachers—the philosophical moves implicated in efforts to establish an uncontested hegemony of the secular—a world in which all that resists the closures of what Taylor calls the "immanent frame" are dismissed, but also light for the continued faithful preaching of the good news of Jesus.

Taylor makes the case that we live in a secular world where belief in God is no longer the default setting. He helps the preacher know better how to bear witness in this secular world. Taylor has couched his philosophy in a story to help us know where we stand, and what is at stake. I agree with Smith's conclusion that Taylor's *A Secular Age* "is an insightful and incisive account of our globalized, cosmopolitan, pluralist present."[136] Reading *A Secular Age* and returning often for its directions is like checking with Siri to make sure you are on the right road in your journey.

The people to whom we attempt to preach inhabit a cross-pressured world, a pluralized, pressurized environment, where believers are riddled with doubts and doubts, at times, are tempted by belief. The cross-pressure of which Taylor speaks is the pressure of several spiritual options that are available to everyone. In this environment, preachers face a growing exclusive humanism that appears to be flourishing without help from Christianity. An expressive, hyped-up individualism mitigates against preacher attempts to create community.

---

134. Smith, *How (Not) to Be Secular*, Kindle ed. loc. 3012.
135. Hart, *Doors of the Sea*, Kindle ed. loc. 89.
136. Smith, *How (Not) to Be Secular*, Kindle ed. loc. 82.

Here then is the strategy for taking on the "smug" intellectualism of the secularist. The preacher now knows that the secular "gospel" is also a "frame," a "spin," a "take" on reality. If faith is only one option among many, then the preacher can make clear that exclusive humanism is also a "take, a construal, a reading."[137] The preacher must keep asking why secularists so confidently assume that their "take" is just the way things are, the only possible conclusion, and the only acceptable framing of reality. The preacher needs to develop confidence, philosophical and theological confidence that what she offers answers the deepest craving and need of human beings.

Smith raises an intriguing question: "Might nonfoundationalism in epistemology already testify to an opening in the immanent frame?"[138] If that is possible, then we have another strong guide in the work of James McClendon. As Hauerwas testifies, "McClendon has been teaching us how to do theology in a world without foundations before anyone knew what anti-foundationalism was. That he has done so is due partly to his philosophical astuteness as developed in his and James Smith's book *Understanding Religious Convictions*. I suspect, however, his 'anti-foundationalism' owes more to his determined stance to do theology in the baptist tradition. The baptist tradition never sought a 'worldly' foundation since it knew there is no foundation other than Jesus Christ."[139]

Philosophically the preacher embracing an anti-foundational stance will realize that postmodernism is more ally than enemy and that the post-truth age offers the preacher multiple opportunities to bear witness with St. Paul and all the saints to "the resurrection of Jesus." In wondrous and delightful ways this puts us back in Kenneth Burke's famous metaphor of the parlor scene. Preachers are as welcome to speak in the parlor as any other current or past speaker. Here is where the action takes place. All the other rooms in the house empty into the parlor where the contest continues with passion. Long live the philosophers!

---

137. Smith, *How (Not) to Be Secular*, Kindle ed. loc. 2042.
138. Smith, *How (Not) to Be Secular*, Kindle ed. loc. 2155.
139. Hauerwas, *In Good Company*, 33.

Chapter 4

What the Rhetoricians Teach Us about Preaching

Homiletics belongs in the family of rhetoric. A long, difficult family dispute pushed rhetoric out of the home. Rhetoric became the "prodigal son" of the family. I am bringing homiletics home again. This chapter says, "Quickly, bring out a robe—the best one—and put it on him; put a ring on his finger and sandals on his feet. And get the fatted calf and kill it and let us eat and celebrate; for this son of mine was dead and is alive again; he was lost and is found!"[1]

Not everyone in the family of preachers will welcome or attend the homecoming party. Some will become angry and refuse to go in. Like the father persuading the older brother to accept his sibling back into the family, I want to address my claim that rhetoric is homiletical; homiletics is rhetoric. As Karl R. Wallace says, "The substance of rhetoric: good reasons. My position is this. First, rhetorical theory must deal with the substance of discourse as well as with structure and style. Second, the basic materials of discourse are (1) ethical and moral values and (2) information relevant to these. Third, ethics deals with the theory of goods and values, and from ethics rhetoric can make adaptations that will result in a modern system of topics."[2]

I propose the rich literature of homiletics with contributions from selected rhetorical theorists. My underlying affirmation: Rhetoric makes preaching human. After all, Jesus is the Word, and he is an embodied Word. Preaching is rhetoric.

---

1. Luke 15:22–23.
2. Wallace, "Substance of Rhetoric," 240.

Let's start by asking, "What is rhetoric?" What is the relationship between rhetoric and preaching? Plato said rhetoric was "the art of enchanting the soul with words."[3] Socrates, in *Phaedrus*, asks, "Is not rhetoric, taken generally, a universal art of enchanting the mind by arguments?"[4] Aristotle defined rhetoric as the "faculty of finding in any given situation the available means of persuasion."[5] Francis Bacon portrayed rhetoric as the "application of reason to the imagination for the better moving of the will."[6] Twentieth-century rhetoricians have given more precise definitions to rhetoric. Kenneth Burke says, "Rhetoric is rooted in an essential function of language itself, a function that is wholly realistic and continually born anew: the use of language as a symbolic means of inducing cooperation in beings that by nature respond to symbols."[7] I. A. Richards argued that rhetoric was "the study of misunderstanding and its remedies."[8] Wallace: "The giving of good reasons."[9]

In my understanding, rhetoric is argument. The Bible is a sustained argument that life as perceived by the world is not life as intended by God. God is the original persuader. Influenced by Plato's doctrine of true forms, I believe God's creative power is persuasive, not coercive. The rhetorical energies of the Bible are argument and persuasion. Rowan Williams says, "It's as though the ancient Hebrews really understood a God who could do whatever he liked and damn the consequences and the God who showed himself to be a God of commitment and forgiveness, ready to be argued with, ready to be recalled to his true nature."[10]

For rhetorical scholars, rhetoric plays a major role in the construction of reality. Rhetoric functions to differentiate (name and label and classify world objects); preserve (ensure that ideas can stay alive until they are validated); associate (relate things to produce new items of knowledge; evaluate (critically test those ideas we differentiate, preserve, and associate); and place ideas in a perspective (help audiences understand relationships).

---

3. Plato, *Phaedrus*, Kindle ed. loc. 103. "Is not rhetoric, taken generally, a universal art of enchanting the mind by arguments; which is practiced not only in courts and public assemblies, but in private houses also, having to do with all matters, great as well as small, good and bad alike, and is in all equally right, and equally to be esteemed—that is what you have heard?" Plato, *Phaedrus*, Kindle ed. loc. 90.

4. Plato, *Phaedrus*, Kindle ed. loc. 90.

5. Aristotle, *Rhetoric*, 6.

6. Bacon, *Selected Writings of Francis Bacon*, 100.

7. Burke, *Rhetoric of Motives*, 43.

8. Richards and Constable, *Philosophy of Rhetoric*, 3.

9. Wallace, "Substance of Rhetoric."

10. Williams, *Tokens of Trust*, 18.

The skills required of preachers are rhetorical ones. Each of the rhetorical scholars mentioned in this chapter—including Chaim Perelman, Ernesto Grassi, Sara Ahmed, and George Lakoff—offers a different perspective on rhetoric. Perelman focuses on epidictic speech and values as a starting point for his examination of rhetoric. Grassi is best categorized as developing an epistemological focus. Ahmed and Lakoff focus on emotions, feelings, and affect theory.

In this chapter, I will focus on the primary claim that preaching is rhetoric and, as a result, the sermon is a sustained argument. Then, I will present a more detailed look at the work of Ernesto Grassi and Chaim Perelman. Following Grassi, I argue that rhetoric is indispensable to all meaning and that it has special relevance to preaching. Rhetoric is the ground of society, the primal language of humanity, and it is a humanistic discipline. As such, rhetoric is indispensable to the preacher's practice. The content of every sermon depends upon the preachers' use of ingenium. "Rather than an isolated art, confined to a specific domain, rhetoric is ingenious activity itself, whose 'essential characteristic [is] celeritas, manifesting in discerning . . . speech.' The root of this discerning speech is metaphor, which is not merely one of the tropes available to clever orators and writers but rather 'a fundamental contribution to the structure of our world . . . Rhetoric understood as ingenium makes meaning."[11]

Buttrick, in an understatement, says, "Let's not disparage rhetoric."[12] Once preachers were trained in rhetoric. Nancey Murphy has also engaged the discipline of rhetoric in her *Reasoning and Rhetoric in Religion*. Murphy includes studies of St. Augustine, John Broadus, and Thomas Long in her work. In addition, Fred Craddock and Thomas Long have made substantial contributions to the relationship between philosophy, rhetoric, and homiletics.

Rhetoric may be viewed as the incubator of Christian preaching from the end of the first century until the works of Whatley in the nineteenth century. Plato and Aristotle informed Christian theology. A theologian was defined as a Platonist or an Aristotelean. Aquinas, who may have out-Aristotled Aristotle, referred to the rhetorical master as "the philosopher." Yet this wellspring of rhetorical wisdom has been dismissed as lacking homiletical significance no longer necessary for undergirding the preaching enterprise.

My 1990 dissertation, "The Epistemic Power of Metaphor: A New Homiletics" argued that homiletics is rhetoric.[13] In it I suggested that meta-

11. Crusius, foreword in Grassi, *Rhetoric as Philosophy*, xv.
12. Buttrick, *Homiletic*, Kindle ed. loc. 380.
13. Published as *The Creative Power of Metaphor*.

phor helps preachers create Christian community as a way-of-being in the world.[14] This is the ongoing dance with metaphors.

Lakoff, in *Metaphors We Live By*, claims that one of our everyday metaphors is "Argument is war."[15] Lakoff notes that this metaphor of argument/war appears in a wide variety of conversational expressions: "Your claims are indefensible. He attacked every weak point in my argument. His criticisms were right on target. I demolished his argument. You disagree? Okay, shoot! If you use that strategy, he will wipe you out!" Note the war language in those expressions. Preachers seem to have developed layers of niceness that preclude warlike metaphors. And yet in 2016 Americans elected a president whose entire vocabulary was filled with war metaphors. Rhetorical scholar Robert Ivie says, "Demolition was the guiding trope of Trump's apocalyptic rhetoric."[16] Weaponized rhetoric is now part of the evangelical arsenal.

GENERAL OBSERVATIONS ABOUT THE SERMON AS ARGUMENT

We live at a point in history where the demand for individual freedom has been coupled with the notion of common sense to the point that what passes for common sense threatens to cut off at the knees action to prevent existential threats to human survival. The preacher must swim against the strong currents of both the demand for absolute freedom and the notion of common sense that defies truth and reason. This trend has reached such epidemic proportions that Hauerwas makes the shocking statement: "No task is more important than for the Church to take the Bible out of the hands of individual Christians."[17]

An argument moves from a basic claim to a persuasive conclusion. This movement puts the preacher in the company of creation. Rowan Williams reminds us that movement and energy are at the heart of creation. "The scientist, of course, will tell us that at the heart of every apparently solid thing is the dance of the subatomic particles."[18] The preacher should be delighted that this sort of talk puts movement and energy at the center, but will want to add that at the heart of the sermon is the potential of the outpouring of life from God. Williams continues, "It's a vision present in many of our prayers as well as hymns, and it's there too in the Bible, most of all in what are usually called

14. Kennedy, *Creative Power of Metaphor*, 64–65.
15. Lakoff and Johnson, *Metaphors We Live By*, 4.
16. Ivie, "Rhetorical Aftershocks of Trump's Ascendancy," 62.
17. Hauerwas, *Unleashing the Scripture*, 15.
18. Williams, *Tokens of Trust*, 36.

the 'Wisdom Books' of the Old Testament and the Apocrypha—Proverbs, bits of Job, some of the Psalms, the Wisdom of Solomon, the Wisdom of Jesus son of Sirach, and so on."[19] Motion, energy, emotion—these are the essential ingredients to the creativeness of the sermon.

In arguing, the preacher engages in persuasion. The preacher's goal is to persuade people to a new way of thinking. Both biblical definitions of "to repent" are in play when persuasive preaching occurs: "to turn" and "to change the mind." St. Paul says, "Therefore, knowing the fear of the Lord, we try to persuade people, but we ourselves are well known to God, and I hope that we are also well known to your consciences."[20] Luke offers a picture of Paul's preaching: "Every Sabbath he would argue in the synagogue and would try to convince Jews and Greeks."[21]

Christian preachers make one primary claim in every sermon: "Jesus is Lord." This primary claim unsettles all imperial claims to truth and power. This claim opposes the claim of the powers and principalities that they control what passes for truth. The claim of the preacher is a counterclaim to that of the world.

Two primal claims face us: "Jesus is Lord" and "Caesar is Lord." When the first Christians made the claim "Jesus is Lord," they did so in full awareness of a dominant counterclaim: "Caesar is Lord!" In Thessalonica, a group of Jews organized a mob and dragged Jason and some other believers before the city authorities, alleging, "these people who have turned the world upside down have come here also, and Jason has entertained them as guests. They are all acting against the decrees of Caesar, proclaiming that there is another king, Jesus."[22] Caesar, like his Old Testament predecessor Pharaoh, is a metaphor for all the evil that opposes God in the world. Jesus confronts the forms, presuppositions, values, and claims that "Caesar" and Pharaoh have staked. There is always a Caesar at the center of the world of power. Caesar/Pharaoh is clearly a metaphor. "He embodies and represents raw, absolute, worldly power. He is, like Pilate after him, a stand-in for the whole of the empire. As the agent of the 'empire of force,' he reappears in many different personae."[23]

The preacher, equipped with the gathered materials of analogy, metaphor, simile, example, and illustration—a veritable army of tropes—makes

19. Williams, *Tokens of Trust*, 36–37.
20. 2 Cor 5:11.
21. Acts 18:4.
22. Acts 17:6–8.
23. Brueggemann, *Truth Speaks to Power*, 17. Brueggemann says, "I take the generative phrase from James Boyd White, *Living Speech: Resisting the Empire of Force.*"

the claim of the gospel knowing that it is contestable and elusive. Yet despite all the twists and turns, the preacher remains confident that she/he speaks truth. The tropes chosen by the preacher are a way of naming the world. As Burke puts it, "Such naming is done, not for the sheer glory of the thing, but because of its bearing upon human welfare."[24] This suggests that the most complex and sophisticated sermons can be legitimately considered as "proverbs writ large."[25]

By "proverb" I also mean metaphor. The point of view offered is that metaphors are strategies for dealing with the situations that confront the preacher. The preacher develops strategies for dealing with the situations that confront the congregation. Another name for strategies might be arguments or attitudes. Remember that "strategy" is itself a military metaphor suggesting the positioning of troops in the most advantageous of way. The preacher's claim reveals the sermon's strategy.

This is the question the preacher must ask of every piece of material: "Will this preach?" Here the question becomes, "What do we have to go on?" Even if the congregation shows up on Sunday with no criticism, no demands for clarification, the preacher owes it to her own sermon to ask, "What have I got to go on?" If challenged, it is the preacher's task "to produce whatever data, facts, or other backing she considers relevant and sufficient to make good the initial claim."[26]

Preachers make assertions in sermons. This is a commitment to a particular claim. The preacher's job is to establish the veracity of her claim. In other words, she "must be able to establish it."[27] The preacher has to make good on the assertions by showing that they are justifiable. "How is this to be done? Unless the assertion was made quite wildly and irresponsibly (always a possibility in a sermon or political speech), we shall normally have some facts to which we can point in its support."[28]

The preacher's argument will include examples, images, and illustrations that are "visual arguments." The preacher needs to be well prepared with a wealth of metaphor, analogy, symbols, and all kinds of depiction. Metaphor possesses the emotional power to invoke a new reality for the congregation—the coming of the unexpected kingdom of God into human consciousness. In short, metaphor possesses epistemic, reality-creating power.

---

24. Burke, "Literature as equipment for living," 293.
25. Burke, "Literature as equipment for living," 293.
26. Toulmin, *Uses of Argument*, 13.
27. Toulmin, *Uses of Argument*, 90.
28. Toulmin, *Uses of Argument*, 90.

Is the new reality created by metaphor evolutionary or revolutionary? Is it persuasive or coercive? Here the preacher moves from the paradigm that the purpose of the sermon is to get a person to "repent" and have the revolutionary experience of becoming a Christian to the idea that "repentance" is not a one-shot, one-time experience, but a lifetime of confession and change.

For example, a progressive Christian sees developing ethical consciousness as a viable and useful tool of biblical interpretation. The moral development of humanity for example led to evolutionary changes that moved from slavery as ordained of God to slavery as an inhumane, immoral, and unlawful practice. In areas that still create difficulty for churches—such as the ordination of women and gay marriage—the ethical consciousness of progressives led to both the ordination of women and the acceptance of gay marriage. The argument over the validity of ethical consciousness as a tool for biblical interpretation remains a tense debate among evangelicals and progressives.

For example, the arguments over slavery continued for more than two centuries. In the years prior to the Civil War, Protestant preachers in the South labored mightily to produce "biblical" justifications for slavery. The book of Genesis records an instance of Noah cursing his son Ham's descendants to be slaves. Although there is no biblical evidence that Ham was the "father" of African peoples, various Jewish, Christian, and Islamic writers came to believe that he was, and their association helped to justify centuries of African enslavement. Poor Ham had to bear the burden of slavery as ordained of God deep into the nineteenth century. David Goldenberg in *The Curse of Ham: Race and Slavery in Early Judaism, Christianity and Islam*, looks at how a misinterpreted Bible story has been used to justify centuries of African slavery. Goldenberg's investigation covers a 1,500-year period, from ancient Israel (around 800 BCE) to the eighth century CE, after the birth of Islam. By tracing the development of anti-Black sentiment during this time, Goldenberg uncovers views about race, color, and slavery that took shape over the centuries—most centrally, the belief that the biblical Ham and his descendants, the black Africans, had been cursed by God with eternal slavery. He opens his work with a recitation of Genesis 9:18–25, the story of Ham seeing his father, Noah, naked. Goldenberg says, "This biblical story has been the single greatest justification for Black slavery for more than a thousand years. It is a strange justification indeed, for there is no reference in it to Blacks at all."[29] Here the preacher should also read J. Kameron Carter's *Race: A Theological Account*, which traces the rise of racism

---

29. Goldenberg, *Curse of Ham*, 1.

and white supremacy to second-century Gnosticism and their undoing of the Jewishness of Jesus.[30] Carter argues, "In making Christ non-Jewish . . . He became white."[31]

We are still dealing with the ramifications of these deeply embedded racial attitudes. In addition, we now must deal with a furious reaction against even the idea of "racism" from conservative politicians and evangelicals. The arguments are fierce as words like "wokeness" and "critical race theory" explode in political diatribes. American historian David Blight should have the attention of every preacher:

> If you repeat the terms "voter fraud" and "election integrity" enough times on the right networks you have a movement. And "replacement theory" works well alongside a thousand repetitions of "critical race theory," both disembodied of definition or meaning, but both scary. Liberals sometimes invite scorn with their devotion to diversity training and insistence on fighting over words rather than genuine inequality. But it is time to see the real enemy—a long-brewing American-style neo-fascist authoritarianism, beguilingly useful to the grievances of the disaffected, and threatening to steal our microphones midway through our odes to joy.[32]

Eddie Glaude seems to be shouting, "There are those among us willing to turn their backs on democracy to safeguard their privilege. We won't allow it. No more sweet-talking. No more dancing. No one can be comfortable. And no individual or organization can say they alone represent black people. 'We are the leaders we've been looking for.' Together, we must close the value gap and uproot racial habits by doing democracy, once again, in black. If we fail this time—and if there is a God I pray that we don't—this grand experiment in democracy will be no more."[33] Preaching operates at a crossroads where there are moments when theological, cultural, or biblical or ethical issues arise and one or several thinkers come to view accepted concepts in ways that differ from those in which concepts have traditionally been viewed.

Despite the testimony of history and the African American prophetic tradition, politicians and preachers push back to deny systemic racism as a problem. They resist the pressures toward anti-racism in all its emotional,

---

30. Carter, *Race*, 7.
31. Carter, *Race*, 7.
32. Blight, "Trump Has Birthed a New 'Lost Cause' Movement."
33. Glaude Jr., *Democracy in Black*, 236.

disciplinary, and professional aspects. The emotional aspects derive from the sense of shame that is invoked in the process of arguing for a change.

A major topic for preachers today should be the explosive clash between shame and dignity playing out in our churches and politics. The pedagogy of shame has a long history in Christian preaching. Elspeth Probyn writes that rather than seeing shame as a toxin to be purged from the social body, we should think of it as a necessary element of embodied interliving. I would add, shame is a necessary component of pedagogy. Many scholars, including Probyn, Eve Kosofsky Sedgwick, and Megan Watkins have commented on the affective dimensions of pedagogy.[34] The question of the role of shame in preaching recalls centuries of preachers dealing in shame in negative and positive ways. Not all shame is bad. Silvan Tomkins proposes that parents form their children's behaviors by shaming them around particular actions, clipping certain desires and allowing others to flourish.[35] The chisel that is used to sculpt civilized subjects is shame, which chips away at some desires and produces disciplined bodies.

This is where rhetoric loops back in to impact the pedagogy of preaching. Schaefer notes, "Pedagogy is not just something that happens to kids. We are always being taught by people around us. Progressive politics—in particular the politics of antiracism, gender emancipation, queer emancipation, and of new horizons of political enfranchisement—is organized around a retraining and a reteaching of bodies. Therefore, progressive politics is a project intimately associated with shame."[36] As critical race theorist Sharon Patricia Holland argues, racism is not simply a neutral exercise of opinion. It is maintained by a formation of pleasure,[37] what Tomkins might identify as the thrill of contempt.[38] Holland calls this racism's "own erotic life" and Schaefer refers to it as the "hedonicity of hate."[39] It is precisely because racism (and other forms of racialization) is pleasurable that the effort to unravel it is so perilous. Progressive pedagogy's goal is to eliminate this erotics or jouissance by blocking the circuit of desire for conservatives. Like a beta blocker—a drug that prevents the stimulation of the adrenergic receptors responsible for increased cardiac action—progressives use the

---

34. Probyn, "Teaching Bodies"; Sedgwick, "Teaching/Depression"; Watkins, "Desiring Recognition, Accumulating Affect"; Watkins, "Pedagogic Affect/Effect"; Watkins, "Thwarting Desire."
35. Tomkins, *Affect Imagery Consciousness*, xxxvii.
36. Schaefer, "Whiteness and Civilization."
37. Holland, *Erotic Life of Racism*, 107.
38. Schaefer, *Religious Affects*, 123
39. Holland, *Erotic Life of Racism*, 107; Schaefer, *Religious Affects*, 123.

injection of shame to prevent the stimulation of pleasure felt by racists, sexists, and homophobes.

Shame saturates contemporary politics and church life. "Bodies that once felt like the unchallenged masters of their space—white bodies, male bodies, cis bodies, straight bodies, rich bodies, citizen bodies—are being confronted, more and more, with a demand to respond to the violence trailing in the wake of the comforts and pleasures they enjoy."[40] This effect is amplified by the increasing opposition by the former masters of shame (the evangelicals) by insisting they are not racists. They repudiate progressive shame altogether rather than responding to the evolutionary challenge of repenting—changing their minds and actions. I contend that much of the emotional anger and fear comes out of this ongoing battle between shame and its refusal. The attempt to rip systemic structures of degradation and abuse from speech has produced a fierce refusal of culpability by evangelicals.

The preacher faces these competing emotional arguments in every sermon. It impacts every church in America. "A pastor asked me the other day, 'What percentage of churches would you say are grappling with these issues?' And I said, 'One hundred percent. All of them,'" Russell Moore, editor at *Christianity Today*, says. "I don't know of a single church that's not affected by this."[41]

THE SERMON AS ARGUMENT

In the Old Testament there are narrative passages where Abraham and Moses argue with God. The psalmists argue with God. Job argues with God. Jonah argues with God. Jeremiah argues with God. Sustained arguments across Scripture's narratives are sufficient evidence that the sermon may at times appear as an argument with God, with the congregation, with a secular world, or even with the devil. Stanley Hauerwas "believes sermons should be arguments."[42] I agree. The seminary is a school of rhetoric

Albert Jonsen's thesis is that ethicists "invent and improvise arguments" in much the same way that classical musicians extemporize on particular musical scores. Both move—make judgments, execute actions—from themes already laid down. While improvisation allows and indeed encourages the virtuoso to stray, wander, explore, it nonetheless demands that she remain close to home. Improvisation "departs from the composition and must return to it; and, indeed, even as it flows from the artist's virtuosity,

---

40. Schaefer, "Whiteness and Civilization," 9.
41. Alberta, "How Politics Poisoned the Evangelical Church."
42. Hauerwas, *Cross-Shattered Church*, 21.

it must remain at least remotely true to the composer's inspiration."[43] All of which is to say that improvisation is a difficult art because it is under constant negotiation.

Rhetorical invention is a feature of the preacher's craft in ways like the improvisation and invention of the musician during a performance. Invention describes the argumentative, persuasive core of rhetoric. More precisely, invention entails all the thinking, reading, and gathering of materials by the preacher. Invention is a "living entity" within the preacher's mind—with her every moment of every day. The preacher has to always be inventing for the next sermon. The best preachers, with manuscript in front of them in the pulpit, will improvise. Preachers invent and improvise arguments from texts, topics, ideas, concepts already part of the tradition. In the same manner, musicians extemporize the melodies, keys, and rhythms of their tradition. The invention of the concerto form for orchestra and solo instrument in the seventeenth and eighteenth centuries, for example, "allowed the soloist an opportunity to show technical skill by departing from the composer's notation and playing freely for some time."[44]

Rowan Williams says, "When you see a great performer at work realizing a piece of music, you are looking at one human being at the limit of their strength and concentration. All their strength, their freedom, and you could even say their love is focused on bringing to life the work and vision of another person."[45] The preacher at work realizing a biblical text is completely free and at the same time captured by the words of the text. During the performance of the sermon, the preacher—the whole of her being, her life, her freedom, her skill—is lifted up to the third heaven as this mysterious, different rendition of the text comes to life. The vision and imagination of the text's composer comes through, but the human particularity of the preacher is not removed. The preacher and the text become "consubstantial" thus freeing the preacher to improvise, create, and make known to others a new song.

The primary use of argument is to justify a claim. This means producing reasons for a claim after the fact of arriving mentally at that claim. For the preacher, this means that prior to the sermon the preacher has a claim that will be the subject of the sermon. A sound argument stands up to criticism because it has produced a strong claim. For example, in my sermon, "Being Born Again and Again and Again," I make the claim that "being born again" is a metaphor that includes the possibility of multiple experiences of

---

43. Jonsen, quoted in Hauerwas, *Performing the Faith*, 242.
44. Hauerwas, *Performing the Faith*, 80.
45. Williams, *Tokens of Trust*, 72.

being born again. The entire sermon is built around that major claim and the counter claims of evangelicals about the nature of being born again.

If the preacher's claim is that Darwin's theory of evolution is a useful explanation for the existence of human life on earth, in what ways can the preacher justify her claim? What is the backing for this claim from Scripture and science? What are the oppositions that are likely to block the preacher's argument—oppositions that may have been pre-formed in the minds of some members of the congregation?

Here are a pair of examples of extended arguments that a preacher may use. These examples are in essay form rather than sermon form but provide the same concepts.

CHALLENGING THE CLAIMS OF EVANGELICALS

Evangelicals make incredulous claims—claims so huge people think they must be right otherwise they would be unbelievable. For example, some Christians are fond of saying they "hate what God hates." The presumption that someone "hates what God hates" turns out to be exactly that: a presumption. We don't know the mind of God in any way that might be considered complete. If we claim that we know the mind of God revealed in Scripture, we are not in a better position because our own prejudice in reading and interpreting the Bible may skew our understanding of what God hates.

I challenge the presumptions of anyone claiming they hate what God hates. Such a statement is a product of bad religion. The first indication of bad religion is the presumption that a preacher knows what he is talking about when he claims God is a hater. Williams says that "bad religion is about not trusting God."[46] Fred Craddock says, "There's the gulf of bad religious experiences. Some people have had terrible religious experiences."[47] Imagine being a young person who is gay, who loves Jesus, loves the church, has trusted Jesus as Savior, has been baptized, and sits in church on Sunday and hears the preacher condemn being gay as an abomination and adds that "God hates gays." Imagine that young man's broken heart for a moment.

I challenge the presumption that they know what they say when they say "God." Hauerwas says, "For it turns out that we are most likely to take God's name in vain when we assume we can know what we say when we say 'God.'"[48] I accuse evangelicals of taking God's name in vain when they

---

46. Williams, *Tokens of Trust*, 9.
47. Craddock, *Cherry Log Sermons*, 51.
48. Hauerwas, *Working with Words*, 79.

attempt to put in God's mouth their hateful language about gays. The word "God" can be easily hijacked for nefarious purposes. It can be used to legitimate power over people who are unable to defend themselves, to legitimate social formations that tempt Christians to abandon Christianity for secular power.

For God's sake, we put "In God we trust" on our money. This is not the God of the Bible, but the god of America and capitalism. We added "one nation under God" to our pledge of allegiance. Today Christian nationalists used the Pledge of Allegiance as their creed. The use of God in these political contexts makes God a useful commodity. It is thus acceptable in public forums of the state because there is no specific faith tradition attached to it. How easy it is for people to corrupt the word "God."

It is ironic that evangelicals, charged with proclaiming the gospel of Jesus, are more likely to invoke the American god—the generic god that can be given any meaning that anyone desires. This helps legitimize the violence of the state. Hauerwas makes clear, "If you are to minister to a church that is an alternative to a nation-state that has co-opted the word 'god' as a means of legitimating the violence it calls peace, you should insist that it makes all the difference that when the church says 'peace' the peace that is said requires that we also say 'Jesus.'"[49]

Second, I challenge the presumption that evangelicals know what God hates. This is not to ignore that there are biblical attempts to delineate what God hates. Proverbs 6, for example, provides a list of what God hates: "There are six things that the Lord hates, seven that are an abomination to him: haughty eyes, a lying tongue, and hands that shed innocent blood, a heart that devises wicked plans, feet that hurry to run to evil, a lying witness who testifies falsely, and one who sows discord in a family."[50]

That list may surprise those who think God hates gays. The list sounds more like a typical day in Washington, DC, doesn't it? The idea that God hates the way we do politics is not that far-fetched. Zechariah pinpoints God's hatred in the political realm: "These are the things that you shall do: speak the truth to one another, render in your gates judgments that are true and make for peace, do not devise evil in your hearts against one another, and love no false oath, for all these are things that I hate, says the Lord."[51]

The biblical witness seems clear that God hates idolatry: "Yet I persistently sent to you all my servants the prophets, saying, "I beg you not to do

---

49. Hauerwas, *Working with Words*, 91.
50. Prov 6:16–19.
51. Zech 8:16–17.

this abominable thing that I hate!"[52] The metaphorical truth of the Scripture is that God treats idolatry as adultery. God's people have committed multiple adulteries; they are serial adulterers. Preachers confront idolatry as the primary rebellion of people against God.

Amos also has a clear vision of what God hates: "I hate, I despise your festivals, and I take no delight in your solemn assemblies. Even though you offer me your burnt offerings and grain offerings, I will not accept them, and the offerings of well-being of your fatted animals I will not look upon. Take away from me the noise of your songs; I will not listen to the melody of your harps. But let justice roll down like water and righteousness like an ever-flowing stream."[53] Psalm 11:5 claims that God hates violence. God hates wickedness. Malachi says that God hates divorce. "For I hate divorce, says the Lord, the God of Israel, and covering one's garment with violence, says the Lord of hosts. So take heed to yourselves and do not be faithless."[54]

Third, I challenge the presumption that God hates any human beings or any entity in God's created world. God's agenda is open for all to see: peace and praise. There's no hate in the Godhead. The love between the persons of the Trinity is at the very heart of the Christian faith. The New Testament writers have nothing to say about what God hates. John insists that God is love. "God is light and in him there is no darkness at all."[55] This matters because hate originates in darkness, in rebellion against God's purpose of peace and praise.

Finally, I challenge the presumption that preachers have the right to say, "I hate what God hates." When preachers make hateful, demeaning, judgmental statements they usually put the blame on God. When Wiley Drake prayed for God to kill President Obama,[56] he claimed that people should not be mad at him because he was merely saying what God said. This is a false claim because God has not said that God wishes for the death of anyone. Drake, like other preachers before him, and politicians like Lauren Boebert,[57] are using verses from Psalm 109:8–13. This is one of the imprecatory prayers whose purpose is to show the depth of human agony and despair when faced by implacable and unjust rulers. These psalms are

---

52. Jer 44:4.
53. Amos 5:21–24.
54. Mal 2:16.
55. 1 John 1:5.
56. Allen, "Wiley Drake Lifts Call for 'Imprecatory Prayer' against President Obama."
57. Balevic, "Lauren Boebert Receives Cheers at a Christian center after Saying She Prays that Biden's 'Days Be Few and Another Take His Office.'"

gut-wrenching, human prayers and not the utterances of the God of love. The presumptions of Drake and Boebert are presumptions.

Franklin Graham used the same excuse. After using the Bible to defend his harsh statements about gays, Graham doubled down by dragging God into the arena of the accusation of hate. Graham points out, "They say, 'Well, you're offending a lot of people. I'm not offending them, but God's offending them, because it is what God says. But my message is not against gay people, or people that think differently or worship differently from us. My message is about love.'"[58] It's hard to decipher Graham's talking out of both sides of his mouth, but I am concentrating on his presumption that God is offended by the presence of gay people. This is an unbiblical, unchristian, and hateful statement from Graham. He makes it worse by insisting that his message is about love.

If we feel obligated to make presumptions, then let's go with the realism of Job and Psalms, which both depend upon the presumption that God is God, and we are not. Let's own up to our shortcomings and our lack of knowledge. We don't always know the mind of God. It is hard to be patient with the arrogant presumptions of those who speak of God with such certainty. I have lost all patience and Christian charity for these merchants of hate, as well as the perorations and tirades of preacher moralists, gravely and condescendingly informing us that they and they alone know what God hates. But obviously, it is hard not to hear disquisitions on the hatefulness of God confidently delivered by persons who have made no discernible effort to ascertain who God is.

It seems a curious delusion—but apparently it is one shared by a great number of the more passionate evangelicals—to imagine that Christianity has never at any point during the two millennia of its intellectual tradition chosen mercy and grace, empathy, and compassion over prejudice and hatred. The Bible has been read for too many centuries by those with the power to authorize appalling abuse, mistreatment, and even murder of Jews, women, and gay people.

To badmouth God as a hater doesn't inspire a positive response to the Christian faith; it freezes people's hearts. To claim God is a hater is first and foremost to put the preacher on a pedestal as if he is Moses returning from Sinai with the Ten Commandments. Instead, he is just a little man, a cipher in the gears of injustice.

Enough of the presumptions of evangelicals. The time has come to fight the cruelty imposed on others in the name of God. As surely as we finally mustered the courage to condemn slavery, now we must show the

---

58. Kennedy, "Franklin Graham Says He's not a Preacher of Hate."

same courage and the same willingness to speak up for all Others who have been so shamed, so harmed, and so horribly treated for so long.

CONTRAPUNTAL CLAIM: GOD'S CONCERN FOR THE GENTILES MIRRORS GOD'S CONCERN FOR ALL OF HUMANITY

The preacher, with strong backing from biblical texts, can offer the counterclaim that God loves all humanity, including foreigners. The book of Jonah provides the contrapuntal for the notion that God only loves Israel. The accepted frame—God only loves Israel—was not open for discussion. Jesus' sermon at the synagogue in Nazareth shows the power of framing. Any arguments to the contrary fall on deaf ears—especially conservative deaf ears—brains with frames that don't fit the claim of God caring for all foreigners.

Jesus provides specific historical examples as grounds for his claim: The widow of Zarephath in Sidon and Naaman the Syrian leper. No one in the audience would have disputed the examples Jesus uses. But look at the outcome: "When they heard this, all in the synagogue were filled with rage. They got up, drove him out of the town, and led him to the brow of the hill on which their town was built, so that they might hurl him off the cliff." Preaching against embedded racist nationalism is not the easy thing we may have presumed.

If a congregation is convinced that God doesn't love foreigners, the same sort of frame may be in place for how God relates to immigrants, women, minorities, gays, and transgender people. Frames are not changed by a single sermon. The outcome of one powerful sermon insisting on a truth people are not prepared to hear is predictable: rage.

A preacher or professor with the highest possible credentials will experience this kind of reaction to any attempt to change the framing of an evangelical audience. Francis Collins, despite the authenticity of his credentials as a leading scientist and faithful Christian, has faced hostile congregations when he has been a guest speaker. Why? Many conservative evangelicals have rejected Collins because they have a frame that accepts the first three chapters of Genesis as literal. When Collins, after giving his Christian testimony, states that he believes in evolution and does not read the first chapters of Genesis literally, he faces abusive treatment. In *The Language of God* he recalls speaking at a national gathering of Christian physicians. Some in attendance walked out "shaking their heads in dismay" when he confessed to being an evolutionist.[59] People have stormed out of Southern Baptist churches when they discovered that he accepted evolution. Others came to the microphone after his talk and implied that, in accepting evolution, he was "under the influence of the devil." And, though Collins regularly receives critical email from nonbelievers, the "nastiest" messages come from fellow Christians, "infuriated that someone who claims to be a believer could say these things about the truth of the evolutionary process." He has even been "excommunicated" a couple of times, which, given that he is Protestant, is technically impossible.[60]

SECOND SAMPLE CLAIM: GLOBAL WARMING

The emotional environment of preaching has become one of precarity. People feel they are losing something essential to life. They exist in precarity. Climate change denial is the most epic form of fake news our culture has even known. Not only will preachers who address global warming from a creation/stewardship perspective have trouble gaining adherents, but the pushback will be substantial. Evangelical preachers have made climate change a comedic topic—poking fun at the idea. It is unprecedented in its extremity and absurdity. It's like having a dance on the deck of the Titanic before the ship sank.

Climate change denial has allied with one of the newest and most dangerous of evangelical virtues, "freedom." "Climate-denial pretends to give the denier a power greater than that of nature... To give the denier freedom from truth itself, in the case of the most consequential truth at present bearing down upon humanity."[61] The preacher deals with people "unwilling to be 'bound' by anything, not even truth itself."[62]

One of the casualties of this loss of accepting the truth is the undermining of the rhetorical trope of ethos—credibility. "How dare you interfere with my right to burn coal / to pollute."[63] Climate-deniers say to scientists, "Who are you to tell me that I should believe in global warming?" This attitude now passes for common sense in much of America. Conservatives push back against all efforts to mitigate global warming. The right wing Frank Luntz, who publishes books used as training manuals for conservatives, "persuaded conservatives to stop talking about 'global warming,'

59. See Stephens and Giberson, *Anointed*, 54–55.
60. Stephens and Giberson, *Anointed*, 55.
61. Read, "What Is New in Our Time," 81.
62. Read, "What Is New in Our Time," 81.
63. Read, "What Is New in Our Time," 84.

because it sounded too scary and suggested human agency. Instead, he brought 'climate change' into our public discourse on the grounds that 'climate' sounded kind of nice (think palm trees) and change just happens, no human agency."[64] It is the same attitude that denied COVID and birthed the anti-vax movement. The preacher already faces a difficult task in attempting to proclaim the dangers of greed, the unfettered pursuit of Mammon, and the love of money. Now, the preacher has to face the truth-deniers as well. People are denying, as if it's a joke, the most crucial truth about the world today—that pollution is on the verge of collapsing our planet—while continuing to make more money and make humanity more precarious.

Along with this sense of cultural precarity, decades of climate and geological research have coalesced in consensus about a different type of precarity that threatens not just publics, but humanity as a species: the Anthropocene. "In the Anthropocene," note G. Mitchell Reyes and Kundai Chirindo, "the precarity that had been the nearly exclusive preserve of people occupying the bottommost rungs of human society is becoming generalized to most if not all humans—though not in equal measure."[65] This means humans now face precarity at the biological or species scale. It indexes the fact that we (and our various publics) "have now ourselves become a geological agent disturbing [the] parametric conditions needed for our own existence."[66] In other words, humanity through climate change renders *all* publics precarious. This is an opportunity for scholars and for preachers to rethink our theories in light of the human species (in imminent danger). What might it mean to think about preachers as those who warn, not of hell fire and brimstone, but of the precarity of the planet in light of human agency?[67]

Climate change denial prepared the ground for the growth of the fake news and "post-truth" landscape as we now know it. The denier is involved in a kind of fantasized power over reality itself in the form of ultimate reality. The preacher needs the courage to address the sense of the "fantastical" that inhabits the evangelical framing.

We are in danger of losing the public sphere because of the constant exposure to new forms of propaganda: personalized propaganda. Personalized propaganda mixes with the rise of individualist ideology to create even more precarity for the planet and for democracy. The advent of Fox News,

---

64. Lakoff, *Don't Think of an Elephant*, 20.

65. Kundai, "Precarious 'Publics.'" See also Reyes and Chirindo, "Theorizing Race and Gender in the Anthropo-cene," 436.

66. Chakrabarty, "Climate of History," 218.

67. Chirindo, "Precarious Publics." I am indebted to Chirindo for raising my own environmental consciousness.

social media, and other conduits for expressive individualism has created a powerful enemy for preachers: propaganda.

The Old Testament words for propaganda were "false prophets." "Your prophets have seen for you false and deceptive visions; they have not exposed your iniquity to restore your fortunes but have seen oracles for you that are false and misleading."[68]

Ezekiel offers searing critique on false prophets and false witnesses:

> Mortal, prophesy against the prophets of Israel who are prophesying; say to those who prophesy out of their own imagination: "Hear the word of the Lord!" Thus says the Lord God, "Alas for the senseless prophets who follow their own spirit and have seen nothing! Your prophets have been like jackals among ruins, O Israel. You have not gone up into the breaches, or repaired a wall for the house of Israel, so that it might stand in battle on the day of the Lord. They have prophesied falsehood and lying divination; they say, 'Says the Lord,' when the Lord has not sent them, and yet they wait for the fulfillment of their word! Have you not seen a false vision or uttered a lying divination, when you have said, 'Says the Lord,' even though I did not speak?"[69]

Such warnings may sound dire, but exposure to personalized propaganda continues to bombard the "truth shield" of the public sphere. Paul promised us that the "belt of truth"[70] would protect us from harm. The emergence and hegemony of Facebook, Twitter, Instagram, and their unscrupulous purveyors of propaganda and fake news have put preachers on the defensive. The danger, and here the preacher must step up in the pastoral role of "rebuking,"[71] is that we are losing the public sphere. Truth now exists in a state of precarity. "The truth [cannot] be spoken by someone who still lives in falsehood."[72]

The language, the quotes, the memes, the slogans begin to "think for us." They are implanted in the mind as viruses that attack the truth and replace it with propaganda and conspiracy. The words are repeated endlessly until we think arguments can be won by slogans.

Historian Timothy Snyder, warning of the dangers of tyranny, says, "Most of the power of authoritarianism is freely given. In times like these, individuals think ahead about what a more repressive government will

68. Lam 2:14.
69. Ezek 13:2–7.
70. Eph 6:14.
71. 2 Tim 4:2.
72. Wittgenstein, *Culture and Value*, 35.

want, and then offer themselves without being asked. A citizen who adapts in this way is teaching power what it can do."[73] Satan, having lost his prize in the wilderness, has now claimed a significant portion of Jesus' followers with the lure of power.

Authoritarian pastors who "lord it over" congregations have learned a secret. People are remarkably receptive to obedience. Often, control is handed over to the authority figure without question or critical reflection. This is what rhetoricians term "ultimate identification." Followers, according to political scientist Ann Ruth Willner, perceive the authoritarian leader as "superman" (or "God's anointed"), they follow "blindly," they "unconditionally comply," and they "give unqualified emotional commitment."[74]

Willner describes what occurs in the unmediated relationship between followers and "the" leader. The followers abdicate judgment to the leader. Belief and obedience are almost automatic. Followers accept and believe that the past was as the leader portrays it, that the present is as he depicts it, and that the future will be as he predicts it. And they follow without hesitation his prescriptions for action.[75] If this is anywhere close to reality, we are quite close to a neo-fascist situation here.

The "cuckoo birds" of religious and political propaganda have deposited their eggs of "propaganda" in the nest of democracy and faith. In nature, the cuckoo eggs hatch earlier than the host eggs, and the cuckoo chick grows faster; in most cases, the chick evicts the eggs and/or young of the host species. By the time anyone knows there's a "cuckoo egg" in the nest, it is too late to act.

The crucial point is that everything depends on how far people abandon themselves to propaganda. In my view, this is the central struggle in life and faith—the struggle to discern the difference between genuine truth and fake truth, between what really does and doesn't make sense. The reality is that we are not as different from the climate-denying evangelicals as we like to think we are. We are perhaps living in "soft denial." "We are not facing reality, not changing our lives as climate-reality demands."[76] In a general sense, the preacher now faces ongoing challenges to her/his truth claims.

Joel Backstrom argues that "truth becomes a problem . . . where matters are morally-existentially charged, and so self-deception becomes tempting. To the extent that our life is marked by injustice and destructiveness, it is

---

73. Snyder, *On Tyranny*, 17.
74. Willner, *Spellbinders*, 8.
75. Willner, *Spellbinders*, 7.
76. Read, "What Is New in Our Time," 84.

... also marked by systematic falsification, a conspiracy to deny the truth about it, about us."[77]

Our culture has cultivated a rank contempt for truth that requires counterclaims from those who preach. There are national leaders who have deliberately advanced a "consumer" attitude toward truth. The attitude of individualism and consumerism combine to create precarity. The love of truth and reason collies with love for big business, wealth, the love of Mammon, and the demand of having the right to your own opinion no matter what. The evangelicals have become the most "postmodern" of all Americans. They have produced an extreme form of individualized relativism; an unthinking production of the worst element of our time—the perverse and deadly denial of ecological constraints. Instead of being the enemy of our secular age, the evangelicals have become the ultimate bastard child of the 1960s. Such irony!

The essential move for the preacher is to struggle against the befogging of her own understanding. There has to be clarity that begins with humility. "A philosophical problem has a form: I don't know my way about."[78] Then the preacher takes a stand and makes a mark in the name of truth.

For example, William Sloane Coffin Jr. determined that his long-term strategy was nuclear disarmament; Martin Luther King Jr.—civil rights; Will D. Campbell—reconciliation. Now, preachers have a calling to embrace the challenges of global warming and the changing and reining in of human appetites that are rooted and grounded in the ancient cardinal vices, especially greed.

There is a sense in which we live in pre-truth times. It isn't that one just hasn't yet arrived at truth, but that one actively tries to keep it away. This manifests itself as all kinds of stupidity and failures of understanding, but the root problem isn't intellectual. "What makes a subject hard to understand—if it's something significant and important" is rather, as Wittgenstein says, "the contrast between understanding the subject and what most people want to see. Because of this the very things which are most obvious may become the hardest of all to understand."[79] Only insofar as people are just and good, insofar as they don't fear each other and disgust themselves, but long wholeheartedly to know each other and themselves, can truth in the full sense be lived and spoken between them.

---

77. Backstrom, "Pre-Truth Life in Post-Truth Times," 97.
78. Wittgenstein, *Philosophical Investigations*, 11.
79. Wittgenstein, *Culture and Value*, 17.

RHETORIC AS THE GROUND FOR HOMILETICS: ERNESTO GRASSI

An Italian humanist philosopher/rhetorician may seem an unusual source to discover homiletical wisdom. But given the inhumanness of some American Christianity, a humanist philosopher can become a light for our journey. In *Rhetoric as Philosophy*, Grassi argues that rhetorical speech is the primary and original form of speech. It is tied to the act wherein the premises of thought are created. "It is this original, prophetic sense of the word, the word that connects the world to a transcendent order of reality, that is at the basis of rhetoric."[80] Rhetoric is no mere act of persuasion, a language of emotions, or a way of communicating truth established by logical thought. Rhetoric connects with imaginative speech and ingenuity to disclose the reality signified in terms of new situations. Grassi offers a humanistic conception of rhetoric that parallels the doctrine of incarnation in Christian theology. He insists that rhetoric is the ground of being, language the presupposition of religion, and that ingenium and metaphor empower the process of humanization. In his appeal to the primacy of metaphoric/poetic speech over scientific speech, Grassi opens the door to preaching that no longer has to be restricted by proofs, rationalizations, and unchanging principles.

Grassi says that "insight into relationships basically is not possible through a process of inference, but only through invention and discovery."[81] This is a continuous theme in Grassi: invention is primary over purely rational thought. For the preacher, this offers a freedom from imposing the scientific method on the Bible—a book filled with symbolic, metaphorical texts.

This symbolism presents an epistemological challenge to fundamentalists and literalists. George Marsden notes that fundamentalism was the result of an application of the scientific method to the Bible. The fundamentalists patched together nineteenth-century American values about truth, morality, and freedom with rational thought and produced a biblical literalism that has reduced the power of preaching to this day even in progressive churches.[82] The bold attempt to force the symbolic, metaphorical, rhetorical language of the Bible into scientific rationalism, Scottish common sense philosophy, and American common sense, has reduced the power of rhetoric as the true ground for homiletics.

---

80. Grassi, *Rhetoric as Philosophy*, 35.
81. Grassi, *Rhetoric as Philosophy*, 7.
82. Marsden, *Fundamentalism and American Culture*, 220–21.

Walter Brueggemann addresses the issue: "The gospel is thus a truth widely held, but a truth greatly reduced. It is a truth that has been flattened, trivialized, and rendered inane."[83] (This premise receives backing from Fred Craddock's *Overhearing the Gospel*.)[84] Brueggemann explains what happens when flat prose is imposed on the symbolic language of the Bible: "But more than that, our technical way of thinking reduces mystery to problem, transforms assurance into certitude, revises quality into quantity, and so takes the categories of biblical faith and represents them in manageable able shapes."[85] Robert Lifton, in his *Living and Dying*, has written of a "symbol gap" when "there are no religious symbols that are adequate to mediate experience. In such a gap, we become numb, and when numb, are capable of brutality. Positivistic, technical reason urges and embodies the banishment of liberated, liberating symbols."[86] The scientific method is anathema for interpreting Scripture.

Here's the plan: a cursory overview of Grassi's rhetorical stance followed by unpacking the significance of Grassi for preachers. Grassi presents three limitations of the scientific paradigm. It seeks to discover first principles with no attempt to understand the origins of the system. The result is that all reality is rational and that what cannot be numerically verified is not real, knowable, or worth studying. Lastly, Grassi says that the scientific paradigm is concerned only with universals and not with individual cases or situations.

Grassi's humanism has a great deal of influence on me. I was born left-handed and for many years I was a left-handed baseball pitcher. I am too old for baseball now, but for the record, I am still throwing "breaking pitches" from the left. Therefore, I value ideologies from the left more than those from the right. Without the influence of Grassi I would have never understood rhetoric and its importance for homiletics. Working with images and metaphors, rhetoric "makes manifest," revealing relationships and making connections. "Rhetorical language determines the premises themselves, that is, the dominant assumptions, first assertions, or hypotheses of formal discursive systems."[87] His insistence that rhetoric is the ground of being, that humanism trumps the scientific method, that ingenium and metaphor are the gateway to our well-being, combine to make Grassi an essential read for preachers.

---

83. Brueggemann, *Finally Comes the Poet*, Kindle ed. loc. 38–39.
84. Craddock, *Overhearing the Gospel*.
85. Brueggemann, *Finally Comes the Poet*, Kindle ed. loc. 40.
86. Lifton, *Living and Dying*, 137.
87. Grassi, *Rhetoric as Philosophy*, 97.

I often make use of Grassi's direct opposition to the scientific tradition, his basic concern that rhetoric is the means by which the human world appears and reveals itself, the necessity of examining particulars of human experience rather than being hidebound by the words encased in a leather-bound version of the King James Bible, and his emphasis on poetic language—tropes and metaphors. To trope, for Grassi, is to fight the dangers of a scientific and technological world. Grassi works to make humans more human.

Yet it remains an uphill struggle to persuade preachers that rhetoric has the primary place in homiletics. As Grassi confesses, "The problem confronting us is that our rationalistic scientific ideal of knowledge equates the rigor of objective thought with the provable and excludes every form of figurative, poetic, metaphorical, and rhetorical language from the theoretical sphere."[88] Despite these obstacles, the humanist tradition breaks with the primacy of logic and proofs and its language. It takes rhetoric as the starting point for philosophizing.

In a move that has importance, especially for preachers, Grassi refers to Dante's notion that the poet as orator is shown in all its power. Dante, after all, defines poetic language as "a rhetorical idea presented in music."[89] "According to Dante's definition language arises as a question or an answer in the context of some material or spiritual imposition of need."[90] This produces the production of meanings to sensory appearances. The divine manifests itself in this original tension.

Grassi's evaluation of Dante deserves a closer look. Dante "claims that 'true,' 'authentic' language can never be 'artificial' or 'fixed' but only one in which men work, act, and live—that language in which they express their strivings and passions that stem from a concrete situation."[91] He means here the native tongue of a particular people in all its historicity. For Christians, that is a reminder that the Greek New Testament, the native tongue of Christianity, was written in koine Greek—the street language of Athens.

Language arises as a question or answer. I believe that the language of theology, rhetoric, and philosophy arose in an unhistorical time from an unexpected source. The serpent in the garden of Eden started the game of language with a question, "Did God say?" All language since has been the attempt to answer that question.

---

88. Grassi, *Rhetoric as Philosophy*, 76.
89. Grassi, *Rhetoric as Philosophy*, 76.
90. Grassi, *Rhetoric as Philosophy*, 76.
91. Grassi, *Rhetoric as Philosophy*, 78.

For Dante the theory of language occurs in the story of the construction of the tower of Babel. The mythology of Babel tells us that there was only a single language for all humanity. This original language is fragmented by rebellion against God and work—the variety of differently structured activities. Here, for Dante, is the origin of language and work. This development of different languages is hard work; it requires effort. Here is the origin of history.

The universal language that existed prior to history was crystallized or set in stone, a language with fixed rules. For Dante, this universal language was Latin—a language constructed in a purely rational way and therefore ahistorical. The Christians who later invented the idea of "the literal word" of God conceived their language in the same way. It is a language they consider safe from historical changes. The task of the preacher is therefore rhetorical. She tropes the original language, or more precisely, re-tropes it, repurposing it to meet changing situations. In this way faith can be propelled forward by formulating meanings different from those already in circulation.

The relevance of Dante derives from his consciousness of his mission as a poet. He claims that authentic language can never be artificial, but only one in which men work, act, and live—that language in which they express their deepest emotions that stem from lived experiences. In other words, the poet and the preacher will speak from the native tongue in all its humanness and historicity. "The people's tongue is all the closer to us the more we are associated with it. For it is this alone that is then close to us, and not in any accidental way, but because it is connected with the people that are closest to us, our relatives, fellow-citizens, and our own people. This is our native tongue, which is not just close to us personally, but near to everyone of us."[92]

Dante describes the hunt for the right words as a hunt for a panther that is hidden in a thicket, in the bush of different dialects. His metaphor visualizes the multiplicity of formulations that result in different rhythms, standards, and orders that are all necessary to make possible a community's shared vocabulary. The hunt for the panther is dangerous because of how difficult it is for the preacher to be objective. For Dante the true language can only be found in work, in communication with others, and in the face of his own feelings. His thesis therefore is that the poet is the one who creates the meaning of reality through his own search for the true language. As Walter Brueggemann expresses it, "Finally comes the poet." Having noted that Dante believes the poet must be an orator, I am also suggesting that the preacher must be a poet.

---

92. Alighieri, *Convivio (The Banquet)*, 41.

The poet/orator/preacher creates the meaning of reality in the constant search for new tropes, new readings. "The language needed for this task," Grassi claims, "must use images and metaphors because this is the only way it can affect the passions. The poet must be an orator."[93]

The picturesque language of the preacher is metaphorical. The primacy of directive, revelatory, metaphorical language over argumentative, deductive, rational speech cannot be made clearer. This metaphorical language must be illuminating because it brings people into higher truths by the virtue of the "illuminating brilliance" of its creative poetic power.[94] Students of preaching read complex and difficult academic works in theology, ethics, and biblical studies. Putting that complexity into understandable, metaphorical language—the original tongue of the people—makes for a lifetime of hard translation. The task of the preacher is that of paraphrase. I refer to this as a popular or common paraphrase. Buttrick notes that the average seminary graduate has a vocabulary of about twelve thousand words whereas the average congregation will have a vocabulary of 7,500 words. He concludes that the words used for preaching, "the common shared vocabulary of a congregation," will consist of about five thousand words.[95] The challenge of the preacher is the unending task of increasing the shared vocabulary of preaching in line with the symbolic language of the Bible. And as Ellen Davis says, "The most difficult aspect of the Bible's literary complexity is its use of symbols."[96]

For the Greeks the term "metaphor" originally signified a concrete activity, that of carrying an object from one place to another. As the Gibeonites became "woodcutters and drawers of water for all the congregation, as the leaders had decided concerning them" the metaphor carries meaning from one place to another. Preachers should happily and humbly accept the metaphorical title of "Water Carriers for Jesus." Keep in mind, that in our modern understanding, "to carry the water" indicates a subservient position, to do the bidding, the menial tasks, and frequently the dirty work, of a more powerful person.

In the new world of Jesus' kingdom, "carrying the water" is a position of influence and standing. Carrying the water for the congregation becomes a useful work metaphor for the preacher. In the wilderness, after all, the people cried, "We thirst." "But the people thirsted there for water, and the people complained against Moses and said, 'Why did you bring us out of

---

93. Grassi, *Rhetoric as Philosophy*, 79.
94. Grassi, *Rhetoric as Philosophy*, 81.
95. Buttrick, *Homiletic*, Kindle ed. loc. 2439.
96. Davis, in Davis and Hays, eds., *Art of Reading Scripture*, 14.

Egypt, to kill us and our children and livestock with thirst?"[97] The woman at the well speaks for all humanity: "Sir, give me this water."[98]

In symbolic, metaphorical language we never encounter abstract human beings, but on the path of life, we encounter those who, like ourselves, find themselves through work, in temporal and spatial relationships. "The concepts through which we come to understand and 'grasp' each situation come from our ingenious, metaphorical, fantastic capacities that convey meanings in the concrete situations with which we are confronted."[99]

The metaphorical form of biblical language is the primary language of preaching. It is the only framework within which we can work out meanings and purposes of texts. Rhetorical language is primary for the preacher and now acquires an importance whereby it realizes a new model of thought. This is the framework in which rhetoric gains its contemporary theoretical importance for preaching.

In a practical way, Ellen Davis has identified four principles, what she defines as "critical traditioning," that apply to the preacher willing to dance with the metaphors: Texts of Scripture are difficult and present ethical problems for interpreters. Difficult texts are worthy of charity from interpreters. Ethical consciousness is a legitimate interpretative tool for preachers. Here Davis cites Stephen Fowl's suggestion that the issue of "how and under what circumstances homosexuals are to be recognized and included in the church"[100] be investigated in a manner analogous to the first Jewish Christians' discernment about gentile inclusion, as recorded in Acts 10–15. "The validity of a given interpretation does not depend on the interpreter's proximity to the authorial source, since an authoritative text is one authorized for repeated rereading and reinterpretation within the faith community."[101]

GRASSI AND HUMANISM

The work of ingenium is revealed through the work of the preacher. To accomplish this difficult work requires what Vico calls "the act of Hercules." For the preacher this means both work and the taking of pains, which is the double meaning of the word "labor." Without work, the taking of pains, and extreme labor of the mind and the heart, a sermon arrives stillborn.

97. Exod 17:3.
98. John 4:15.
99. Grassi, *Rhetoric as Philosophy*, 100.
100. See Fowl, *Engaging Scripture*, 127.
101. Davis and Hays, eds., *Art of Reading Scripture*, 179.

I have no patience with the old insistence that the conclusions of the mind are eternally valid, absolutely true. Preachers who insist on certainty never reach me. The truths we seek "always emerge within limited situations bound in space and time; i.e., they are probable and seem to be true only within the confines of 'here' and 'now,' in which the needs and problems that confront human beings are met."[102]

Preachers have issues that are rhetorical as well as theological. There's our loss of confidence in the power of words. There's also the idea that we don't really expect God to show up. The novel *Revelation* is the story of a preacher to whom God actually speaks and the chaos that then surrounds the preacher and his congregation.[103] Author Peggy Payne sheds light on the tendency of preachers to say, "God told me" or "God spoke to me last night."

We also have trouble trusting those to whom we preach. There's trouble in the covenant between preacher and people. People may think they are critics and not participants. They think the preacher is supposed to say only what the people already know and believe. The truth of the gospel is no easy thing to say to a congregation that presumes it is already righteous.

Grassi seeks to reclaim the humanism of rhetoric. I make a similar move in my attempt to project preaching as a human act, an act of flesh and blood. The humanist philosophy of Renaissance philosophy (especially in Italy) was partially repressed through the funeral pyres of the Inquisition. In some ways, this almost complete allegiance to Descartes and the philosophy of rational certainty continues to plague preaching.

The capacity that allows the human world to appear is characteristic of fantasy and is expressed originally in metaphors. The preacher must traverse this strange land of fantasy. The journey requires a Herculean act. The notion of the fantastic used here derives from literary theory. The genre of the fantastic is a celebration of ambiguity, something indefinite, a moment of hesitation and indecision. Todorov finds the fantastic suspended between the uncanny—the bizarre and ultimately untrue—on the one hand and the marvelous—the extraordinary but ultimately credible—on the other. When we encounter an extraordinary event, for the moment that we cannot decide whether we are hallucinating or witnessing a miracle, we are participants in the fantastic. It is a moment of epistemological uncertainty.[104] The literary fantastic, while it raises emotions and exploits attitudes, stubbornly refuses to render final judgments that would allow us to direct them.[105]

---

102. Grassi, *Rhetoric as Philosophy*, 10.
103. Payne, *Revelation*, Kindle ed. loc. 71.
104. Todorov, *Fantastic*.
105. Darsey, "Joe McCarthy's Fantastic Moment."

"Long ago God spoke to our ancestors in many and various ways by the prophets, but in these last days he has spoken to us by a Son, whom he appointed heir of all things, through whom he also created the worlds."[106] Paul outlines how Jesus entered the play: "For while we were still weak, at the right time Christ died for the ungodly."[107]

As Shakespeare describes the drama of God and humanity, "All the world's a stage, and all the men and women merely players. They have their exits and their entrances, and one man in his time plays many parts."[108] The preacher's task, in union with Father, Son, Holy Spirit, and church, is to play her role as herald, prophet, preacher and tell the story of God become man for the salvation of all humanity.

GRASSI'S CONTRIBUTIONS TO PREACHERS

Grassi helps the preacher understand that rhetorical speech is the primary and original form of speech. "Rhetoric possesses this original, prophetic sense of the word that connects us to the original word—'In the beginning was the Word.'"[109] Rhetoric connects with imaginative speech and ingenuity to disclose the reality signified in terms of new situations.

The key term in Grassi's rhetoric is "ingenium." It refers to a capacity to creatively shape the world. Ingenium is a way of "knowing" that exceeds ingenuity, mental cleverness, wit, or insight. Karen Foss summarizes ingenium as the "process by which humans move from the natural realm to the human one . . . Ingenium allows humans to deal with the changing situations of nature and thus make the transference from the world of senses to the world of intellect and interpretation."[110] Ingenium helps us decipher the world in order to discover reality and for the Christian, in the discovery of reality, ingenium becomes the origin of community. Preaching, for me, is the ecstasy of discovery, of being alive, of finding the path that leads to life.

Grassi shows us that metaphor provides for the operation of ingenium and allows for the transfer of meaning and for connection between the world of nature and the human realm. "Thus metaphor, as a process of transfer, has the ability to transform things—to create new relationships."[111] Since metaphor produces knowledge, we are released from the illusion that

---

106. Heb 1:1–2.
107. Rom 5:6–21.
108. Quoted in Taylor, *Scarlet Thread*, 22.
109. John 1:1.
110. Foss, Foss, and Trapp, *Contemporary Perspectives on Rhetoric*, 140.
111. Grassi, *Rhetoric as Philosophy*, 50.

rational, fixed truth is the only truth. The preacher is freed from describing facts or proving beliefs to the joy of creating images. As Jacob Bronowski says, "All our ways of picturing the invisible are metaphors, likenesses that we snatch from the larger world of eye and ear and touch."[112]

Grassi presents a notion of "folly" that feels remarkably like the concept of "folly" in St. Paul. Grassi reverses our current reliance on the scientific paradigm by choosing rhetoric as a way of "folly"—a way that seems foolish to the world.

With the nerve of a Hebrew prophet, Grassi warns that humanity is committing technological suicide. Even if science were to solve all problems, answer all questions, and verify every hypothesis, there is still no guarantee that this would make us more humane or that humanity would survive.

The threat we face is that of overdependence on the scientific paradigm, a convenient forgetting that science itself is rhetorical, metaphorical. There is no room for an attitude of superiority and arrogance on the part of those who believe in the primacy of rationality to solve all problems. There is no place for the same sense of superiority and arrogance on the part of those preachers who dismiss all legitimate advances of science. This should remind us of what Charles Taylor says that his point is rather to show that proponents on all sides are throwing "huger rocks . . . than are safe for dwellers in glass houses"[113] and "both sides need a good dose of humility"[114] concerning how "'fragile' their positions are and how deeply each is implicated in histories of violence."[115] Grassi offers us an alternative to the reduced, flat, rational paradigm. He offers the way of "folly" to help us discover values that can unify our lives. Like St. Paul, Grassi is an evangelist/poet/rhetor/prophet in the sense that his language is indicative, declarative, inventive, imaginative, and pathetic in character.

CHAIM PERELMAN

Chaim Perelman's *The New Rhetoric* offers preachers multiple insights into the art of preaching. Three important lessons for the preacher are rooted in Perelman's new rhetoric: The Jewish mode of argument in the pursuit of justice; the sermon as epidictic speech; and the celebration of the audience and community. Perelman developed a rhetorical philosophy intended to produce justice. David Frank says, "When Perelman turned to Jewish thought,

---

112. Bronowski, *Science and Human Values*, 52.
113. Taylor, *Secular Age*, 624.
114. Taylor, *Secular Age*, 675.
115. Hauerwas, *Working with Words*, 181.

he did so to chart a path between dualisms and to create a philosophical rhetoric that aspires to Tsedek, the Jewish conceptualization of justice."[116] The nucleus of Perelman's rhetoric is justice and its justification through epidictic argument.

THE JEWS AND JUSTICE

Preaching starts with the Jews. Justice for the oppressed made up the content and theme of the earliest preaching. The writers of the first five books of the Bible portrayed Moses as the first preacher of Israel. Whatever we decide about the identity of Moses, he is a metaphor for "preacher." In his first sermon, Moses preached to Pharaoh: "Let my people go." Leviticus, Numbers, and Deuteronomy expand on that first sermon with volumes of sermons attributed to Moses. The sermons in Leviticus are rooted in issues of justice: aliens, widows, orphans, and the poor. Elijah and Elisha caring for widows are archetypal Hebrew stories. Jesus uses the stories of Elijah and Elisha as illustrations in his sermons. The expositors of the Law were preachers.

The Hebrew prophets preached to God's people. Hosea preached, "Come, let us return to the Lord; for it is he who has torn, and he will heal us; he has struck down, and he will bind us up."[117] Jonah preached to the foreign city of Nineveh: "Another forty days and Nineveh is inverted."[118] The prophets preach to all nations to be just and righteous. Cornel West reminds us, "There is nothing tribalistic or nationalistic about prophetic witness. Xenophobic prejudices and imperialistic practices are unequivocally condemned."[119] Justice is the aspiration and goal of Jewish preaching.

Preaching speaks truth to power. West moves seamlessly from the ancient prophets to contemporary ones: "This profound tradition should inform and embolden the struggle against the callous indifference of the plutocratic elites of the American empire about the sufferings of our own poor and oppressed peoples. It should also help to illuminate the effects of our imperialism on the poor and oppressed peoples around the world."[120]

Connecting rhetoric to the argumentation of Judaism and her rabbis has major advantages for preachers. With substantial assistance from David A. Frank, rhetorical scholar, and Ellen Davis, Old Testament scholar, I offer preachers a way of preaching that connects with Jewish reading of Scripture

---

116. Frank, "New Rhetoric," 312.
117. Hos 6:1.
118. Jonah 3:4.
119. West, *Democracy Matters*, 18.
120. West, *Democracy Matters*, 19.

and argument. Frank's analysis of Perelman produces two arguments: Judaism and talmudic habits of argument are crucial; *The New Rhetoric* offers a philosophical rhetoric designed to seek justice and to develop its justification. Justice and its justification are the nucleus of Perelman's *New Rhetoric*, "a theory of justice,"[121] according to Crosswhite. Farrell writes that for Perelman justice is "the principal aim of all practical reasoning."[122] By embracing Judaic forms of preaching and argument, Christian preachers return to their roots. As Hopkins put it, "Mine, O Lord of life, send my roots rain."[123] The preacher who drinks from Jacob's well finds the words of life. As God opened the eyes of the outcast Hagar, the preacher versed in the Hebrew Scripture will see a well of water, and filling their jars with water, he will provide drink for God's children.[124]

Justice is the primary aim of preaching. The preacher calls out the sources of injustice. Preachers of justice will not shy away from targeting the human idolatry of relying only on military power. Aggressive militarism wastes resources that would build communities, reduce poverty, and make possible more just modes of life. The preacher is God's Zechariah when the nation is tempted by aggressive militarism and war. "This is the word of the Lord to Zerubbabel: Not by might, nor by power, but by my spirit, says the Lord of hosts."[125]

West sees aggressive militarism as a dogma endangering our nation's life. "Fashioned out of the cowboy mythology of the American frontier fantasy, the dogma of aggressive militarism is a lone-ranger strategy that employs 'spare-no-enemies' tactics. It guarantees a perennial resorting to the immoral and base manner of settling conflict, namely, the perpetration of the very sick and cowardly terrorism it claims to contain and eliminate."[126] Hosea makes clear that military alliances will not stay the judgment of God: "When Ephraim saw his sickness, and Judah his wound, then Ephraim went to Assyria, and sent to the great king. But he is not able to cure you or heal your wound."[127]

The preacher can never lose sight of the reality that the Romans brutally executed Jesus because he threatened the authoritarianism and militarism of the empire. Jesus, the new suffering servant, the stand-in for the

---

121. Crosswhite, "Reason as Justice," 1.
122. Farrell, *Norms of Rhetorical Culture*, 205.
123. Quoted in Taylor, *Secular Age*, 764.
124. Gen 21:19.
125. Zech 4:6.
126. West, *Democracy Matters*, 5.
127. Hos 5:13.

whole people of God, is pictured dramatically in the metaphorical language of Isaiah 53: "Surely he has borne our infirmities and carried our diseases; yet we accounted him stricken, struck down by God, and afflicted. But he was wounded for our transgressions, crushed for our iniquities; upon him was the punishment that made us whole, and by his bruises we are healed."[128] There is no stronger biblical trope standing against aggressive militarism with more power than that of the suffering servant.

In Numbers 22, there's a story of comedic genius that mocks military dependence over faith in God: Balaam's donkey standing in the middle of the road to block Balaam from his attempt to curse a military foe. Even the donkey has enough sense to oppose military intervention. In the genre of comedy, the appearance of a donkey elicits laughter. When the donkey talks wisely, the joke explodes with laughter. The donkey of Balaam rivals the great fish that swallowed Jonah for comedic genius. Perhaps the primordial metaphor for the comedic folly of the preacher remains Balaam's ass. After all, the ass speaks—a true Feast of Fools.

Mikhail Bakhtin has noted that during the Middle Ages and into the Renaissance, folly in the writings of Rabelais and in the form of "Carnival celebrated temporary liberation from the prevailing truth and from the established order; [they] marked the suspension of all hierarchical rank, privileges, norms, and prohibitions. Carnival was the true feast of time, the feast of becoming, change, and renewal."[129]

Another way the preacher can herald the quest for justice is to speak to the plight and value of all sorts of peoples. With the good news of Jesus, the preacher can speak to all the wounded and offended issues of identity that now haunt American Christianity. Issues related to homosexuality, women, minorities, and immigrants are identity issues. White males in particular feel threatened by diversity, openness, and a progressive agenda of acceptance of all Others. Here the preacher, informed by the Jewish tradition, can blend all human faculties, including empathy, understanding, and emotion with the reasonable.

The preacher names and condemns all the idols of our culture. The condemnation of idolatry requires all the preacher's resources because idolatry is such a subtle wickedness. We mostly think that we are no longer guilty of idolatry, as if it were an ancient sin now conquered. Yet idolatry is every love of the heart that is greater than our love for God. Idolatry sits on the throne of all empires, idolatry resides in the lap of luxury and greed, idolatry is the golden calf of excessive, unregulated capitalism. The preacher,

---

128. Isa 53:4–5.
129. Bakhtin, *Rabelais and His World*, 10.

with the boldness of Jesus, will preach the dangers of wealth without fear. As Cornel West puts it, "The golden calf of wealth, along with the blood-soaked flag that envelops it, is the true idol of empires, past and present."[130]

The preacher faces a daunting challenge in naming American Christianity's addiction to "greed." If people believe we no longer worship idols, show them the golden goose—the contemporary version of the golden calf. Our culture has a litany designed to protect the golden goose. American historian Robert McElvaine says, "'Don't kill the goose that lays the golden eggs' is one of the favorite sayings of champions of high profits, low taxes on the rich, concentrating wealth and income at the top, and the rest of the tenets of trickle-down economics. But when profits become too high and taxes on the very rich too low, the geese get obese, eventually stop laying eggs, and develop coronary problems."[131]

The economic, sociological, political experiences of the preacher must be part of her preaching. Perelman's experience of World War II and the Nazis factored into his writing of *The New Rhetoric*. That background now becomes crucial for preachers today in need of facing the growing precarity of a new fascism in American politics. Timothy Snyder notes, "The European history of the twentieth century shows us that societies can break, democracies can fall, ethics can collapse, and ordinary men can find themselves standing over death pits with guns in their hands. It would serve us well today to understand why."[132] He advises: Do not obey a voice of charisma and power without thinking about what he or she is saying. Do not obey the voice in advance. Take responsibility for the face of the world beginning in your local neighborhood because all politics is local. And defend and maintain ethics. Why? Because character still matters. Believe in truth: pursue it, follow it, keep it. Listen for dangerous words and refuse to follow the slinger of such words. Keep your cool when the unthinkable happens. Be a patriot in its deepest, truest sense. The true patriot carries on a love argument with the nation. And a true preacher resists the powers and the principalities.

As Kenneth Burke warned of the influence of Hitler, "Let us try also to discover what kind of 'medicine' this medicine-man has concocted, that we may know, with greater accuracy, exactly what to guard against, if we are to forestall the concocting of similar medicine in America."[133] The preacher's task is to forestall fascism in America, not throw more wood on the

---

130. West, *Democracy Matters*, 18.

131. McElvaine, "Great Depression," Kindle ed. loc. 641. McElvaine, "Their Party Crashed."

132. Snyder, *On Tyranny*, 11.

133. Burke, "Rhetoric of Hitler's 'Battle,'" 33.

incipient fires of paramilitary, authoritarian religious movements, and political utilitarians.

PREACHING PRECARITY WITHOUT SCARING THE "HELL" OUT OF PEOPLE

A resounding theme in the preaching of the Hebrew prophets is the precarity of the people of God. Preachers of the gospel now share that national precarity with the prophets. Here I join the metaphorical with precarity. The prophets often used tropes to shock the people into a recognition of how precarious their very existence was.

Francois Pierre-Louis explained, "The American public doesn't understand that democracy is a fragile system that can wither away if you don't take care of it."[134] Freedom House, in its *Freedom in the World 2021* report, shared this concern. "Even before 2020 Trump had presided over an accelerating decline in U.S. freedom scores, driven in part by corruption and conflicts of interest in the administration."[135] They concluded that democracy itself had been rendered vulnerable. "The expansion of authoritarian rule, combined with fading and inconsistent presence of major democracies on the international stage, has had tangible effects on human life and security."[136]

Why should this matter to preachers? In *Precarious Rhetorics*, Wendy Hesford, Adela Licona, and Christa Teston suggest that one cause of the growing sense of precarity felt around the world is the growth of right-wing nationalist populism.[137] White, middle-class Americans have been swayed by populist, nativist claims that the foundational institutions of the nation have forsaken them. They are convinced by the misinformation that diversity is an evil, immigration is an invasion of a criminal horde, globalization is a devil that has left them behind. Feelings of anxiety, fear, anger, and revenge bubble over in the cauldrons of the nationalist populists. The affective label for all these feelings is precarity. Many Americans feel exposed to, vulnerable to, dependent upon, and impinged upon by others. "This cultural . . . precarity . . . is an inescapable face of being human and of the publics human constitute."[138] The evangelicals have embraced right-wing

---

134. PBS NewsHour, "December 15, 2020," directed by Chris Alexander.
135. Quoted in Repucci and Slipowitz, *Freedom in the World 2021*, 9.
136. Repucci and Slipowitz, *Freedom in the World 2021*, 3.
137. Hesford, Licona, and Teston, *Precarious Rhetorics*, 1.
138. Chirindo, "Precarious Publics," 432.

nationalist populism and preachers need the right words and materials to counter these idolatries.

Taking up the challenge of the precarity of humanity will require that preachers augment our theology with more of a philosophical and rhetorical emphasis. It requires a rethinking of some assumptions taken for granted in American churches. This includes revising our understanding of the role of tropological invention beyond the popular philosophies of the day. For the preacher, precarity becomes an incentive for invention.

This should not represent a huge jump for preachers. For centuries the church insisted that humans existed in precarity as "sinners in the hands of an angry God." Threats of hell loomed large in much Christian preaching partly because people didn't enjoy much of a lifespan. The fear of hell was the most precarious sermon that a preacher could produce. With the advent of modern unbelief, a demise in belief in hell, and longer lifespans, the notion of spiritual precarity in the threat of hell has basically disappeared. This doesn't, however, eliminate the precarity. Now, precarity comes from other sources and it is more frightening than ever. This is multiplied by the number of preachers who routinely make fun of scientific warnings about humanity being on the brink of destruction. Evangelicals are jealous of keeping all "apocalyptic messages" within their own end-time framework. Maybe this accounts, in part, for the evangelical hatred of science. The "sermons" of science are much more frightful and threatening than any sermon on people dying and going to hell.

THE PROPHETS AND PRECARITY

The Hebrew prophets lived in an age of precarity among a people of precarity. Indeed, they lived precarious lives. Since we inhabit an age of precarity, our preaching turns naturally and hopefully to the Old Testament. This presents a challenge, however, because many preachers feel an unease with Hebrew texts. Ellen Davis says, "That some difficulty exists is evidenced by the fact that there is not a lot of Old Testament preaching done these days, at least not in European-American churches. And even when an Old Testament text is treated, often little is attempted with it—little, that is, in terms of serious reckoning with the text itself. In most cases, there is a brief reference to a familiar biblical figure or story as illustrative of the sermon's main point, which is somewhere outside the text and the biblical story."[139]

---

139. Davis, *Wondrous Depth*, Kindle ed. loc. 114.

The prophets often used symbolic tropes to reveal the precarious state of the nation. Jeremiah used a "potter's earthenware jug."[140] He used it to warn that God was bringing disaster upon the people. God's words graphically describe the coming precarity: "And I will make this city a horror, a thing to be hissed at; everyone who passes by it will be horrified and will hiss because of all its disasters. And I will make them eat the flesh of their sons and the flesh of their daughters, and all shall eat the flesh of their neighbors in the siege, and in the distress with which their enemies and those who seek their life afflict them."[141] God instructed Jeremiah: "Then you shall break the jug in the sight of those who go with you, and shall say to them: Thus says the Lord of hosts: So will I break this people and this city, as one breaks a potter's vessel, so that it can never be mended."[142] "Thus says the Lord of hosts, the God of Israel: I am now bringing upon this city and upon all its towns all the disaster that I have pronounced against it, because they have stiffened their necks, refusing to hear my words."[143]

These symbolic actions and the rhetorical tropes that the prophets used are written large all over the books of the prophets. Hosea acted out a fleshly, material, bodily trope. He married a "wife of whoredom"[144] at God's command. His children by his whore of a wife were given tropological names. The first child's name was Jezreel because God says, "In a little while I will punish the house of Jehu for the blood of Jezreel, and I will put an end to the kingdom of Israel."[145] The second child, a daughter, was given the name of Lo-ruhamah, meaning "for I will no longer have pity on the house of Israel or forgive them."[146] Then a third child, a son, was born and named Lo-ammi, meaning "for you are not my people and I am not your God."[147] (This is not a recommendation for preachers to use their children in sermons.) The prophet's wife, Gomer, left him to be a prostitute in a pagan temple. Hosea purchased her for fifteen shekels of silver. The story is a metaphor of God loving, forgiving, and taking Israel back. The tropes of the prophets are powerful assets for the preacher.

James Arnt Aune explains that tropes are strategies of invention used by rhetorical innovators by formulating meanings different from those

---

140. Jer 19:1.
141. Jer 19:8–9.
142. Jer 19:10.
143. Jer 19:15.
144. Hos 1:2.
145. Hos 1:4.
146. Hos 1:6.
147. Hos 1:10.

already in circulation. "Meaning, any meaning," says Aune, "occurs as part of an agon or struggle with previous meaning."[148] To trope is to fight a war for the salvation of people from precarity. Turning back to God depends then on memes: new words, new meanings, new actions for old words, phrases, and metaphors. Jeremiah and Hosea not only evoked the message of God to Israel, they troped it, giving it a new urgency to bring the people back to God.

The tropes used by the prophets demonstrate they did not believe in a bad-tempered, capricious, wrathful God who needed placating. Instead, they used the most vivid metaphors and visual symbols to show the most true thing about God: forgiveness. As Rowan Williams puts it, "What the Bible puts before us is not a record of a God who is always triumphantly getting his way . . . but a God who gets his way by patiently struggling to make himself clear to human beings, to make his love real to them."[149] In Hosea's case he lives the reality of the "broken heart" of the preacher.

The Hebrew prophets, living on the edge, employ every rhetorical strategy, offer all the bold, stark tropes available, to persuade the people to turn back to God. This is always a major task for those who preach. The people to whom we preach are as embedded in political tribes, group instinct, and nationalistic pride as those to whom the prophets preached. Reading the prophets of the Old Testament together with Amy Chua's *Political Tribes: Group Instinct and the Fate of Nations*[150] and David Livingston Smith's *Less than Human*[151] provide the preacher with a deeper understanding of the current state of precarity in our nation.

Isaiah, the Hebrew prophet, embodied his tropes by walking around naked to send the message that the king of Ethiopia would go into captivity "naked and barefoot."[152] Now, there's a commitment to tropological messages that would be a bridge too far. The exaggerated nature, however, points to the seriousness of the preacher's task.

Alongside the prophetic troping of precarity for the nation, there is the prophetic sense of justice. Presenting a system dedicated to justice, *The New Rhetoric* acknowledges and embraces the interests of the Other, difference, alterity, indeterminacy, and pluralism, yet retains the possibility of genuine argument. *The New Rhetoric* maintains this possibility because as a system of thought it oscillates between the Other and sameness, the particular and

---

148. Aune, "Burke's Late Blooming," 329.
149. Williams, *Tokens of Trust*, 16.
150. Chua, *Political Tribes*.
151. Smith, *Less Than Human*.
152. Isa 20: 4.

the universal, refusing to settle on an absolute or on one side of a polarity. Justice and its justification, Perelman recognized, requires an enlarged sense of reason that avoids binary thinking and includes intellect and sentiment. Preachers have yet to realize the potential of *The New Rhetoric*, to appreciate its vision, or to hear its prophetic voice offering an alternative to violence and absolute chaos.

PERELMAN'S RHETORIC OF JUSTICE AND BLACK PREACHING

When sermons tend toward the "happy, sappy" genre, paying attention to issues of justice can be a challenge. Thomas Long says, "The faithful preacher cannot always speak a pastoral word that makes life healthier and more manageable but may only declare the trustworthiness of Christ, celebrate the signs and wonders in the present, and point to the future, which belongs to God."[153]

Preaching keeps company with justice because preachers are called by God, and God is a God of justice. "For God will lead Israel with joy, in the light of his glory, with the mercy and righteousness that come from him."[154] West says, "The Jewish invention of the prophetic commitment to justice—also central to both Christianity and Islam—is one of the great moral moments in human history."[155]

The preacher should never make the mistake of substituting liturgy for justice, words for action. God's language is justice; God's actions are just. Again, West rings out the powerful reality of the prophetic: "This was the commitment to justice of an oppressed people. It set in motion a prophetic tradition based on the belief that God had imparted this love of justice because God is first and foremost a lover of justice. The Judaic prophetic commitment to justice is therefore predicated on the divine love of justice."[156]

If we put on sackcloth and ashes without removing the yoke from the neck of the oppressed, we face Jesus' condemnation of the Pharisees: "Woe to you, scribes and Pharisees, hypocrites! For you tithe mint, dill, and cumin and have neglected the weightier matters of the law: justice and mercy and faith. It is these you ought to have practiced without neglecting the others. You blind guides! You strain out a gnat but swallow a camel!"[157] When

---

153. Long, *Witness of Preaching*, 36.
154. Bar 5:9.
155. West, *Democracy Matters*, 17.
156. West, *Democracy Matters*, 17.
157. Matt 23:23–24.

preachers substitute liturgy for justice, God and the prophetic tradition have left the building. But wait: the prophetic without liturgy can become mere scolding with no roots in the fear of God. The Pharisees fasted without offering their untouched food to the hungry. "God is silent because they do not speak God's language."[158]

The prophetic voice is not the only voice of the preacher, but it should be, at times, a dominant voice. Ours is an age that cries out for the voice of the prophetic. God wanders our secular age of oppression, violence, and aspirational fascism, crying once more, as in the days of Isaiah, "Whom shall I send, and who will go for us?"[159] When the preacher demands justice, there will be other preachers counseling restraint. There will be cowardly voices clamoring, "Now is not the time." As Kenyatta Gilbert defines justice as "the prophetic voice [that] mediates God's activity to transform church and society in a present-future sense based on the principle of justice," then justice is always "go" time.[160]

When it comes to justice, the preacher never lacks materials or issues that demand sermons. Pick any age and watch the sermon topics that gravitate in the orbit of justice multiply. Review our own history and see as God raises up generation after generation those willing to speak truth to power. Gilbert does a masterful job of retelling this history of prophetic preaching in the Black prophetic tradition. After the Civil War, issues of justice included a failed Reconstruction period, widespread agricultural depression, the rise of Jim Crow laws, and America's entry into World War I. Black clerics in these dark years, such as Baptist pastor Reverend Adam Clayton Powell Sr., AME Bishop Reverdy Cassius Ransom, and AME Zion pastor Florence Spearing Randolph rose up to speak truth to power within their northern congregations and to the wider public sphere. Their prophetic preaching named the dehumanizing effects of substandard housing, racial and gender discrimination, and unstable employment as realities contrary to God's will. Their preaching criticized the dominant social forces afflicting Black life in the United States and, simultaneously, offered words of promise from Scripture. Among other themes of spiritual uplift, their prophetic words of a hopeful future that God would one day give essentially functioned to help migrants forge a vital link between their former southern lives and their new lives in the industrial North. These preachers were guided by both a vital hermeneutic of God's good intention for creation and the resolute conviction that listeners in their northern Black congregations needed a way to

---

158. Taylor, *When God is Silent*, 66–67.
159. Isa 6:8.
160. Gilbert, *Pursued Justice*, Kindle ed. loc. 63.

articulate their misery in order to be freed from America's forged cultures of silence.[161]

The prophets assumed the seemingly impossible task of proclaiming divine justice that criticized the corruption of the established government and the idolatrous practices of temple worship.[162] The issues piled up at the prophet's door until he could no longer keep silent: the unfair distribution of material resources, unfairness to one's neighbor, unrighteousness toward God, the improper use of the created order, and personal irresponsibility for communal wellness. The prophet hears what everyone else fails to hear. Jeremiah cries, "My anguish, my anguish! I writhe in pain! Oh, the walls of my heart! My heart is beating wildly; I cannot keep silent, for I hear the sound of the trumpet, the alarm of war."[163] The sorrow of Jeremiah is part of the cross that the prophet always carries for there has always been a cross in the heart of God, and the prophets have been the beating heart of God's mercy, love, grace, and justice.

In every age, and yes, in ours now, the inequities are glaring. In our mostly unregulated free market, the aims of society are military power and economic efficiency; injustice will follow without fail. Glen Tinder argues that the pursuit of perfect or equal justice in a society governed by fallen people inevitably leads to inequities. Whether it is a determined free-market system or welfare state, if the practical aims of society are military and economic efficiency, infringements on justice are ineluctable.[164]

Gloria Albrecht argues that the "beloved community" is actualized at the site of one's dangerous memory of struggle against domination and acts of resistance. Through the dangerous memory of suffering and resistance, she writes, "the subversive hope for justice" is nourished.[165] I believe that Jesus captures the entirety of the prophetic message with the text he chose for his inaugural sermon: Isaiah 61:1–2. Luke records Jesus reading the sermon text: "He stood up to read, and the scroll of the prophet Isaiah was given to him. He unrolled the scroll and found the place where it was written: 'The Spirit of the Lord is upon me, because he has anointed me to bring good news to the poor. He has sent me to proclaim release to the captives and recovery of sight to the blind, to let the oppressed go free, to proclaim the

---

161. Gilbert, *Pursued Justice*, Kindle ed. loc. 148–56.
162. Gilbert, *Pursued Justice*, Kindle ed. loc. 1135.
163. Jer 4:19.
164. Tinder, *Political Meaning of Christianity*.
165. Albrecht, *Character of Our Communities*, 68.

year of the Lord's favor.'"[166] Jesus turned to the prophet for his text because he had breathed the air of the prophets since childhood.

Here is the paradigm for preaching. Justice—political, cultural, economic, national—for everyone. In 1836 Reverdy Cassius Ransom declared that preachers "must proclaim liberty to the captives—those that are socially, economically, and politically disinherited—with authority of a divine justice that will not rest until every fetter of injustice and oppression is broken."[167]

African American preachers paint vivid tropes of injustice and its remedy—the justice of God. For example, in "Why Dives Went to Hell," by Dr. Benjamin Mays, the preacher argues the rich man went to hell "because he had no social conscience."[168] No empathy. Decent? Yes. Respectable? Yes. A good man? Yes. Pillar of community? Yes. Nice home? Yes. But he went to hell.[169] Or more accurately, his life was hell. A life without empathy is hell. Kenyatta Gilbert, commenting on the sermon, says, "The central issue of 'Why Dives Went to Hell' is economic justice, specifically the exploitation of the poor and marginalized."[170]

A second vivid example of preaching economic justice may be found in Samuel DeWitt Proctor's "The Bottom Line." Jesus has a bottom line. We should understand. After all, we are a bottom-line people. Nothing matters as much as the bottom line. Corporations live or die on the bottom line. CEOs rise and shine or fall and disappear on the bottom line. The bottom line is the final total of an account, balance sheet, or other financial document. Proctor proclaims, "It is embarrassing to see how straightforward Jesus was in setting out the basic requirements of God for his people and how confusing and complicated we have made it. We have seen Europe soaked in blood over religious wars . . . burning scholars at the stake, beheading so-called heretics, imprisoning Bible translators . . . And yet Jesus, in simple clarity, gave us the bottom line: "I was hungred and ye gave me meat; I was

---

166. Luke 4:16–19.

167. Ransom, "Church That Shall Survive," quoted in Gilbert, *Pursued Justice*, Kindle ed. loc. 1687.

168. Mays, "Why Dives Went to Hell." This sermon was delivered on September 21, 1980 at Hillside Chapel and Truth Center in Atlanta, Georgia, where Rev. Barbara King served as pastor. It was also delivered on August 17, 1980 at Second Baptist Church in Los Angeles, California. An early version was preached on August 21, 1955. Mays Collection, Moorland-Spingarn Research Center, Washington, DC. Quoted in Gilbert, *Pursued Justice*, Kindle ed. loc. 4057.

169. Mays, "Why Dives Went to Hell," quoted in Gilbert, *Pursued Justice*, Kindle ed. loc.

170. Gilbert, *Pursued Justice*, Kindle ed. loc. 2354.

thirsty, and ye gave me drink ... I was in prison, and ye came ... That's the very bottom line."[171]

Racial injustice walks hand in hand across the American landscape. Amos asks, "Can two walk together unless they be agreed?"[172] "Economic disparity resulting in harrowing poverty partners with racial injustice to create a near monopoly of white power in America. Cornel West names this "America's weak will to racial justice"[173]

James Cone wrote passionately and eloquently about the horrors of racial injustice. In his studies at graduate school, he faced the kind of ideas that he says were

> forcing me to realize the bankruptcy of any theology in America that did not engage the religious meaning of the African American struggle for justice. What I studied in graduate school ignored white supremacy and black resistance against it, as if they had nothing to do with the Christian gospel and the discipline of theology. Silence on both white supremacy and the black struggle against racial segregation made me angry with a fiery rage that had to find expression. How could any theologian explain the meaning of Christian identity in America and fail to engage white supremacy, its primary negation? I concluded that it was my responsibility to address the great contradiction white supremacy poses for Christianity in America.[174]

If you aren't preaching anti-racism, you are not preaching. If the tone of my writing sounds at times somewhat critical, preachy, or even sermonic, I can only ask forgiveness. The theme of injustice lends itself to such affects (emotions).

Faithful preaching for racial justice extracts a price, because the opposition to it—the power of injustice rooted in white supremacy—is so prevalent, cunning, and subtle. West has noted that there is an insidious and largely unseen effort to silence the Black prophetic tradition. "This tradition," he says, "which stretches back to Sojourner Truth and Frederick Douglass, has consistently named and damned the cruelty of imperialism and white supremacy. It has done so with a clarity and moral force that have eluded most other critics of American capitalism."[175]

---

171. Proctor, "Bottom Line," in Proctor and Watley, eds., *Sermons from the Black Pulpit*, 88.
172. Amos 3:3 KJV.
173. West, *Democracy Matters*, 216.
174. Cone, *Cross and the Lynching Tree*, 18–19.
175. West, "Cornel West and the Fight to Save the Black Prophetic Tradition."

West calls the Black prophetic tradition "the leaven in the American democratic loaf."[176] He names the prophets holding back the currents of fascism. "What has kept American democracy from going fascist or authoritarian or autocratic has been the legacy of Frederick Douglass, Harriet Tubman, Sojourner Truth, Martin King, Fannie Lou Hamer. This is not because black people have a monopoly on truth, goodness or beauty. It is because the black freedom movement puts pressure on the American empire in the name of integrity, decency, honesty and virtue."[177]

Racial injustice hides within an imperial system, a corporate state that denies racism while condoning and practicing racism. West says,

> Garvey used to say that as long as black people were in America the masses of black people, the poor and the working class, would never be treated with respect, decency or fairness. That has always been a skeleton in the closet, the fundamental challenge to the black prophetic tradition. It may very well be that black people will never be free in America. But I believe, and the black prophetic tradition believes, that we proceed because black people are worthy of being free, just as poor people of all colors are worthy of being free, even if they never will be free. That is the existential leap of faith. There is no doubt that with a black president the black masses are still treated unfairly, from stop and frisk to high unemployment, indecent housing and decrepit education.[178]

The preacher challenges the claim of white politicians and preachers that racism is a part of America's past. It's a residual evil that has been wiped out, according to the proponents of the theory. This material makes the case that preaching and the churches in America are still racist. Racism, not in the obvious context of white robes and hoods, or the bad thoughts and deeds of intentional individuals, but in the systemic, cultural, and political sense. I am not addressing race as a package of individual attitudes, rhetoric, and actions, but racism as the core and center of white American philosophy. Stuart Hall describes race as "one of those major or master concepts that organize the great classificatory systems of difference that operate in human societies. Race is the centerpiece of a hierarchical system that produces differences."[179]

---

176. West, "Cornel West and the Fight to Save the Black Prophetic Tradition."
177. West, "Cornel West and the Fight to Save the Black Prophetic Tradition."
178. West, "Cornel West and the Fight to Save the Black Prophetic Tradition."
179. Hall, *Fateful Triangle*, 32–33.

Race functions as "a system of meaning, a way of organizing and meaningfully classifying the world."[180] In this sense, race is a huge structure of meaning/group consciousness/world-making that seeps into, emerges from, and articulates to a host of significations.[181] This is what Eduardo Bonilla-Silva defines as the "racial structure." The structure, invisible to sight, infuses our social system as white supremacy, forming "the totality of the social relations and practices that reinforce white privilege."[182] These invisible structures that I have previously dubbed "the Harry Potter cloak of invisibility" enable people to maintain racist attitudes while denying that they are racists. Uncovering the social, economic political, religious, social controls responsible for the reproduction of racial privilege in a society requires the patience of a chef peeling an orange from the inside out.[183]

The task of the preacher here is to do the hard work of offering alternative gospel tropes and messages to what is now accepted in culture as common sense—ways of talking about, making sense of, or calculating ways to pretend racism no longer exists. By engaging the ordinary world outside the sanctuary, preachers are encouraged to not speak in pious, holy rhetoric, in esoteric language disconnected from the people in the street. The church is, after all, predominantly white, highly regulated by various visible and invisible hierarchies, and full of divisions, fissures, cracks, and imperfections that rough up the reputation of the church. It is a site where it is easy for the banality of racism to circulate, be refined, and mostly dismissed.

The critical work of the preacher begins here with defining racism. Michael Omi and Howard Winant define racism as a "racial project [that] creates or reproduces structures of domination based on racial significations and identities."[184] Ibram X. Kendi defines racism as "a marriage of racist policies and racist ideas that produce and normalize racial inequities."[185] Here it is essential that we do not mistake racism as individual prejudice, but see it as systemic, institutional, as part of the air we breathe. Our culture tends to obsess on individual outbursts of discrimination. We have developed a way of responding to a racist claim by shaming the person involved in the rhetorical mistake. The person then insists that she is not a racist and that she was only joking or that everyone knows she is not a racist. The result is that the idea that racism is just people having fun or people making

---

180. Hall, *Fateful Triangle*, 33.
181. Wanzer-Serrano, "Rhetoric's Rac(e/ist) Problems," 468.
182. Bonilla-Silva, *Racism without Racists*, 9.
183. Bonilla-Silva, *Racism without Racists*, 9.
184. Omi and Winant, *Racial Formation in the United States*, 128.
185. Kendi, *How to Be an Antiracist*, 8.

racist statements becomes ingrained in communal consciousness. A person can be without a shred of racism as an individual but participate in system racism within the culture.

White critical race scholar Robin DiAngelo makes this painfully clear for us, writing, "As a product of my culture, my racial illiteracy has rested on a simplistic definition of a racist: an individual who consciously does not like people based on race and is intentionally hurtful to them. Based on this definition, racists are purposely mean. It follows that nice people with good intentions who are friendly to people of a different race cannot be racist. Not only does this definition hide the structural nature of racism, it also enables self-delusion."[186] The preacher has a responsibility here to speak to those with eyes but who do not see. Such self-delusion is what allows politicians to protest against any hint of racism by screaming words like "wokeness," "critical race theory," or "replacement theory."

White people tend to talk about merit, but as Delgado points out, "merit sounds like white people's affirmative action . . . a way of keeping their own deficiencies neatly hidden while assuring that only people like them get in."[187] In an atmosphere that is the intellectual and spiritual home that is fundamentally racist, what are we to do? Start where Kendi starts: become antiracist.

> It's not enough to be "not racist." "I'm not racist" and "There's no racism in America" are the cop-out brothers to color blindness. The language of color blindness—like the language of "not racist"—is a mask to hide racism. "Our Constitution is color-blind," U.S. Supreme Court Justice John Harlan proclaimed in his dissent to *Plessy v. Ferguson*, the case that legalized Jim Crow segregation in 1896. "The white race deems itself to be the dominant race in this country," Justice Harlan went on. "I doubt not, it will continue to be for all time, if it remains true to its great heritage." A color-blind Constitution for a White-supremacist America.[188]

How can the preacher break from the modern, Western, colonial, anti-Black, racist structures of American Christianity? We must produce an antiracism that is "a powerful collection of antiracist policies that lead to racial equity and are substantiated by antiracist ideas."[189] We must name and shame racism based on biology, ethnicity, body, culture, behavior, color, space, and class. We can use all our critical thinking faculties, all our passionate

---

186. DiAngelo, "White People Are Still Raised to be Racially Illiterate."
187. Delgado, "Rodrigo's Chronicle," 1364.
188. Kendi, *How to Be an Antiracist*, 10.
189. Kendi, *How to Be an Antiracist*, 20.

commitment to the reconciling ways of Jesus to tear down the house of race once and for all and replace it with a true antiracist structure.

This is a good beginning. Perelman's rhetoric insists that rhetoric begins with a recognition of the human other—the beginning of justice. We now turn to the epidictic as the form of discourse through which Perelman believes justice may be achieved.

THE EPIDICTIC SERMON

Rhetorical tradition limits epidictic speeches to ceremony, declamation, and demonstration, most often the rhetoric of funerals and other formal events. It is one of the three branches of speech outlined by Aristotle. Perelman, in *The New Rhetoric*, offers a much higher status to epidictic speech. The goal of epidictic speech is contemplative rather than pragmatic because it prompts the audience to think, to reflect, or to embrace a new idea. It is a sort of speech that shapes and cultivates the basic codes of value and belief by which a society or culture lives. Aristotle recognized the importance of ceremonial speaking as a way not of training speakers or entertaining audiences but of reinforcing public values.

There is something poetic and deeply religious in Perelman's prosaic account of argumentation. In a secular age riddled with doubters, Perelman offers preachers a model for preaching. His insistence on the recovery of epidictic speech as argument rather than as ceremony presents a homiletical ethnography of our secular culture.

Perelman names and expands what some of our best speakers, orators, and preachers testify to—epidictic speech is persuasive. Two of the most famous epidictic speeches in American history are President Abraham Lincoln's "Gettysburg Address" and the Rev. Dr. Martin Luther, King Jr.'s "I Have a Dream" speech.

I advocate for the epidictic as a primary form of the sermon. Perelman views epidictic speech as a central part of the art of persuasion. This matters to preachers because the epidictic sermon "strengthens the disposition toward action by increasing adherence to the values it lauds."[190]

There is a lingering fear that the epidictic will only be regarded as a spectacle, as the preacher showing off rhetorical agility. Jacques Bossuet in his *Sermon on the Word of God* says, "You should now be convinced that preachers of the Gospel do not ascend into pulpits to utter empty speeches to be listened to for amusement."[191]

190. Perelman, *New Rhetoric*, 50.
191. Bossuet, *Sermon on the Word of God*, 148–49.

Perelman's conception of the epidictic helps outline the discursive foundations of genuine argument. He insists that rhetoric begins with a recognition of the human other. The best metaphor I have found in Scripture that can animate the preacher is the cry of the Israelite slaves in Egypt: "The Israelites groaned under their slavery and cried out. Out of the slavery their cry for help rose up to God. God heard their groaning, and God remembered his covenant with Abraham, Isaac, and Jacob. God looked upon the Israelites, and God took notice of them."[192] As God heard the groaning of the slaves, the preacher is called to hear the cries of the Others: women, Jews, slaves, colonized peoples, African Americans, homosexuals, immigrants. And the preacher, like Moses, is to give voice to the Others. And that is to be the voice of liberation. Preaching articulates the voices of the previously voiceless, nameless, homeless, powerless—that is true proclamation.

THE EPIDICTIC SERMON PREACHES VALUES

Perelman shows that the function of the epidictic speech is to appeal to "common values, undisputed though not formulated, made by one who is qualified to do so, with the consequent strengthening of adherence to those values with a view to possible later action."[193] George Lakoff makes the same argument by insisting that progressives must state their deepest values and repeat them again and again.

Lakoff is adamant about the value of values: "It is vital—for us, for our country, and for the world—that we understand the progressive values on which this country was founded and that made it a great democracy. If we are to keep that democracy, we must learn to articulate those values loud and clear. If progressives are to win in the future, we must present a clear moral vision to the country—a moral vision common to all progressives. It must be more than a laundry list of facts, policies, and programs."[194]

EPIDICTIC AS EDUCATIONAL

Preachers concerned with teaching basic Christian pedagogy will learn to value the epidictic sermon. "The epidictic served as a community creating discourse that could be used to evoke action against injustice."[195] Weil points

---

192. Exod 2:23–25.
193. Perelman, *New Rhetoric*, 53.
194. Lakoff, *Don't Think of an Elephant*, Kindle ed. loc. 181.
195. Frank, "New Rhetoric," 321.

to the importance of education in the growing of roots. "Education—whether its object be children or adults, individuals or an entire people, or even oneself . . . consists in creating motives. To show what is beneficial, what is obligatory, what is good—that is the task of education."[196] Perelman draws from Weil's advocacy of education that "the epidictic is essential from an educational point of view."[197]

Education as it is embodied through the epidictic performs the function of creating communal motives and roots. The community and audience, rather than the individual and speaker, are seen as creators and arbiters of social values. Communities are formed and identified through epidictic discourse, which in *The New Rhetoric* functions to establish roots for communities and audiences. Perelman's rhetoric repudiates narcissism and solipsism, insisting that rhetoric begin with a recognition of the human other.

The preacher spends much time and energy attempting to create community, communal motives, and roots. This doesn't suggest that community is a strong enough metaphor to account for the church. The church is much more than a community. Hauerwas asserts, "Community is far too weak a description for that body we call church."[198]

I have resisted, for example, the current plague of Christian nationalism, which has swallowed "hook, line, and sinker" the necessity of involvement in conservative politics, but I have come to an uneasy acceptance of their insistence that preachers can't stay on the sidelines. An evangelical pastor says, "The battle lines have been drawn. If you're not taking a side, you're on the wrong side."[199] Any time that we offer reasons why someone has done a good or courageous thing, we are reasoning epidictically. We present a virtue, and we show how someone has exhibited it. Thus, epidictic oratory exercises a strong influence in all the spheres of public life (political speeches, addresses at festivals or social gatherings, funeral orations, etc.), making this type of oratory indispensable.

Hauerwas argues that one of the essential tasks of the preacher is to be a teacher of language—in particular the language of Christianity. "Scripture, of course, is the source as well as the paradigm of Christian speech. What we say must be said faithful to the language of Scripture. That is a complex task because it is by no means clear how the many ways of expression in Scripture are to be said coherently."[200] "In epidictic oratory, the speaker turns

---

196. Weil, *Need for Roots*, 189–90.
197. Perelman, *New Rhetoric and the Humanities*, 6.
198. Hauerwas, *In Good Company*, 25.
199. Alberta, "How Politics Poisoned the Evangelical Church."
200. Hauerwas, *Working with Words*, 88.

educator."²⁰¹ The preacher can't be a prophet in every sermon. Hauerwas observes, "You can become a scold urging the church to become more socially active in causes of peace and justice. This may earn you the title of being 'prophetic,' but such a strategy may contribute to the incoherence of the ministerial task."²⁰² The preacher/teacher/instructor offers a pedagogy that differs from that of the secular culture.

Before noting the advantages of epidictic, there is one hazard that needs to be noted. The preacher will be tempted, in these intensely political times, to be a propagandist rather than an educator. The preacher teaching the meaning of baptism to his congregation is an educator. The preacher addressing secular political issues without a grounding in Scripture becomes a propagandist.

Perelman explains the difference between education and propaganda:

> Epidictic discourse, as well as all education, is less directed toward changing beliefs than to strengthening the adherence to what is already accepted. Propaganda, on the other hand, profits from the spectacular aspect of the visible changes it seeks to, and sometimes does, bring about. Nevertheless, to the extent that education increases resistance to adverse propaganda, the two activities may advantageously be regarded as forces working in opposite directions. Moreover, as we shall see later, all argumentation can be considered as a substitute for the physical force which would aim at obtaining the same kind of results by compulsion.²⁰³

The epidictic, according to Perelman, is essential in forming the community of minds.²⁰⁴ Unlike deliberative and forensic discourse, epidictic oratory plays a critically important educational function by "bringing about a consensus in the minds of the audience regarding the values" that are celebrated in persuasive discourse. "The orator's aim in the epidictic genre is not just to gain a passive adherence from his audience but to provoke the action wished for, or, at least, to awaken a disposition so to act. This is achieved by forming a community of minds, which Kenneth Burke . . . 'calls identification.'"²⁰⁵ The preacher seeks identification with the congrega-

---

201. Perelman, *New Rhetoric*, 51.

202. Hauerwas, *Working with Words*, 85.

203. Perelman, *New Rhetoric*, 54.

204. Perelman, *New Rhetoric*, 6–7.

205. Perelman, *New Rhetoric*, 6–7. See Burke, *Rhetoric of Motives,* for more details on "identification," 21.

tion without producing an unmeditated relationship with the people. The preacher is a servant leader and not an authoritarian one.

Being an educator is high praise for the preacher. Hauerwas, speaking to a seminary graduating class, says, "For I want to suggest to you that one of the essential tasks of those called to the ministry in our day is to be a teacher. In particular, you are called to be a teacher of language. I hope to convince you if you so understand your task you will discover that you have your work cut out for you. But that is very good news because now you clearly have something to do."[206] As Perelman says, "The speaker engaged in epidictic discourse . . . does not arouse controversy, is not attacking or defending . . . but simply promoting values that are shared in the community."[207]

In this context, the preacher approaches the status of "the beloved," since he or she is assured in advance of the goodwill of his congregation. Keep in mind that this places us in the realm of Aristotle's ethos—the preacher must have a high reputation. Our secular culture no longer gives a fig leaf for character. Aristotle's ethos has been replaced with pathos. Even evangelicals have deserted the notion of high character for the prospect of winning elections with any old kind of powerful candidate. Perelman insists that "In the epidictic, more than in any other kind of oratory, the speaker must have qualifications for speaking on his subject and must also be skillful in its presentation."[208]

In writing an epidictic sermon, the preacher will need to know his congregation. By knowing the congregation, the preacher will have surmised the thoughts that are already in the hearts of his people even though they have not been expressed publicly. When the congregation hears the preacher expressing thoughts they have but haven't previously shared, the preacher is listened to with respect and the emotional impact of the values expressed are dramatically increased—some thirty, some sixty, some one hundredfold. The appeal to common values lays out the necessity of the preacher as a good listener, observer, and fellow communicant with the thoughts and feelings of his congregation. The love of the people makes possible the preaching of sermons that move the hearts and minds of the congregation.

As with the search for justice in the Jewish tradition, the search for truth was contested and elusive. Majority rule, while privileged, was held in check by dissenting voices that could at some future point move the community, through persuasion, in a different direction. In the Jewish legal

---

206. Hauerwas, *Working with Words*, 86.
207. Perelman, *New Rhetoric*, 52.
208. Perelman, *New Rhetoric*, 52.

model, humans were held accountable to and by God. God's law, or Torah, "may not be heaven," but God and the heavenly voices were members of the community and presented arguments to the human audience. Human reason must also attend to, but not be bound by, heavenly voices and the universal.

Judaism and rhetoric are natural allies for the preacher, for they aspire to both nonviolence and spiritual freedom. "One can indeed try to obtain a particular result either by the use of violence or by speech aimed at securing the adherence of minds. It is in terms of this alternative that the opposition between spiritual freedom and constraint is most clearly seen."[209]

THE UNIVERSAL AUDIENCE AND THE CREATION OF COMMUNITY

When a speaker is addressing an audience, the members of the audience normally become a unity, with themselves and with the speaker. If the speaker asks the audience to read a handout provided for them, as each reader enters his or her own private reading world, the unity of the audience is shattered, to be re-established only when oral speech begins again. Printed handouts and PowerPoint presentations isolate audience from content. Walter Ong says, in effect, that there is no collective noun or concept for readers or viewers corresponding to "audience." The collective "readership"—"this magazine has a readership of two million"—is a far-gone abstraction.[210]

Perelman's commitment to his community of origin can be traced to the Jewish view of the relationship between the individual and the community. In the Jewish tradition, communal obligations take precedence over individual rights, asserting the notion that "to be one who acts out of obligation is the closest thing there is to a Jewish definition of completion as a person within the community."[211] Cover explains that the "principal word in Jewish law, which occupies a place equivalent in evocative force to the American legal system's 'rights,' is the word 'mitzvah' which literally means commandment but has a general meaning closer to 'incumbent obligation.'"[212] In Jewish thought, obligation to the community is a central, unifying principle.

Individualism, in its Christian and free-market consumer ideologies, gives people a kind of fantasized power over reality itself. For example,

---

209. Perelman, *New Rhetoric*, 55.
210. Walter J. Ong, quoted in Long, *Witness of Preaching*, 263.
211. Cover, "Obligation," 67.
212. Cover, "Obligation," 65.

climate denial seems to give the denier a power greater than that of nature.[213] The attraction is the promise of ultimate freedom. What is at stake here for the preacher is shaming, and condemning the attitude of individualism or consumerism that has now invaded truth itself. There are immense challenges facing us as peoples and as a species. Decades of climate research have reached a consensus about a precarity that threatens humanity as a species. We now face precarity at the species scale. We "have now ourselves become a geological agent disturbing [the] parametric conditions needed for our own existence."[214]

PREACHING PRECARITY WITHOUT SCARING THE "HELL" OUT OF PEOPLE

One way for preachers to account for the role precarity plays in the church is by looking beyond the American political confines so dominant in our public sphere. I draw on epistemic tropes of biological change to highlight an opportunity for preachers to foreground precarity's role in sermons for "precarious publics" that make up the audiences of preachers.

We are losing the "word" battles. As observed earlier, it was Frank Luntz who persuaded conservatives to stop talking about "global warming" because it sounded too scary and suggested human agency. Instead, he brought "climate change" into our public discourse on the grounds that "climate" sounded kind of nice (think palm trees) and change just happens, with no human agency. Luntz suggested Orwellian language. He praised "clean coal" and "energy independence." Conservative legislation that increases pollution is called the Clear Skies Act.[215]

The obscene lust for absolute freedom renders all humanity precarious. Precarity has proved an important issue of creation and stewardship for Christians. This begs a question of the preachers, congregations, and denominations: where might we look for clues about how precariousness relates to discursive logics our work has a stake in? The prophets preached in the face of overarching moments of precarity. We are now facing precarity that threatens our planet's existence. This is no time for individual "cowboys" thumbing their noses at science, refusing to obey instructions about COVID, debunking the truth claims of science, and shouting, "How dare you interfere with my 'freedom' to burn coal / ignore COVID restrictions / to drive / to fly; how dare you interfere with my 'right' to pollute?" These

---

213. Read, "What Is New in Our Time," 81.
214. Dipesh Chakrabarty, quoted in Chirindo, "Precarious Publics," 432.
215. Lakoff, *Don't Think of an Elephant*, 20.

slogan questions would have seemed bizarre until recently but can now pass for common sense.

Viewed rhetorically, an audience is drawn from a universal human community and constitutes "the ensemble of those whom the speaker wishes to influence by his argumentation."[216] Accordingly, the values and knowledge of the audience take priority over those of the speaker: "In argumentation, the important thing is not knowing what the speaker regards as true or important, but knowing the views of those whom he is addressing."[217] Perelman's focus on the community and the audience brings his view of the epidictic into relief: "Such discourse has defined the Jewish community, as the various rituals that involve the Jewish calendar, worship, and rites of passage, embody and communicate fundamental communal values."[218] Indeed, modern Jewish identity is a direct result of epidictic discourse, and Perelman's vision of community and values must have been affected by Jewish communicative practices.

Politically, evangelicals attempt to wrest control of the "universal audience," and claim it as their own. They pretend not to be a "particular audience," and demand that everyone else, who is inclined to dissent, should bow to their concept of the "universal audience." This is not only kidnapping, but also the murder of reason and argument. Perelman concludes that "each individual, each culture, has thus its own conception of the universal audience."[219] Evangelicals possess an insatiable appetite for power, but not shared power. They desire "sequestered power."[220] They are concerned to have power over the reading of biblical texts and their universal meanings. They use a rhetoric of violence to achieve this power over others. They seek to control what is uncontrollable because their power move usurps the power of God. There's a biblical metaphor for the evangelicals—the tower of Babel. As Will Campbell observed, "Anyone who has ever read the story of the Tower of Babel can understand what their creation did, does now and will do."[221]

Evangelicals think that what they have decided is the truth is for their exclusive use in controlling all others. They push and push and they never stop pushing. They are like Pharisees adding rules for Sabbath observance.

216. Perelman, *New Rhetoric*, 19.
217. Perelman, *New Rhetoric*, 23–24.
218. Frank, "New Rhetoric," 231.
219. Perelman, *New Rhetoric*, 33.
220. Griffiths, *Intellectual Appetite*, 20.
221. Campbell, "I Love My Country," 45.

For example, they managed to overturn *Roe vs. Wade.* Now, they push to eliminate abortion completely. Then they push to outlaw the sale of abortion pills. Then they push to indict for murder women who have abortion. They keep all the satisfaction, the grueling, self-righteous satisfaction that they are only doing God's will, to themselves. Therefore, it is a sequestered power intended only to empower evangelicals. They assume they are the masters of the universe, and they are also masters of the truth.

Evangelicals create wars about issues to distract themselves from the loneliness that is the necessary result of their desire to possess all the power. Such a lust for power is a form of greed. The opposite of this "sequestered power" would be a "participatory, democratic power" shared with all, especially the "least of these." Griffiths argues that the studious "do not seek to sequester, own, possess, or dominate what they hope to know; they want to participate lovingly in it, to respond to it knowingly as gift rather than as potential possession, to treat it as icon rather than as spectacle."[222] For the studious what they know can be loved and contemplated, but not dominated by sequestration. "The studious, therefore, accept as a gift what they have come to know which means they assume that which they know is known in a common making possible a shared life."[223] These are the Christians willing to share the power. The extent to which we are gripped by power is determined by how much power we are willing to give away. "The studious Christian, therefore, seeks," in Griffiths' words, a "participatory intimacy driven by wonder and riven by lament,"[224] which makes it impossible for them to seek ownership of what they have been given.[225] For Christians believe that all creatures have been brought into being by God out of nothing. Accordingly, the studious recognize that only God possesses or owns any creature. Only God, therefore, has the power to sequester any being into privacy or to grant it public display.

For example, in the sequestered world of evangelicals, gays are excluded. The holiness of God is not shared with this outsider group. This is the opposite of participatory intimacy that includes everyone. Why should it matter so much to evangelicals about homosexuals? Lakoff claims that it is a question of male identity within the "strict father" metaphor that dominates the evangelical world.[226] I would extend that to include that it is the self-satisfaction they derive from the use of their "sequestered power." They

---

222. Griffiths, *Intellectual Appetite*, 26.
223. Hauerwas, *Working with Words*, 136–37.
224. Griffiths, *Intellectual Appetite*, 128–29.
225. Hauerwas, *Working with Words*, 137.
226. Lakoff, *Political Mind*, Kindle ed. loc. 1310.

possess a lack of charity and are fearful of intimacy. Those who preach need to go in a different direction.

Perelman quotes Plato's admonition in the *Phaedrus* that a true rhetoric would aspire to convince the gods themselves.[227] There exists the temptation, within closed communities of faith, to not interpret the meanings of the divine with the idea that human flaws and interest will affect the values and judgments produced by these reduced, sterile interpretations. Evangelical preachers can't stand to be told that don't have as much epistemic right as anyone else on any topic that they like to think they understand or have some "rights" in relation to. They have a tendency to apply their literalism and certainty to every discipline rather than sticking only to the Bible.

In my reading of preaching, everyone is invited into the arguments, but no one is privileged as possessing the definitive answers or complete insight. Preaching is too tentative, too riddled with the possibility of error, to be granted an overwhelming epistemic power. As Davis insists, "Using the text to confirm our presuppositions is sinful; it is an act of resistance against God's fresh speaking to us; an effective denial that the Bible is the living word of God."[228] Bonhoeffer calls this practice the art of reading Scripture "for ourselves" in order to maintain our ideology.[229]

Perelman's new rhetoric becomes an alternative to the dangers of Enlightenment thinking. Evangelicals, who have abandoned Enlightenment thinking by appealing to the emotions in their values, have nevertheless maintained an Enlightenment understanding that their values are the only reasonable ones, the only acceptable ones, and that all thinking persons should adopt the same ideology. Perelman's new rhetoric offers the preacher another way, a "third way" between the certainty of the Enlightenment and the radical skepticism of some postliberal Christian thought. "Our local and global communities need a philosophical system that allows humans to disagree and remain in relationship."[230]

Sermons should be arguments that challenge people. The more the preacher reads, thinks, writes, the more his argumentative skills increase. The preacher becomes like the man born blind (John 9) in the ability to make impressive improvement in sustained persuasive arguments.

But it is not enough to affirm pluralism. One must resist the pressures that grind all genuine disputes into calm "conversations."[231] The preacher

---

227. Perelman, *New Rhetoric*, 7.
228. Davis and Hays, eds., *Art of Reading Scripture*, 16.
229. Dietrich Bonhoeffer, cited in Davis and Hays, eds., *Art of Reading Scripture*, 16.
230. Frank, "New Rhetoric," 328.
231. Hauerwas, *In Good Company*, 104.

does not enter the pulpit to offer calm conversations but to announce a word from the Lord that has the potential for repentance. Socrates knew this phenomenon well: dialectic, that is argument, is a process of sorting through a host of opinions to discern what is true in each, in search of that which is most true, most good. The good. The Jewish influence needs a rediscovery in Christian preaching. The Jewish approach to interpretation eliminates the reductionistic approach of literalism. Too much Christian preaching has relied on apodictic logic. This is the logic assumed to be beyond dispute. This is what evangelicals call "Thus saith the Lord," or "the biblical view."

We inhabit a world of pluralism in need of justice. Evangelicals believe that the only answer here is to oppose pluralism rather than do the hard work of creating justice in a world where Christians are no longer in charge of the levers of power. The influence of Judaism is critical for preachers. A tradition that routinely offers multiple meanings to texts can be a relief for preachers who are fearful that they may depart from the only acceptable reading. It also gives freedom from fear of the congregation. When a congregation learns that there is freedom and truth in a new, fresh readings of texts, they are more accepting of the preacher's task of bringing a word from the Lord that may contradict common sense and old ideas in the church.

HOW PERELMAN HELPS THE PREACHER

I believe that Perelman offers us a just politics and a justice that is deeply grounded in Jewish understandings of justice and righteousness. Christian preachers are allowed the pilgrimage back to our roots in our study of *The New Rhetoric*. Our salvation is of the Jews, and in our current mess/malaise, the concept of justice from the rabbis may again be our salvation Perelman helps the preacher provide a rhetoric that invites people to argue about values, to do so with diverse others, and to use definitions of reason that include all human faculties of understanding and compassion.

Jewish faith insists on justice for all. Davis says, "Christian confessional interpretation of the Bible has historically been dangerous, even deadly, to Jews."[232] She then adds that "Christian biblical interpretation is dangerous when it is pursued in ignorance or disregard of the long history of Jewish interpretation, and also Jewish martyrdom. These two must be considered together, because they are inextricably bound in the minds and lives of many Jews."[233]

---

232. Davis and Hays, eds., *Art of Reading Scripture*, 24.
233. Davis and Hays, eds., *Art of Reading Scripture*, 23.

The physical, bodily, fleshly nature of preaching reveals itself in the metaphor of martyr (witness). Preaching produces suffering bodies. Reynolds Price relates an experience with an editor at *Time* magazine. He was asked to write a cover story about Jesus for one of *Time*'s end-of-millennium issues. He submitted a lengthy essay. He says that a sentence dealing with his view of how the Great Commission saying in Matthew 28 had been anti-Semitic. He says, "As my essay proceeded through the immense machinery of *Time*'s various departments, I received numerous edits and proofs; and I began to notice that one of my sentences, a sentence of great importance to me, disappeared each time I resubmitted it." The managing editor of *Time*, whose name suggested an eastern European Jewish heritage, repeatedly cut the sentence. Price then told his editor, "Tell your managing editor that the sentence in question is intended for his great-grandfather." Thereafter the disappearing sentence silently resurfaced and appeared in my essay as it ran in *Time* on 6 December 1999." Price then added these words to his essay: "Given the gleaming confidence of those words, and in light of the ghastly failures of Jesus' followers, that last command goes on contributing heavily to the evils of national and religious warfare, institutional and individual hatred, imperialism and enslavement—and all in the name of a teacher who, to our knowledge, never refused a single person who approached him honestly."[234]

Perelman has also constructed a theory of argument that is noncoercive and nonviolent. He has given us systems of logic and argument that are nonformal and allow for non-foundational judgment. Our communities are desperate for a nonviolent system of adjudicating value disputes. With his commitment to justice, Perelman embraced the interests of the Other, difference, diversity, alterity, indeterminacy, ambiguity, contingency, and pluralism within the framework of genuine argument. This has inestimable value for the preacher because it offers a way out of dualism, of binary thinking, of "us" vs. "them" polarities. What a joy to see the vision and hear the prophetic voice offering an alternative to violence and absolutes. Let us heed the voice that cries, "Let justice take the lead."

---

234. Price, *Serious Way of Wondering*, 37–38.

Conclusion:
For God's Sake Feel the Sermon

RATHER THAN OFFERING A summary of the chapters on novelists, poets, philosophers, and rhetoricians, my closing remarks are reflective and motivational. I offer them as the stick that stirs the gumbo that is the sermon. I am aware that this has been an unusual approach to homiletics. I have chosen to bring to the table a variety of other disciplines that have long informed, aided, and given inspiration to preaching. The picture I painted offers a daunting challenge and some will not wish to rise to the challenge. Good preaching is incredibly hard. I choose to bless all the hard effort of preparing the sermon with the most powerful of Aristotle's three pillars of rhetoric: Ethos. I suggested that the ethos of the preacher—ego-integrity, confidence, credibility, and character were essential to the preacher's work. I now want to tie this sense of ethos to all the hard work of the preacher as reader, thinker, writer, and speaker.

Faithful preaching turns out not to be a technique but a rhetorical attitude. The task of inventing the sermon requires a fierce boldness. This puts us in the Aristotelian realm of ethos. The preacher's ethos—character, attitude, approach, integrity—is prequel to any act of preaching. A certain ethos will be required to face the challenges of a secular age. An attitude that suggests power, courage, and boldness has to show up every morning in the mind of the preachers.

At some point, every preacher needs a dominant thematic metaphor for her or his reason for preaching. I have such a metaphor. The Greeks coined the perfect word for the attitude of the preacher: parrhesia. In the New Testament parrhesia is most often translated as "bold," as in bold speech. The bold speakers of the gospel that populate the pages of the book of Acts are my heroes. Safety and timidity are crimes preachers should never commit unless they desire only praise or elevation by a congregation to the status of "beloved." A preacher must willing wrestle with all the mysteries and strangeness of life, with all the power and ambiguity of Scripture, and anyone who does not wish to accept that dangerous, bone-chilling calling should write technical manuals or sell burial insurance instead. The idea of a sermon should stir the blood. There's no weakness here. "It should be instinctual, incurable, unanswerable, and a calling, not a choice."[1] As the writer of Proverbs puts it, "The righteous are as bold as a lion."[2]

THE FEAR OF PREACHING

Nothing cripples the preacher like fear. It's like contracting a virus that puts the preacher in the intensive care ward with a medical chart that reads that chances of survival are slim. Fear wrecks the career of aspiring preachers before it can grow wings to fly. It is a common malady in all of life. The fear of speaking in public is known as glossophobia. There's an interesting contrast here with glossolalia. Around 75 percent of the population struggles with a fear of public speaking to a certain degree. That means over 200 million people feel nervous about talking to others.[3]

No progress can be made in preaching until the preacher rids herself or himself of the nagging fear. Make no mistake. Fear dogs the preacher even in sleep. Fear of how the congregation will respond. Fear that the preacher can't say what he or she has learned to be true. "Don't tell your congregation" was a typical trope among seminary professors of the Southern Baptist tribe in the 1970s. The assertion smacks of a certain fearfulness. A sense of being muzzled, held back. Marney said that the preacher had to decide whether to be a "successful blesser of a successful culture" or not.[4]

Beneath the fear there's an attitude that becomes a place of ease and comfort for many preachers. I call this the Valley of Passivity. There exists a sentimental nihilism within the ranks of the preachers. Sentimentalism not only afflicts some sermons, but it is also a way of life for preachers who know the truth but fail to act consistently on the truth. They have limits to how much they will preach the social gospel, promote racial equality, and support the LGBTQ community. They enjoy their comfortable lives, their standing as the pastor in the community. They see themselves as courageous bleeding hearts who abhor evil, but they refuse to speak of the true horrors of it. They lack the courage to condemn social evils because they fear social shunning. West says, "Such cowardly lack of willingness to engage in truth

---

1. Conroy, *My Reading Life*, 315.
2. Prov 28:1.
3. https://www.creditdonkey.com/fear-of-public-speaking-statistics.html
4. Marney, *Priests to Each Other*, 10.

telling, even at the cost of social ills, is the fundamental characteristic of sentimental nihilism."[5] In a word, such preachers are passive.

James Cone holds up Reinhold Niebuhr as an archetypal representative of white liberal preachers/theologians. Even though Niebuhr was particularly sensitive to the evils of racism, he was hesitant, moderate, and passive in every other sense. In a long passage worth our attention, Cone remarks,

> On the one hand, [Niebuhr] says that "in the matter of race we are only a little better than the Nazis"; and, on the other, he is urging "sympathy for anxious [white] parents who are opposed to unsegregated schools." In terms almost as severe as those of Malcolm X, Niebuhr speaks about "God's judgment on America." He calls "racial hatred the most vicious of all human vices," "the dark and terrible abyss of evil in the soul of man," a "form of original sin," "the most persistent of all collective evils," and "the gravest social evil in our nation." But, unlike Malcolm, Niebuhr also says that the founding fathers, despite being slaveholders, "were virtuous and honorable men, and certainly no villains." "They merely bowed to the need for establishing national unity" based on "a common race and common language." He even says that the 1896 Supreme Court doctrine of "separate but equal," which made Jim Crow segregation legal in the South, "was a very good doctrine for its day," since it allowed "the gifted members" among ex-slaves, a "culturally backward" people, to show, as a few had done in sports and the arts, "irrefutable proof that these deficiencies were not due to innate inferiorities."[6]

In my view these latter views amount to a moral justification of slavery and Jim Crow. More to the point, my commitment is eliminating passivity from the emotional equipment of the preacher. In that light, I want to consider the opposite of passivity as the essential pathos of the preacher. An attitude of boldness runs through the Bible—a Mississippi River of courage against all oppressors, all evil, and all kingdoms of this world.

THE RHETORICAL ATTITUDE OF PREACHING IS KNOWN AS PARRHESIA

Before parrhesia can live in the heart and mind of the preacher, the demons of anxiety and insecurity have to be expelled. There's the insecurity that comes from not knowing exactly what a preacher is supposed to do. Stanley

---

5. West, *Democracy Matters*, 37–38.
6. Cone, *Cross and the Lynching Tree*, 65–66.

Hauerwas says, "As a result, many who enter the ministry discover after a few years of doing the best they can to meet the expectations of those they serve, expectations such as whatever else you may do you should always be nice, end up feeling as if they have been nibbled to death by ducks."[7] This is the anxiety that causes preachers to hesitate to bring up certain topics from the pulpit—the anxiety of keeping one's position.

There's the insecurity of influence. Harold Bloom writes of this form of anxiety for poets. He argues that poets suffer the anxiety of their precursors. "Authentic, high literature relies upon troping, a turning away from not only the literal but from prior tropes."[8] In preaching, the more a denomination has doctrinal strictures, set positions on social issues, and built-in resistance to the new, the more anxiety the preachers of these denominations will experience.

Bloom says strong poets make poetic history by "misreading one another, so as to clear imaginative space for themselves." The very mention of "misreading" produces anxiety among Southern Baptists and other varieties of evangelicals. Misreadings are not allowed. Disagreement with precursors is not encouraged. Bloom states, "My concern is only with strong poets, major figures with the persistence to wrestle with their strong precursors, even to the death." A preacher will need to drink deep from the eternal pond of parrhesia to break the shackles of precursors and to be liberated from fear of the audience.

Great preaching is defined by a rhetorical attitude of confidence, boldness, fearlessness, and courage. Michel Foucault, in his lectures on "fearless speech," says, "Parrhesia is translated by 'free speech.' The parrhesiastes is the one who uses parrhesia, i.e., the one who speaks the truth. This makes the rhetorical trope of parrhesia a perfect fit for preaching. In a bit of frivolity, note that the general meaning of parrhesiazesthai is 'to say everything.'"[9] This certainly may apply to some preachers on some Sunday mornings. The one who uses parrhesia says everything he has in mind; he does not hide anything but opens his heart and mind completely to other people. The preacher and the congregation have a relationship that affords the preacher the right to say whatever he wants to say. "The parrhesiastes uses the most direct words and forms of expression he can find."[10] A primary characteristic of parrhesia is frankness.

Foucault points out two types of parrhesia. One is the pejorative sense of "chattering," the saying everything one has in mind without qualification.

---

7. Hauerwas, *Working with Words*, 84–85.
8. Bloom, *Anxiety of Influence*, xix.
9. Foucault, *Fearless Speaking*, 12.
10. Foucault, *Fearless Speaking*, 12.

CONCLUSION: FOR GOD'S SAKE FEEL THE SERMON

This suggests droning on an on until doomsday about nothing. One of the characters in Lisa Alther's *Original Sins* comments on an East Tennessee preacher: "The pastor droned on.... Mother and I endured the eternal sermon with downcast eyes.... Our pastor sure could talk, but to his credit, he didn't pound on hellfire and abuse. His topics were drier: church dogma."[11] Plato uses this type of parrhesia when he criticizes the democratic constitution where everyone has a right to tell fellow citizens anything—even the most stupid or dangerous things for the city.[12]

The positive sense of parrhesia—"to tell the truth"—dominates the literature of the Greeks and Romans of the classical era. "The parrhesiastes says what is true, because he knows that it is true; and he knows that it is true, because it is really true."[13] Here a danger appears for the preacher because the preacher may be tempted to say more than he or she knows. "Thus says the Lord" may become a cover for "In my opinion, brothers and sisters." In true parrhesia there is an exact coincidence between belief and truth.

There is an additional rhetorical aspect to parrhesia. The courage of the preacher serves as an emotional proof. To say something dangerous requires sincere courage. Dangerous speech is speech different from what the majority believes. Danger is a second characteristic of parrhesia. Risk or danger in speaking the truth is part of the equation for parrhesia. When a preacher addresses a congregation and tells them that Christian nationalism is idolatry and patriotism is not a Christian virtue, then the preacher speaks the truth and this act is a risk.

The preacher must find the exact words and tones to help Americans know that the flag can become an idol. Frederick Douglass, speaking from the African American prophetic tradition, disrupts notions of nationalism and patriotism: "I have no love for America, as such. I have no patriotism. I have no country."[14] Douglass let his righteous anger flow in metaphors of degradation, chains, and blood. "The institutions of this country do not know me, do not recognize me as a man," he declared, "except as a piece of property." All that attached him to his native land were his family and his deeply felt ties to the "three millions of my fellow-creatures, groaning beneath the iron rod ... with ... stripes upon their backs."[15] Demanding his birthright as an American, he felt like the "veriest stranger and sojourner."[16]

11. Alther, *Original Sins*, 246–47.
12. Plato, *Republic*, 577b. Cf. also *Phaedrus*, 240e.
13. Foucault, *Fearless Speaking*, 14.
14. Blight, "Frederick Douglass's Vision for a Reborn America."
15. Blight, "Frederick Douglass's Vision for a Reborn America."
16. Blight, "Frederick Douglass's Vision for a Reborn America."

This leaves no doubt that the parrhesiastes takes risks. Having imbibed the same waters that filled Will D. Campbell, I have accepted risk as the cost of preaching. "God has called you," Will said, "to smash the images erected which have become more important than God himself."[17] These are rhetorical risks because they involve words, language, speech. If, in a sermon, a preacher risks losing his popularity because his political opinions are contrary to those of the congregation, he uses parrhesia, dangerous parrhesia. The use of parrhesia usually occurs when a person who is in a "one-down" relationship with a more powerful person dares to speak in ways that will offend or anger the more powerful person. Christian preaching in the New Testament that is directed at governors, kings, and emperors is exactly that kind of parrhesia.

Perhaps the boldest parrhesiastes I have encountered is Duncan Gray, Episcopal priest, Will Campbell's friend, who served an Episcopal parish in Oxford, Mississippi during integration. Gray, confronting General Walker from Texas, a segregationist leader, told the general: "My name is Duncan Gray. I am the rector of the local Episcopal church. This is my home, and I am deeply hurt to see what is happening to the university and the state. I am here to do anything I can do to stop the rioting and keep any more people from getting hurt or killed."[18]

Here is one of the sweet ironies of my life. Campbell, an iconoclastic Anabaptist, taught me the radical liturgy of *The Book of Common Prayer*, and Duncan Gray taught me the meaning of parrhesia. Campbell says that reading through *The Book of Common Prayer* he was struck by how often the words "joy" and "joyous" appeared. And that Duncan Gray was described by those who knew him, as joyous. "His wife said, 'He is the most joyous person I have ever met.'"[19] The powers and the principalities always fall at last to the power of joy and love.

I argue that parrhesia is the defining attitude of Christian preaching in the book of Acts. Risking death became the act du jour for Christian preachers in Acts. "When you accept the parrhesiastic game in which your own life is exposed, you are taking up a specific relationship to yourself: you risk death to tell the truth instead of reposing in the security of a life where the truth goes unspoken."[20] When the preacher prefers herself as a truth-teller rather than as a person who is false to herself, she is a faithful parrhesiastes.

---

17. Campbell and Goode, *Crashing the Idols*, vii.
18. Campbell, *And Also with You*, 26.
19. Campbell, *And Also with You*, 246.
20. Foucault, *Fearless Speaking*, 17.

A third characteristic of parrhesia is criticism. The criticism flows in two directions. The preacher faces the prospect of being criticized by the congregation. The other direction is the criticism the speaker delivers of the congregation. "This is the way you behave, but that is the way you ought to behave." Parrhesia is a form of criticism of the more powerful. "The parrhesiastes is always less powerful than the one with whom he speaks. The parrhesia comes from 'below,' and is directed towards 'above.'"[21] The explicit danger here is if the fearful preacher uses his or her charisma to create a "total identification" with the congregation.

The faithful parrhesiastes speaks as a minority voice: he discloses a truth that threatens the majority, the powerful. In a system where power may be exercised to protect the powerful from the truth. Even in a democratic society, power may be aligned against the speaking of the truth.

The final characteristic of parrhesia is duty. The speaker of truth is not forced to speak but is free to stay silent. No one forces him to speak. Why then does the speaker insist on telling the truth? One reason: he feels it is his duty to do so. In the Bible, there are those who speak out of being commanded to speak by God. There are these terrible arguments between God and the person God has chosen to be a faithful parrhesiastes. For example, the friends of Job would qualify as unfaithful parrhesiastes whereas Job is the faithful parrhesiastes.

Parrhesia doesn't travel alone. Somehow it transfers the responsibility from the speaker to the audience. The boldness of the preacher can become the boldness of the congregation. Rather than search for certainty and sincerity in the claims of the speaking voice, audiences who model their communicative habits on the Socrates of the dialogues accept the responsibility to listen critically, make judgments, and take accountability for their roles in democratic deliberations. The Socratic commitment to questioning requires a relentless self-examination and critique of institutions of authority, motivated by an endless quest for intellectual integrity and moral consistency. A bold and courageous clergy willing to speak against idolatry, fake news, conspiracy theories, and misinformation is an absolute necessity in our culture. Parrhesia—fearless speech—is the lifeblood of any authentic clergy.

The concept of parrhesia can become a tool of manipulation in the hands of the powerful whenever audiences acquiesce to figurative claims of sincerity without examining the claim critically. Preachers can easily give the appearance of being faithful parrhesiastes. They are frank and fearless. They stand up to the system and the law. They are unafraid to tell it like it is. They are not captive to the political elites. They are not politically correct.

---

21. Foucault, *Fearless Speaking*, 18.

They are unafraid of criticizing, accusing, blaming, scapegoating, and demonizing others. This negative parrhesia has no place in a preacher's life.

Parrhesia may be analogically conceived as the wearing of the "whole armor of God" for the faithful preacher. This is the rhetorical attitude that opens the doors to bold, effective, and powerful preaching.

Parrhesia often faces stiff opposition from the people in the pews. Preachers feel a lot of pressure to not say everything they learned in seminary. They feel reluctant to speak the truth that may unsettle the congregation. Parrhesia is not the natural match with Christian belief that it should be. A sensitive preacher may be thrown by a member of the congregation jumping up and running out of church when angered by something the preacher says. Or a critical letter may linger in the preacher's mind for weeks. There's no question that preachers need a sensitive spirit rooted in love, but also a certain amount of toughness is required for the faithful parrhesiastic.

Traditionally, preachers were able to negotiate a "parrhesiastic contract" with congregations, thereby mitigating the risk associated with truth-telling. Foucault described this contract as one in which the party with power and in need of truth granted the parrhesiastes the privilege of presenting truths without the threat of punishment. This tacit cultural contract is moral, not legal or institutional, and thus truth-telling still carries some potential for consequence. However, the agreement constructs a sanctioned space for truth-telling that lessens the risk and vulnerability of criticism. A free pulpit offers an avenue by which truth-tellers might render criticism more palatable and help others receive and digest racial truths. This "parrhesiastic contract" has become more difficult to produce among preachers and congregations.

Preachers may be fired for speaking truth counter to the accepted truth of the congregation. This tension has always existed, but the contract was honored, and the humor used to talk about it publicly aided in that ability to treat the contract as flexible. A preacher asked his congregation if there were subjects they didn't want him to address. The chair of the committee said, "Don't talk about sex, money, or politics." The preacher then asked, "What then do you want me to preach?" The reply: "Anything you like, Rev. as long as you preach the gospel." Fearless preaching?

How can we garner the courage to present the parrhesia attitude and acts of the Bible as incarnational offerings of the preacher's own heart? How can we face an angry people filled with a rage for stoning us to death? Acts 19:8 serves as text: "He entered the synagogue and for three months spoke out boldly and argued persuasively about the kingdom of God." As a preacher you are called to be a faithful parrhesiastes. Three rhetorical words: boldly, argued, and persuasively. This is my vision of the preaching event.

PAUL AND THE CHURCH IN THE BOOK OF ACTS

The New Testament book of Acts is a book of parrhesia, faithful parrhesia in the face of imperial power. It is the ultimate face-off between truth and power. For the preacher, the book of Acts is the primary text of the Bible. The account of Luke begins with the commissioning of faithful witnesses to speak confidently and boldly, and the account ends with these words: "proclaiming the kingdom of God and teaching about the Lord Jesus Christ with all boldness and without hindrance."[22] Parrhesia is the dominant rhetorical trope in Acts. Preaching is the primary act in Acts.

Parrhesia plays a major role in the development of Christianity. The New Testament offers an authentic parrhesia like that of the prophets, John the Baptist, Jesus, Paul, and the church in the book of Acts. In the gospel of John parrhesia is linked with the work of Jesus (John 18:20—Jesus answered, "I have spoken openly to the world; I have always taught in synagogues and in the temple, where all the Jews come together. I have said nothing in secret.")

In Acts parrhesia and rhetoric work together as bold proclamation. The parrhesia of the disciples is the essence of their persuasive attempts. Here persuasion is used as synonym for rhetoric. The NRSV translates the word as "convinced." Rudolf Bultmann: "To seek to win men"—to convince them—is "a description of the apostolic calling. One should probably translate: Of course we seek (as we are charged to persuade men—yet in such sort that we can answer for it before God, who sees us through and through. (Acts 18:4)."

Perhaps Acts 28:23–24 best shows what is involved in the parrhesia of Acts: "From morning until evening he explained the matter to them, testifying to the kingdom of God and trying to convince them about Jesus both from the law of Moses and from the prophets. Some were convinced by what he had said, while others refused to believe. So they disagreed with each other." Paul explains, testifies, and tries to convince his audience. Some were convinced and others remained unconvinced. This is the way of parrhesia.

The preachers in Acts display a holy parrhesia. In Acts 4:29–31, the apostles pray, "Lord, look at their threats, and grant to your servants to speak your word with all boldness, while you stretch out your hand to heal, and signs and wonders are performed through the name of your holy servant Jesus. . . . When they had prayed, the place in which they were gathered together was shaken; and they were all filled with the Holy Spirit and spoke the word of God with boldness." The believers pray for parrhesia. The

---

22. Acts 28:31.

parrhesia of the apostle who preaches openly and eloquently to a hostile world is a charisma. A holy parrhesia seeking to offer the gift of salvation to the world differs drastically from a fake parrhesia designed to cling to secular political power.

Here we see followers of Jesus taking upon themselves the role of truth-tellers—a role many Christians are no longer willing to assume because of their conformity to the power of this world. Luke Timothy Johnson says, "At the everyday level, all of them could speak with boldness and bear witness to the good news from God that had touched them."[23]

Paul's closing speech in Acts 26 is the decisive parrhesiastic speech where resurrection truth faces imperial power. In Acts 26, Luke has assembled the Roman governor, the Jewish king, their entourage, and the nobility of the city of Caesarea to hear the word of parrhesia: "a certain dead man, Jesus, was alive."[24] Johnson suggests that "Paul's final defense can be read also as Christianity's first real apologia before the sophisticated Greek world. The speech is both lengthy and the most elegantly constructed of Paul's discourses, with exactly the sort of elevated diction, subtle syntax, and paronomasia that delighted Hellenistic rhetoricians."[25]

Paul's speech is bold, frank, and truthful. He makes plain what is scandalous to the educated Greek world: Jesus was the crucified and raised Messiah. "The experience of the risen Lord bore implicitly within itself all the mandate and significance for Paul's life." In terms of his legal defense, Paul insists that he was only doing his duty. His mission was in direct obedience to God. "He has preached repentance and turning to God and doing the deeds appropriate to conversion."[26]

Festus, not convinced by Paul's arguments, challenges Paul's sanity. "But Paul said, 'I am not out of my mind, most excellent Festus, but I am speaking the sober truth. Indeed the king knows about these things, and to him I speak freely; for I am certain that none of these things has escaped his notice, for this was not done in a corner.'"[27] Paul's is a true parrhesia. All the characteristics of parrhesia are demonstrated in Paul's speech: frankness, truth, danger, criticism, and duty.

Another word for parrhesia is witness. Will Campbell's imaginative novella *Cecelia's Sin* seamlessly connects parrhesia and witness with

---

23. Johnson, *New Testament*, 19.
24. Acts 25:19.
25. Johnson, *Acts of the Apostles*, 440–41.
26. Johnson, *Acts of the Apostles*, 442.
27. Acts 26:25–26.

martyrdom. In an amazing mixture of parrhesia, witness, and martyrdom, Cecelia announces,

> The lowering clouds of despotism and superstition hang dark over all of Europe today. Scenes of violence, of bloodshed and oppression are rampant everywhere. That's the story we have written. But a land which gave us an Erasmus will one day grant us liberty. And when that meridian splendor makes its rounds it will light the way for all the world. Whatever the private interests of the princes, one day they will be a rare occurrence, and the fear they engender will be no more. A people who could snatch this ground from the sea will not let it be forever ruled by tyranny and falsehood. The blood of some may be in vain, but the red blood of Holland's martyrs will paint the corners of the earth. I would die for my Lord anywhere, but I am happy that He will let me die in Amsterdam.[28]

Richard Hays writes, "Luke's Jesus declares himself as the Messiah who by the power of the Spirit will create a restored Israel in which justice and compassion for the poor will prevail."[29]

Rather than being an ally of the world, the church was constituted as an alternative to the politics of death and fear. Rowan Williams says that Augustine's politics presume that the church has a distinctive character. He says, "We can see here how the themes of proper appeal to feeling, the proper formation of desire and delight, the entire pedagogy of the Church's preaching and liturgy, the focal significance of Christ as the source of justice, because he is the embodiment of truth, of true relation to the Father and of self-forgetting compassion and humble acceptance of the constraints of fleshly life, all come together in the vision of fully reconciled social existence."[30] John Milbank argues that the significance of the church lies in its existence as an alternative *civitas*.[31] Hauerwas argues that the church faces "a world that must be witnessed to."[32]

The message of the agent that I have identified as the faithful parrhesia is clear: Jesus is the politics of the new age; he has established a kingdom; he has created a new time that gives us time not only to care for the poor but to be poor. He makes it possible to be nonviolent in a violent world. Jesus is the embodiment of parrhesia: The way, the truth, and the life. He is what Mary

---

28. Campbell, *Cecelia's Sin*, 80.
29. Hays, *Moral Vision of the New Testament*, 115–16.
30. Williams, *On Augustine*, Kindle ed. loc. 129.
31. Milbank, *Theology and Social Theory*, 380–82.
32. Hauerwas, *Working with Words*, 42.

dreamed of: The one who scattered the proud in their imaginations and brought down the powerful from their thrones, sent the rich away empty, lifted up the lowly, and filled the hungry with good things. "The gospel is the proclamation of a new age begun through the life, death, and resurrection of Jesus Christ. The gospel, moreover, has a form, a political form. It is embodied in a church that is required to be always ready to give hospitality to strangers. It is a society called into being by Jesus who gave his people a new way to live."[33] John Yoder put it just right, in my view: [Jesus] "gave them a new way to deal with offenders—by forgiving them. He gave them a new way to deal with violence—by suffering. He gave them a new way to deal with money—by sharing it. He gave them a new attitude toward the state and the 'enemy nation.'"[34]

The reality of faithful truth-telling is written on the bodies of those who have accepted the task of parrhesia with all the attendant pain and demands, up to and including death. The community of the parrhesia is one of crucifixion and this gives rise to another of the primary meanings of the word witness—martyr.

> These are the faithful ones who lived through and died from the *experimentum crucis*. This faithfulness even to the point of death becomes what Luke suggests will be the typical Christian mode of acting and being in the world. There is here a clear line between faithful parrhesia and the reality of trial, suffering, and death. To be a parrhesia in Acts means to 'reenact the life-pattern of the suffering Christ, to suffer for his Name, to be put on trial, to face the possibility of death, and to proclaim the resurrection. In short, it is to embody the cruciform pattern that culminates in resurrection.'"[35]

Risk of life and danger of death are defining characteristics of parrhesia. The Christian parrhesiastes, from Stephen and countless others who met the same violent death, chose a specific relationship with the risen Christ: preferring to be truth-tellers than living beings false to themselves and lapdogs of the powers and principalities.

Marching across the pages of the New Testament from Jerusalem to the "uttermost" parts of the Roman world, parrhesia took on the authorities and powers—the "powers and principalities"—in a cosmic conflagration that makes *Star Wars* look like a tea party. The book of Acts opens with the disciples of Jesus being ordained to be witnesses to the world;

---

33. Hauerwas, *Working with Words*, 123.
34. Yoder, *Original Revolution*, 31–32.
35. Kavin Rowe, *World Upside Down*, 121.

the book of Acts closes with the words: "proclaiming the kingdom of God and teaching about the Lord Jesus Christ with all boldness and without hindrance."

As the story unfolds, the boldness increases as the powers of the pagan world are higher on the political food chain. The witness starts in Jerusalem among the Jews, confronts the Sanhedrin, takes in the story of Stephen and his martyrdom, expands to Samaria, then to the Ethiopian eunuch, spreads to the gentiles, shows the reluctant witness of Peter to Cornelius (a centurion of the Italian cohort), reports the death of Herod killing James and imprisoning Peter, spreads to Cyprus, Antioch of Pisidia, Iconium, Lystra and Derbe, Macedonia, the city council of Philippi, the city authorities in Thessalonica, Berea, Athens (the philosophers), Corinth, the town clerk of Ephesus, to Paul's arrest by the authorities in Jerusalem, to the Roman tribune, to Felix the governor, to the successor of Felix, Festus, to King Agrippa, and finally Paul sails to Rome to face the emperor. The equation is clear: As the power of the opposition increases, the more holy boldness will be required.

Preachers now are facing the collected powers and principalities and more parrhesia than ever will be required. Markus Barth gives a more contemporary description of these enemies in his translation of Ephesians 6:12—"For we are wrestling with . . . . The governments, with the authorities, with the overlords of this dark world, with the spiritual hosts of evil in the heavens."[36] He includes "concrete historical, social, or psychic structures or institutions of all created things and all created life."[37] Now, we face formerly dead enemies, disinterred by religious authorities—racism, sexism, anti-Semitism, homophobia, male superiority, white superiority, and a host of bodies disinterred from the grave to once again challenge the boldness of the preachers.

A congregation receives the word of the Lord from the pastor, and they are to do so in a spirit of openness and with a view toward repentance. Why would a congregation pray for God to cleanse their imaginations of all secular notions by the inspiration of the Holy Spirit, and then close their minds and hearts to the Word of God brought by God's preacher? This is not a sensible way to conduct the business of God. Congregations, not trained in the exegesis of Scripture should always be suspicious of secular interpretations of the Bible. If a congregation comes before the Word in a confessional stance, they will not be suspicious of the preacher's sermon; they will be

---

36. Barth, *Ephesians 4–6*, 758.
37. Barth, *Ephesians 4–6*, 800–801.

suspicious of their own readings. As a people who regularly confess our sins, why should a congregation resist the word that the preacher delivers?

Why do people show up in church loaded with interpretations that they have not reconsidered for years, generations in the church. If you find yourself saying, "I don't care what that preacher says, this is what I believe," the problem is not with the preacher, it is with your interpretation. Worship is not meant as a soothing reinforcement of our secular philosophies; it is a time for the possibility of metanoia—repentance—literally, "change of mind."

For preachers to feel they must couch their language in smooth and soothing words, for preachers to feel afraid of the anger of a congregation, is not the way of the Lord. An unwillingness to provide the pastor with a free pulpit constitutes a crime against the preacher and a rebellion against God. The pastor has every right to say to a congregation: "Whether it is right in God's sight to listen to you rather than to God, you must judge; for we cannot keep from speaking about what we have seen and heard."[38]

A POSTLUDE HONORING ST. PAUL: PRIMAL PARRHESIASTIC

Margaret M. Mitchell relates the story that she placed a caption from Chrysostom on her rather cluttered wall: "Nothing was more ready for combat than Paul's soul." There is still a line of preaching succession that begins with St. Paul and continues to those who now preach. I offer the highest accolades of praise to Paul as the primal parrhesiastic, as the preacher I still hold up as our boldest. As John Chrysostom put it, "I love all the saints, but I love most the blessed Paul, the chosen vessel, the heavenly trumpet, the friend of the bridegroom, Christ. And I have said this, and brought the love which I have for him out into the public eye so that I might make you, too, partners in this love charm."[39]

There is a legend of how Chrysostom, seated at his writing desk hard at work on his homilies, would glance for inspiration at a portrait of the apostle that hung on the wall. According to the tale, the apostle Paul would spring to life in the night and lean over Chrysostom's shoulder whispering exegetical suggestions into his ear. The cover art for Margaret M. Mitchell's *The Heavenly Trumpet* is an artistic depiction of the legend. The cover was

---

38. Acts 4:19.

39. Chrysostom, quoted in Mitchell, *Heavenly Trumpet*, 1.

designed by Lisa Buckley and the cover art is courtesy of Leonidas Ananiades. The painting hangs in the National Library, Athens, Greece.[40]

AN EMOTIONAL APPEAL—A LOVE LETTER TO "THE PARRESIASTES" OF THE AGES: ST. PAUL

I have needed to write the apostle Paul a love letter since I first memorized the Romans Road to Salvation in 1960 as a then thoroughly immersed fundamentalist. Though I had no idea at the time, I had entered the home territory of what would become my literary terrain. While Paul has endured withering criticism for his unyielding teaching about women in the church and seemed to have other issues that made him less than lovable, no one has ever been a more fearless spokesperson for the gospel of Jesus.

The writings of the apostle Paul took full possession of me in a way nothing had before. Later, freed from the evangelical obsession with Paul, I would turn to the teachings of Jesus as a more necessary guide, but for at least two decades I fed on the power and wisdom of this Christian preacher. I stepped into the hard discipline of Paul and could already feel the necessary endurance that would be required to follow him. I caught my breath when I realized that Paul refused to take John Mark on the second missionary journey because Mark quit and went back home during the first journey.

I read for fire. The apostle Paul had my attention from the start with the fire that burned in his gut.

> I regard everything as loss because of the surpassing value of knowing Christ Jesus my Lord. For his sake I have suffered the loss of all things, and I regard them as rubbish, in order that I may gain Christ and be found in him, not having a righteousness of my own that comes from the law, but one that comes through faith in Christ, the righteousness from God based on faith. I want to know Christ and the power of his resurrection and the sharing of his sufferings by becoming like him in his death, if somehow I may attain the resurrection from the dead.[41]

This passionate outburst still leaves me breathless, and I pray that it changes me completely and that I am not the person who first read Paul. Here's what I love: when a great writer turns me into a Jew from Tarsus, who burns with zeal for God's law. Turn me into something else, I cry. Turn me upside down. Challenge me to the total extent of my abilities. Push me to

40. Mitchell, *Heavenly Trumpet*.
41. Phil 3:8–11.

the edge of serious commitment. Make me feel the pain of being stoned, the fear of being chased out of town, the loneliness of being jailed. Put me in front of an angry mob and have me preach Jesus. Stand me in the court of Festus and Agrippa and tell me to hold nothing back. Paul, the parrhesiastic.

There have been subsequent theologians who are far better thinkers and writers than St. Paul. But only a few can match his fearlessness in the face of death. "So I do not run aimlessly, nor do I box as though beating the air; but I punish my body and enslave it, so that after proclaiming to others I myself should not be disqualified."[42] "We are afflicted in every way, but not crushed; perplexed, but not driven to despair; persecuted, but not forsaken; struck down, but not destroyed; always carrying in the body the death of Jesus, so that the life of Jesus may also be made visible in our bodies."[43]

Critics who do not like Paul often despise him, and his very name can produce nausea among the best of them. I am undeterred because the criticism is often deserved. They are just critics, and he is the apostle Paul. When people do not like the writing of St. Paul, their dislike can assume a pure form of hatred. They take a personal offense at some of his insistent words that suggest a patriarchal, misogynistic, male-centered approach.

At his best, Paul never coddles. He demands that you must accede the richness and power of faith taken to their absolute extremes. He can do almost anything to the written word in his letters except hold back. Even when he attempts to hold back there's the sense that he is kicking against the goads, straining against the bridle, ready to explode with admonitions. Paul's parrhesia is a shouted thing. His pulpit was wherever he opened his mouth. He flung words like thunderbolts out toward the unexpecting, unprepared, sensitive young churches.

He inhabits every line he writes and a little of Paul's demanding words go a long way for many readers. If ever a speaker/writer attempted to "say everything," to "tell it like it is," that person was Paul. His courage lay in the fact that he didn't flinch in arguments, debates, and fights. "He kept the howlings and incoherent madness that rise up in nightmare, in the moonless wastelands of sleep when the ores of greatness move through the soft cells of all artists, then disappear when the full light of day is upon us and we blush at the ravings and lunacies of our deepest selves."[44] Paul writes out of the darkness, "For I delight in the law of God in my inmost self, but I see in my members another law at war with the law of my mind, making me captive to the law of sin that dwells in my members. Wretched man that I am!

---

42. 1 Cor 9:26.
43. 2 Cor 4:8–9.
44. Conroy, *My Reading Life*, 249.

Who will rescue me from this body of death?"[45] No one suffered more from the judgment of critics than Paul, yet he never once pulled back or tailored himself to fit the harshness of their anger.

Boys like me—you know the ones—we're the country boys from the Deep South with red clay baked into bare feet, from schools that few have heard of, from towns defined by their nothingness, from regions unpraised and unknown, from histories without stories or records or echoes or honor, are always looking for a hero. St. Paul taught me that if I looked hard enough at the life I was living, if I gave myself to the discipline of parrhesia and intellectual creativity, and commitment to Christ, "the history of the world would play itself out before me within earshot" of my father's garden.[46] All I had to do was be vigilant, disciplined, and courageous. And then out-read everyone. And then speak the truth in love and fierceness.

St. Paul put me on the journey of studying everything the way a scientist labors for a cure for Alzheimer's, the way a lepidopterist pores over the details of a luna moth's wing structure, the way a concert pianist practices and practices for unending hours. For this I am forever grateful.

I stand by my absolute devotion to the man and his letters. Do I not see his flaws? Of course I do, but I see my own with much greater sadness and embarrassment. I still pull guard duty for St. Paul, because like St. Chrysostom I feel Paul standing over my shoulder peering at the words appearing on my computer screen. I think he told more of the truth about God, about Jesus, about the Holy Spirit, about the life, death, crucifixion, and resurrection, about the faith, about the world than anyone else has. Anyone. With every word he writes he gives you the "honest-to-God" truth and demands that you follow without reservation. He stammers, he murmurs, he hunts for the right words, and words spill out of his mind and body as he tries to awaken us to the reality of Christ in us. "When I came to you, brothers and sisters, I did not come proclaiming the mystery of God to you in lofty words or wisdom. For I decided to know nothing among you except Jesus Christ, and him crucified. And I came to you in weakness and in fear and in much trembling. My speech and my proclamation were not with plausible words of wisdom, but with a demonstration of the Spirit and of power, so that your faith might rest not on human wisdom but on the power of God."[47]

When he spots our zeal flagging, he flails his arms, raises his voice, flings us against the wall with his hands to our throats, collars us, makes us look upward out toward the stars and see Jesus in all his magnificent glory.

---

45. Rom 7:22–25.
46. Conroy, *My Reading Life*, 131.
47. 1 Cor 1:1–5.

Let love be genuine; hate what is evil, hold fast to what is good; love one another with mutual affection; outdo one another in showing honor. Do not lag in zeal, be ardent in spirit, serve the Lord. Rejoice in hope, be patient in suffering, persevere in prayer. Contribute to the needs of the saints; extend hospitality to strangers. Bless those who persecute you; bless and do not curse them. Rejoice with those who rejoice, weep with those who weep. Live in harmony with one another; do not be haughty but associate with the lowly; do not claim to be wiser than you are. Do not repay anyone evil for evil but take thought for what is noble in the sight of all. If it is possible, so far as it depends on you, live peaceably with all. Beloved, never avenge yourselves.[48]

That's enough of an assignment to take an entire lifetime. Yes, I see the flaws of St. Paul and I could not care less. I still honor the boy who accepted Paul into my life when I was eleven. I do not know what I would have done if he had failed to find me that year in Junior Sunday school at the Antioch Baptist Church, in Nip 'n' Tuck, Louisiana or where I would be or what I would be doing. I owe my life as a preacher to him, and I will never forget that debt or dismiss his work with my scorn. I thank him with my heart for the fearlessness of his words and the greatness of his spirit and work.

PAUL THE PARRHESIASTIC IN ACTION

Saul was a born parrhesiastic. Convinced of the truth of his family tradition, angered that a new religion seem to endanger his faith, Saul unleashed all his energy as he resolved to stop this new faith in its tracks. "Meanwhile Saul, still breathing threats and murder against the disciples of the Lord, went to the high priest and asked him for letters to the synagogues at Damascus, so that if he found any who belonged to the Way, men or women, he might bring them bound to Jerusalem."[49]

His conversion reads like an assault, a kidnapping. After that day, all of his gifts for parrhesia, had a new master and lord. His name—Jesus. "For several days he was with the disciples in Damascus, and immediately he began to proclaim Jesus in the synagogues, saying, 'He is the Son of God.' All who heard him were amazed and said, 'Is not this the man who made havoc in Jerusalem among those who invoked this name? And has he not come here for the purpose of bringing them bound before the chief priests?' Saul

---

48. Romans 12:12–19.
49. Acts 9:1–2.

CONCLUSION: FOR GOD'S SAKE FEEL THE SERMON

became increasingly more powerful and confounded the Jews who lived in Damascus by proving that Jesus was the Messiah."[50]

Within days of his new mission of speaking the truth fearlessly, enemies plotted to kill him. "His disciples took him by night and let him down through an opening in the wall, lowering him in a basket."[51] All the elements of parrhesia appear when Paul first preaches in Jerusalem. "So he went in and out among them in Jerusalem, speaking boldly in the name of the Lord. He spoke and argued with the Hellenists; but they were attempting to kill him."[52] His bold, risky speech was criticized. His life was in danger. He felt it his duty to speak the truth of Jesus.

Paul checks the boxes for all the characteristics of parrhesia: frank speech, risks, criticism, duty, and boldness. Add to that the fact that Paul had a specific faith relation with the resurrected Jesus Christ.

"But when the Jews saw the crowds, they were filled with jealousy; and blaspheming, they contradicted what was spoken by Paul. Then both Paul and Barnabas spoke out boldly, saying, 'It was necessary that the word of God should be spoken first to you. Since you reject it and judge yourselves to be unworthy of eternal life, we are now turning to the Gentiles.'"[53]

The preacher stands inside and outside of history! The preacher stands with Moses at the Red Sea, with Joshua crossing the Jordan, with Ruth working the fields, with Esther outwitting Haman, with Elijah staring down the prophets of Baal, with David opposing Goliath, with Nathan judging King David, with the hostages in Babylon without a song for their captors, with Ezekiel and the exiles at the River Chebar, with Daniel in the lion's den, with Shadrach, Meshach, and Abednego in the fiery furnace, with Amos preaching in the "king's sanctuary," with Hosea buying back Gomer from pagan priests, with John the Baptist condemning Herod, with the mother hen gathering her brood under her wings, with Jesus on the cross, with Mary Magdalene at the empty tomb, with Stephen as the stones smash into his forehead, with Paul at the Aeropagus, with Titus on Crete with "liars, vicious brutes, lazy gluttons," John on Patmos, and reading the mail of Jesus to the "angels" of the churches—the pastors.

May the parrhesia be with you and in you! May the belt of truth protect you as you speak with boldness. May the courage to face the powers and the principalities be within you! Amen!

50. Acts 9:22.
51. Acts 9:25.
52. Acts 9:29.
53. Acts 13:45–46.

Bibliography

Ahmed, Sara. *The Cultural Politics of Emotion*. Kindle ed. Edinburgh: Edinburgh University Press, 2014.
———. *The Promise of Happiness*. Durham, NC: Duke University Press, 2010.
Alberta, Tim. "How Politics Poisoned the Evangelical Church." *The Atlantic*, June 2022. https://www.theatlantic.com/magazine/archive/2022/06/evangelical-church-pastors-political-radicalization/629631/.
Albrecht, Gloria. *The Character of our Communities: Toward an Ethic of Liberation for the Church*. Nashville: Abingdon, 1995.
Alcántara, Jared E. *The Practices of Christian Preaching: Essentials for Effective Proclamation*. Grand Rapids: Baker Academic, 2019.
Allen, Bob. "Wiley Drake Lifts Call for 'Imprecatory Prayer' against President Obama." *Baptist News Global,* November 20, 2009. https://baptistnews.com/article/wiley-drake-lifts-call-for-imprecatory-prayer-against-president-obama/.
Allen, Wes. *Determining the Form*. Minneapolis: Fortress, 2008.
Alighieri, Dante, *Convivio (The Banquet)*. Los Angeles: Hard, 2009.
Alther, Lisa. *Original Sins*. New York: Open Road Media, 2010.
Ambrose, St. *De Fide (On Belief)*. http://www.newadvent.org/fathers/34041.htm.
Anderson, Floyd. "De Doctrina Christiana: The Convergence of Athens and Jerusalem." *Rhetoric Society Quarterly* XV (1985) 102–4.
Aquinas, Thomas. *Summa Theologica*. Translated by Fathers of the English Dominican Province. Claremont, CA: Coyote Canyon, 2010.
Aristotle, *Rhetoric*. Translated by W. Rhys Roberts. Mineola, NY: Dover, 2004.
———. *Poetics*. Translated by S. H. Butcher. ReadHowYouWant. N.d.
Athanasius. *Athanasius, Letter to Marcellinus, in Athanasius: The Life of Antony and the Letter to Marcellinus*. Translated by Robert C. Gregg. New York: Paulist, 1980.
———. *St. Athanasius on the Incarnation*. London: D. Nutt, 1891.
Augustine. *On Christian Doctrine*. Translated by Durant Waite Robertson. Indianapolis: Bobbs-Merrill, 1958.
Aune, James Arnt. "Burke's Late Blooming: Trope, Defense, and Rhetoric." *Quarterly Journal of Speech* 69 (1983) 328–40.
Backstrom, Joel. "Pre-Truth Life in Post-Truth Times." *Nordic Wittgenstein Review* Special Issue (2019) 97–130.
Bacon, Francis. *Selected Writings of Francis Bacon*. New York: Modern Library, 1955.
Bader-Saye, Scott. *Following Jesus in a Culture of Fear*. Grand Rapids: Brazos, 2007.
Baird, A. C. *Rhetoric: A Philosophical Inquiry*. New York: Ronald, 1965.

Bakhtin, Mikhail M. *Rabelais and His World.* Cambridge: Massachusetts Institute of Technology Press, 1985.
Baldwin, James. "The Creative Process." In *Creative America 1,* 16–21. New York: Ridge, 1962.
Balevic, Katie. "Lauren Boebert Receives Cheers at a Christian Center after Saying She Prays that Biden's 'Days Be Few and Another Take His Office.'" *Business Insider,* June 12, 2022. https://www.businessinsider.com/lauren-boebert-she-prays-psalm-1098-bidens-days-be-few-2022-6.
Barth, Markus. *Ephesians 4–6.* The Anchor Bible. Garden City, NY: Doubleday, 1974.
Bartlett, David L. *What's Good about This News?* Louisville: Westminster John Knox, 2003.
Bauckham, Richard. "Reading Scripture as a Coherent Story." In *The Art of Reading Scripture,* edited by Ellen F. Davis and Richard B. Hays, 38–53. Grand Rapids: Eerdmans, 2003.
Bellinger, William H. *Psalms.* Cambridge: Cambridge University Press, 2014.
Berlant, Lauren. "Trump, or Political Emotions." *The New Inquiry,* August 5, 2016. https://thenewinquiry.com/trump-or-political-emotions/.
Berry, Wendell. "The Responsibility of the Poet." In *What Are People For?,* 86–89. New York: North Point, 1990.
———. *Standing by Words.* Berkeley: Counterpoint, 1983.
Betts, Doris. "This Is the Only Time I'll Tell It." In *The Christ-Haunted Landscape: Faith and Doubt in Southern Literature,* edited by Susan Ketchin, 232–37. Oxford, MS: University Press of Mississippi, 1994.
———. "Interview." In *The Christ-Haunted Landscape: Faith and Doubt in Southern Fiction,* edited by Susan Ketchin, 238–59. Oxford, MS: University Press of Mississippi, 1994.
Bible Portal Staff, "Who was Gamaliel in the Bible (Acts 5)?" *Bible Portal,* October 8, 2022. https://bibleportal.com/articles/who-was-gamaliel-in-the-bible-acts-5.
Biesecker, Barbara. "No Time for Mourning: The Rhetorical Production of the Melancholic Citizen-Subject in the War on Terror." *Philosophy & Rhetoric* 40:1 (2007) 147–69.
Binkley, Timothy. "On the Truth and Probity of Metaphor." *The Journal of Aesthetics and Art Criticism.* 33:2 (Winter 1974) 171–80.
Blackwood, A. W. *The Preparation of Sermons.* Nashville: Abingdon, 1956.
Blake, William. "The Angel that Presided O'er My Birth." https://poets.org/poem/angel-presided-oer-my-birth.
Blight, David W. "Frederick Douglass's Vision for a Reborn America." *Atlantic,* December 2019. https://www.theatlantic.com/magazine/archive/2019/12/frederick-douglass-david-blight-america/600802/.
———. "Trump Has Birthed a Dangerous New 'Lost Cause' Myth." *The Guardian,* January 12, 2022. https://www.theguardian.com/commentisfree/2022/jan/08/trump-has-birthed-a-dangerous-new-lost-cause-myth-we-must-fight-it.
Bloom, Harold. *The Anxiety of Influence: A Theory of Poetry.* Oxford: Oxford University Press, 1997.
Bonhoeffer, Dietrich. *No Rusty Swords.* Translated by C. H. Robertson. London: Collins, 1970.
Bonilla-Silva, Eduardo. *Racism without Racists: Color-blind Racism and the Persistence of Racial Inequality in the United States.* Lanham, MD: Rowman & Littlefield, 2006.

Booth, Wayne. *Critical Understanding: The Powers and Limits of Pluralism*. Chicago: University of Chicago Press, 1979
———. *Don't Try to Reason with Me: Essays and Ironies for a Credulous Age*. Chicago: University of Chicago Press, 1970.
———. *Modern Dogma and the Rhetoric of Assent*. Chicago: University of Chicago Press, 1974.
———. *The Rhetoric of Fiction*. Chicago: The University of Chicago Press, 1983.
———. *A Rhetoric of Irony*. Chicago: University of Chicago Press, 19774.
Bossuet, Jacques Bénigne. *The Sermon on the Mount*. London: Longmans, Green, 1900.
Bosworth, Sheila. "Interview." In *The Christ-Haunted Landscape: Faith and Doubt in Southern Fiction*, edited by Susan Ketchin, 146–71. Oxford, MS: University Press of Mississippi, 1994.
Broadus, John A. *On the Preparation and Delivery of Sermons*. Fourth Edition. Edited by Vernon L. Stanfield. New York: HarperOne, 1979.
Bronowski, Jacob. *Science and Human Values*. London: Faber & Faber, 2011.
Brooks, David. "The Problem with Wokeness." *New York Times*, June 7, 2018. https://www.nytimes.com/2018/06/07/opinion/wokeness-racism-progressivism-social-justice.html.
Brown, Mary Ward. "A New Life." In *The Christ-Haunted Landscape: Faith and Doubt in Southern Literature*, edited by Susan Ketchin, 305–14. Oxford, MS: University Press of Mississippi, 1994.
———. "Interview." In *The Christ-Haunted Landscape: Faith and Doubt in Southern Fiction*. Oxford, MS: University Press of Mississippi, 1994: 319—325.
Brown, Larry. "Interview." In *The Christ-Haunted Landscape: Faith and Doubt in Southern Fiction*, edited by Susan Ketchin, 126–48. Oxford, MS: University Press of Mississippi, 1994.
Brueggemann, Walter. *The Collected Sermons*. Vol. 2. Louisville: Westminster John Knox, 2015.
———. *Finally Comes the Poet: Daring Speech for Proclamation*. Kindle ed. Minneapolis: Fortress, 1989.
———. *The Psalms and the Life of Faith*. Kindle ed. Minneapolis: Fortress, 2004.
———. *Truth Speaks to Power: The Countercultural Nature of Scripture*. Louisville: Westminster John Knox, 2013.
Bullivent, Stephen. *Nonverts: The Making of Ex-Christian America*. Oxford: Oxford University Press, 2022.
Burke, Kenneth. *A Grammar of Motives*, Vol. 177. Oakland: University of California Press, 1969.
———. "Literature as equipment for living." In *The Philosophy of Literary Form* 293-304. Berkeley: University of California Press, 1973.
———. *The Philosophy of Literary Form: Studies in Symbolic Action* 3rd ed. 1941. Oakland: University of California Press, 1973.
———. "The Rhetoric of Hitler's 'Battle.'" *The Southern Review* 5 (Summer 1939).
———. *A Rhetoric of Motives*. Berkeley: University of California Press, 1969.
———. *The Rhetoric of Religion: Studies in Logology*. Berkeley: University of California Press, 1970.
Buttrick, David. *Homiletic: Moves and Structure*. Kindle ed. Philadelphia: Fortress, 1987.

Cahill, Lisa Sowle, and James F. Childress. *Christian Ethics: Problems and Prospects.* Cleveland: Pilgrim, 1996.

Campbell, Will D. *And Also with You: Duncan Gray and the American Dilemma.* Franklin, TN: Providence House, 1997.

———. *Cecelia's Sin.* Macon, GA: Mercer University Press, 1983.

———. "I Love My Country: Christ Have Mercy." *Motive,* 42–47. Division of Higher Education of the Board of Education of The United Methodist Church, Nashville, Tennessee, December 1969.

———. "Interview." In *The Christ-Haunted Landscape: Faith and Doubt in Southern Fiction,* edited by Susan Ketchin, 211–29. Oxford, MS: University Press of Mississippi, 1994.

Campbell, Will D., and Richard C. Goode. *Crashing the Idols: The Vocation of Will D. Campbell (and Any Other Christian for That Matter).* Eugene, OR: Cascade, 2010.

Carter, J. Kameron. *Race: A Theological Account.* Oxford: Oxford University Press, 2008.

Chakrabarty, Dipesh. "The Climate of History." *Critical Inquiry* 35:2 (2009) 197–222.

Chen, Mel Y. *Animacies: Biopolitics, Racial Mattering, and Queer Affect.* Durham, NC: Duke University Press, 2012.

Chesterton, G. K. *Saint Francis of Assisi.* Peabody, MA: Hendrickson, 2008.

Chirindo, Kundai. "Precarious Publics." *Quarterly Journal of Speech* 107:4 (2021) 430–34.

Chouraqui, Andre. "Introduction to the Psalms." *Liturgy O.C.S.O. Journal of Gethsemani Abbey* 13:1 (1979) 3–29. https://cdm16259.contentdm.oclc.org/digital/collection/p15032coll3/id/56/rec/36.

Chua, Amy. *Political Tribes: Group Instinct and the Fate of Nations.* New York: Penguin, 2019.

Claypool, *The Preaching Event.* New York: HarperCollins, 1990.

———. *Tracks of a Fellow Struggler.* Waco, TX: Word, 1974.

Clough, Patricia Ticineto. "Introduction." In *The Affective Turn: Theorizing the Social,* edited by Patricia Ticineto Clough and Jean Halley, 1–33. Durham, NC: Duke University Press, 2007.

Coffin, William Sloane, Jr. *Credo.* Louisville: Westminster John Knox, 2004.

———. "Eulogy for Alex." In *Sermons, Volume II,* 3–5. Louisville: Westminster John Knox, 2008.

Collins, Francis S. *The Language of God: A Scientist Presents Evidence for Belief.* New York: Simon and Schuster, 2006.

Cone, James H. *The Cross and the Lynching Tree.* New York: Orbis, 2011.

Connelly, Thomas L. *Will Campbell and the Soul of the South.* New York: Continuum, 1982.

Conroy, Pat. *Lords of Discipline.* New York: Bantam, 1987.

———. *My Reading Life.* New York: Doubleday, 2010.

———. *The Prince of Tides.* New York: Houghton Mifflin Harcourt, 1986.

Cover, Robert M. "Obligation: A Jewish Jurisprudence of the Social Order." *The Journal of Law and Religion* 5 (1987) 65–74.

Craddock, Fred B. *As One Without Authority: Essays on Inductive Preaching.* Enid, OK: Phillips, 1974.

———. *The Cherry Log Sermons.* Louisville: Westminster John Knox, 2001.

———. *Overhearing the Gospel.* Nashville: Abingdon, 1978.

———. *Preaching.* Nashville: Abingdon, 2010.

Crews, Harry. *Scar Lover.* New York: Simon & Schuster, 1992.

———. "Interview." In *The Christ-Haunted Landscape: Faith and Doubt in Southern Fiction*, edited by Susan Ketchin, 335–51. Oxford, MS: University Press of Mississippi, 1994.
Crosswhite, James. "Reason as Justice: Chaim Perelman and the Justification of Rhetoric." Paper presented to the International Society for the History of Rhetoric, Turin, Italy, 1994.
Crusius, Timothy W. Foreword in Ernesto Grassi, *Rhetoric as Philosophy: The Humanist Tradition*. Carbondale: Southern Illinois University Press. 2000.
Cunningham, David S. *Faithful Persuasion: In Aid of Rhetoric of Christian Theology*. Notre Dame: University of Notre Dame Press, 1990.
Cvetkovich, Ann. *Depression: A Public Feeling*. Durham, NC: Duke University Press, 2012.
Daley, Brian E. "Is Patristic Exegesis Still Usable? Some Reflections on Early Christian Interpretation of the Psalms." In *The Art of Reading Scripture*, edited by Ellen F. Davis and Richard B. Hays, 69–88. Grand Rapids: Wm. B. Eerdmans, 2003.
Darsey, James. "Joe McCarthy's Fantastic Moment." *Communication Monographs* 62:1 (1995) 65–86.
Davis, Ellen F., and Richard B. Hays, eds. *The Art of Reading Scripture*. Grand Rapids: Eerdmans, 2003.
Davis, Ellen F. "Critical Traditioning: Seeking an Inner Biblical Hermeneutic." In *The Art of Reading Scripture*, edited by Ellen F. Davis and Richard B. Hays, 163–80. Grand Rapids: Eerdmans, 2003.
———. *Wondrous Depth: Preaching the Old Testament*. Kindle ed. Louisville: Westminster John Knox, 2005.
Davis, H. Grady. *Design for Preaching*. Philadelphia: Muhlenberg, 1958.
Deleuze, Gilles. *Spinoza: Practical Philosophy*. San Francisco: City Lights, 1988
Delgado, Richard. "Rodrigo's Chronicle." *Yale Law Journal* 101:6 (1992) 1357–83.
DiAngelo, Robin. "White People Are Still Raised to be Racially Illiterate." *NBC News Think* (2018). https://www.nbcnews.com/think/opinion/white-people-are-still-raised-be-racially-illiterate-if-we-ncna906646.
Edgerton, Clyde. *Raney: A Novel*. New York: Algonquin, 1985.
Epstein, Isadore. *The Babylonian Talmud*. London: Soncino, 1960.
Eslinger, Richard L. *A New Hearing: Living Option in Homiletic Methods*. Nashville: Abingdon, 1987.
Fant, Clyde E. *Bonhoeffer: Worldly Preaching*. Nashville: Thomas Nelson, 1975.
———. *Preaching for Today*. New York: Harper, 1975.
Farrell, Thomas B. *Norms of Rhetorical Culture*. New Haven: Yale University Press, 1993.
Fea, John. *Believe Me: The Evangelical Road to Donald Trump*. Grand Rapids: Eerdmans, 2018.
Ferguson, Kitty. *The Fire in the Equations: Science, Religion, and the Search for God*. Grand Rapids: Eerdmans, 1997.
Fitzgerald, F. Scott. *The Curious Case of Benjamin Button and Other Stories*. Garden City, NY: Courier Dover, 2020.
Foucault, Michel. *Fearless Speaking*. Cambridge: Semiotext, 2001.
Foss, Sonja K., Karen A. Foss, and Robert Trapp. *Contemporary Perspectives on Rhetoric*. Prospect Heights, IL: Waveland, 1985.
Fowl, Stephen E. *Engaging Scripture: A Model for Theological Interpretation*. Eugene, OR: Wipf and Stock, 2008.

Frank, David A. "The New Rhetoric: Judaism, and Post-Enlightenment Thought: The Cultural Origins of Perelmanian Philosophy." *Quarterly Journal of Speech* 83:3 (1997) 311–31.

Frost, Robert. *The Poetry of Robert Frost: The Collected Poems.* Edited by Edward Collery Lathem. New York: Henry Holt, 2002.

Funk, Robert W. *Language, Hermeneutic, and Word of God: The Problem of Language in the New Testament and Contemporary Theology.* New York: Harper & Row, 1966.

Gilbert, Kenyatta R. *A Pursued Justice.* Kindle ed. Waco, TX: Baylor University Press, 2016.

Glaude, Eddie S., Jr. *Democracy in Black: How Race Still Enslaves the American Soul.* New York: Broadway, 2016.

Goldenberg, David M. *The Curse of Ham: Race and Slavery in Early Judaism, Christianity, and Islam.* Princeton: Princeton University Press, 2003.

Goodall, Jane, and Phillip Berman. *Reason for Hope: A Spiritual Journey.* New York: Grand Central, 1999.

Gorman, Amanda. "Read the full text of Amanda Gorman's inaugural poem 'The Hill We Climb.'" *CNBC*, January 20, 2021, 2021. https://www.cnbc.com/2021/01/20/amanda-gormans-inaugural-poem-the-hill-we-climb-full-text.html.

Gould, Stephen Jay. *Full House: The Spread of Excellence from Plato to Darwin.* New York: Three Rivers, 1997.

Grady, Davis H. *Design for Preaching*: Philadelphia: Muhlenberg, 1958.

Graham, Franklin. "Franklin Graham Says He's not a Preacher of Hate, so Let's Roll the Tape and See." *Baptist News Global*, June 8, 2022. https://baptistnews.com/article/franklin-grahm-says-hes-not-a-preacher-of-hate-so-lets-roll-the-tape-and-see/.

Grassi, Ernesto. *Rhetoric as Philosophy: The Humanist Tradition.* Carbondale: Southern Illinois University Press,. 2000.

Griffin, David Ray. *Two Great Truths: A New Synthesis of Scientific Naturalism and Christian Faith.* Louisville: Westminster John Knox, 2004.

Griffiths, Paul J. *Intellectual Appetite: A Theological Grammar.* Washington, DC: Catholic University of America Press, 2009.

Grossberg, Lawrence. *Under the Cover of Chaos: Trump and the Battle for the American Right.* London: Pluto, 2018.

Groundwater, Evan. "Review of: *Apocalypse Man: The Death Drive and the Rhetoric of White Masculine Victimhood*." *Quarterly Journal of Speech* 107:3 (2021) 365–68.

Gurganus, Allan. "Interview." In *The Christ-Haunted Landscape: Faith and Doubt in Southern Fiction*, edited by Susan Ketchin, 376–95. Oxford, MS: University Press of Mississippi, 1994.

———. "It Had Wings." In *The Christ-Haunted Landscape: Faith and Doubt in Southern Fiction*, edited by Susan Ketchin, 372–75. Oxford, MS: University Press of Mississippi, 1994.

Hall, Stuart. *The Fateful Triangle.* Cambridge: Harvard University Press, 2017.

Hamer, Fannie Lou. "Testimony Before the Credentials Committee by Fannie Lou Hamer: Say It Plain." www.publicradio.org. https://americanradioworks.publicradio.org/features/sayitplain/flhamer.html.

Hannah, Barry. *Yonder Stands Your Orphan.* New York: Grove, 2002.

Hart, David Bentley. *Atheist Delusions: The Christian Revolution and Its Fashionable Enemies.* New Haven: Yale University Press, 2009.

———. *The Doors of the Sea: Where Was God in the Tsunami?* Kindle ed. Grand Rapids: Eerdmans, 2005.
Hart, Roderick P. *Trump and Us: What He Says and Why People Listen*. Cambridge: Cambridge University Press, 2020.
Hauerwas, Stanley. *A Cross-Shattered Church*. Grand Rapids: Brazos, 2009.
———. *In Good Company: The Church as Polis*. Notre Dame: University of Notre Dame Press, 1995.
———. *Performing the Faith: Bonhoeffer and the Practice of Nonviolence*. Grand Rapids: Brazos, 2004.
———. *Unleashing the Scripture: Freeing the Bible from Captivity to America*. Nashville: Abingdon, 1998.
———. *Working with Words: On Learning to Speak Christian*. Eugene, OR: Cascade, 2011.
Hauerwas, Stanley, and Romand Coles. *Christianity, Democracy, and the Radical Ordinary: Conversations between a Radical Democrat and a Christian*. Eugene, OR: Cascade, 2008.
Havel, Vaclav. *The Power of the Powerless*. Translated and edited by John Keane. New York: Routledge Taylor and Francis, 1985.
Hawking, Stephen. *The Grand Design*. New York: Random House Digital, 2010.
Hays, Richard B. *The Moral Vision of the New Testament: A Contemporary Introduction to New Testament Ethics*. New York: HarperCollins, 1996.
Hemingway, Ernest. *Islands in the Stream*. New York: Random House, 2013.
Hesford, Wendy S., Adela C. Licona, and Christa Teston. *Precarious Rhetorics*. Columbus: The Ohio State University Press, 2018.
Hoffman, William. "The Question of Rain." In *By Land, By Sea*, 160–74. Baton Rouge: Louisiana State University Press, 1988.
Holland, Sharon Patricia. *The Erotic Life of Racism*. Durham, NC: Duke University Press, 2012.
Holling, Michelle A., and Dreama G. Moon. "20/20 in 2020? Refractive Vision, 45, and White Supremacy." *Quarterly Journal of Speech* 107:4 (2021) 435–42.
hooks, bell, and Cornel West. *Breaking Bread: Insurgent Black Intellectual Life*. New York: Taylor & Francis, 2016.
Hopkins, Gerard Manley. *Poems and Prose*. London: Penguin, 2008.
Howell, James. "Christ Was Like St. Francis." In *The Art of Reading Scripture*, edited by Ellen F. Davis and Richard B. Hays, 89–107. Grand Rapids: Eerdmans, 2003.
Huebner, Chris K. *A Precarious Peace: Yoderian Explorations on Theology, Knowledge, and Identity*. Windsor, ON: Herald, 2006.
Hütter, Reinhard. "The Church as Public: Dogma, Practice, and the Holy Spirit." *Pro Ecclesia* 3:3 (Summer 1994) 334–61.
Isaac, Logan M. "'*Biography as Theology*' by James McClendon." May 19, 2005. https://feraltheology.wordpress.com/2015/05/19/biography-as-theology-by-james-mcclendon/.
Ivie, Robert L. "Rhetorical Aftershocks of Trump's Ascendancy: Salvation by Demolition and Deal-Making." *Res Rhetorica* 62 (2017) 61–79.
Johannesen, R., ed. *Contemporary Theories of Rhetoric*. New York: HarperCollins, 1971.
Johnson, Luke Timothy. *The Acts of the Apostles*. Sacra Pagina. Collegeville, MN: Liturgical, 1992.

———. *The New Testament: A Very Short Introduction*. Oxford: Oxford University Press, 2010.

Jones, Edgar Dewitt. *Royalty of the Pulpit*. New York: Harper Row, 1951.

Jonsen, Albert R. "The Ethicist as Improvisationist." In *Christian Ethics: Problems and Prospects*, edited by Lisa Sowle Cahill and James F. Childress, 218–35. New York: Pilgrim, 1996.

Kelly, Casey Ryan. *Apocalypse Man: The Death Drive and the Rhetoric of White Masculine Victimhood*. Columbus: The Ohio State University Press, 2020.

Kendi, Ibram X. *How to Be an Antiracist*. London: One World, 2023.

Kennedy, Rodney. *The Creative Power of Metaphor*. Lanham, MD: University Press of America, 1993.

———. "Franklin Graham Says He's not a Preacher of Hate, so Let's Roll the Tape and See." *Baptist News Global*, June 8, 2022. https://baptistnews.com/article/franklin-graham-says-hes-not-a-preacher-of-hate-so-lets-roll-the-tape-and-see/.

Kenyon, Jane. *Otherwise: New and Selected Poems*. Minneapolis: Graywolf, 1996.

Ketchin, Susan, ed. *The Christ-Haunted Landscape: Faith and Doubt in Southern Fiction*. Oxford, MS: University Press of Mississippi, 1994.

Kierkegaard, Soren. *The Journal of Kierkegaard*. Translated, selected, and with an introduction by Alexander Dru. New York: Harper Torch, 1959.

Kumar, Anugrah. "Mike Huckabee: Climate Science 'Not Settled.'" *HuffPost*, June 21, 2015. https://www.huffpost.com/entry/mike-huckabee-climate-change_n_7632030.

Kundai, Chirindo. "Precarious 'Publics.'" *Quarterly Journal of Speech* 107:4 (2021). DOI: 10.1080/00335630.2021.1983192.

Lakoff, George. *Don't Think of an Elephant: Progressive Values and the Framing Wars—A Progressive Guide to Action*. White River Junction, VT: Chelsea Green, 2004.

———. *The Political Mind: A Cognitive Scientist's Guide to Your Brain and Its Politics*. London: Penguin, 2008.

Lakoff, George, and Mark Johnson. *Metaphors We Live By*. Chicago: University of Chicago Press, 2008.

Lifton, Robert. *Living and Dying*. New York: Praeger, 1976.

Lindberg, David C. *The Beginnings of Western Science: The European Scientific Tradition in Philosophical, Religious, and Institutional Context, Prehistory to AD 1450*. Chicago: University of Chicago Press, 2010.

Lischer, Richard. *The End of Words: The Language of Reconciliation in a Culture of Violence*. Kindle ed. Grand Rapids: Eerdmans, 2008.

Liu, Jennifer. "Read the full text of Amanda Gorman's inaugural poem 'The Hill We Climb.'" CNBC, January 20, 2021. https://www.cnbc.com/2021/01/20/amanda-gormans-inaugural-poem-the-hill-we-climb-full-text.html.

Long, Thomas G. *The Witness of Preaching*. Louisville: Westminster John Knox, 2016.

Louth, Andrew. *Discerning the Mystery: An Essay on the Nature of Theology*. Oxford: Clarendon, 1983.

Lowry, Eugene L. *The Homiletic Plot*. Atlanta: John Knox, 1980.

———. *Doing Time in the Pulpit*. Nashville: Abingdon, 1985.

———. *The Sermon: Dancing the Edge of Mystery*. Nashville: Abingdon, 1997.

Lucas, Stephen. *The Art of Public Speaking*. New York: McGraw-Hill, 2004.

Luhrmann, Tanya M. *When God Talks Back: Understanding the American Evangelical Relationship with God*. New York: Knopf, 2012.

Manning, Erin. *Always More than One: Individuation's Dance*. Durham, NC: Duke University Press, 2013.

Marney, Carlyle. "Fundaments of a Competent Ministry." Lecture, Fort Polk, Leesville, LA, n.d.
———. *Priests to Each Other.* Valley Forge, PA: Judson, 1978
Massumi, Brian. *Parables for the Virtual: Movement, Affect, Sensation.* Durham, NC: Duke University Press, 2002.
McClendon, James Wm. *Systematic Theology, Vol. 1: Ethics.* Nashville: Abingdon, 1986.
———. *Systematic Theology, Vol. 3: Witness.* Nashville: Abingdon, 2010.
McElvaine, Robert S. *The Great Depression: America, 1929–1941.* Kindle ed. Portland, OR: Broadway, 1993.
———. "Their Party Crashed. Ours May Too." September 28, 2008. https://historynewsnetwork.org/article/55079.
MacIntyre, Alasdair. "Poetry as Political Philosophy: Notes on Burke and Yeats." In *On Modern Poetry: Essays Presented to Donald Davie,* edited by Vereen Bell and Laurence Lerner, 145–57. Champaign: University of Illinois Press, 1988.
Marney, Carlyle. "Fundaments of Competent Ministry." Unpublished paper. Fort Polk, Leesville, LA: n.d.
———. *Priests to Each Other.* Valley Forge, PA: Judson, 1978.
Marsden, George. *Fundamentalism and American Culture.* Oxford: Oxford University Press, 2022.
Marsh, John. *In Walt We Trust: How a Queer Socialist Poet Can Save America from Itself.* New York: New York University Press, 2015.
McKenzie, A. M. *Novel Preaching: Tips from Top Writers on Crafting Creative Sermons.* Louisville: Presbyterian, 2010.
Menninger, Karl. *Whatever Became of Sin?* New York: Hawthorn, 1973.
Milbank, John. *Theology and Social Theory: Beyond Secular Reason.* Malden, MA: Blackwell, 1990.
Miller, Donald. G. *The Way of Biblical Preaching.* Nashville: Abingdon, 1957.
Miller, Kenneth R. *Only a Theory: Evolution and the Battle for America's Soul.* New York: Penguin, 2008.
Mitchell, Margaret M. *The Heavenly Trumpet: John Chrysostom and the Art of Pauline Interpretation.* Louisville: Westminster John Knox, 2002.
Morrison, Toni. *Beloved.* New York: Vintage, 1987.
Moss, Otis, Jr. "A Prophetic Witness in an Anti-Prophetic Age." *The African American Pulpit* 7:4 (2004) 68–72.
Moss, Otis, III. *Blue Note Preaching in a Post-Soul World: Finding Hope in an Age of Despair.* Louisville: Westminster John Knox, 2015.
Muller-Fahrenholz, Geiko. *America's Battle for God: A European Christian Looks at Civil Religion.* Grand Rapids: Eerdmans, 2007.
O'Connor, Flannery. *Collected Works: Wise Blood / A Good Man is Hard to Find / The Violent Bear it Away / Everything that Rises Must Converge / Essays and Letters.* New York: Library of America, 1988.
———. *The Habit of Being: Letters of Flannery O'Connor.* New York: Macmillan, 1988.
———. *Mystery and Manners: Occasional Prose.* Kindle ed. New York: Macmillan, 1969.
———. *Wise Blood: A Novel.* New York: Macmillan, 2007.
Oliver, Mary. *Devotions.* New York: Penguin, 2017.
———. *A Poetry Handbook.* Boston: Houghton Mifflin Harcourt, 1994.
Omi, Michael, and Howard Winant. *Racial Formation in the United States.* Oxfordshire: Routledge, 2014.

Ong, Walter J. *Orality and Literacy: The Technologizing of the Word*. London: Methuen, 1982.
Osherow, Jacqueline. *Dead Men's Praise*. New York: Grove, 1999.
Ott, Brian L., and Greg Dickinson. *The Twitter Presidency: Donald J. Trump and the Politics of White Rage*. Oxfordshire: Routledge, 2019.
Payne, Charles. *I've Got the Light of Freedom*. Berkeley: University of California Press, 2007.
Payne, Peggy. *Revelation*. Kindle ed. New York: Simon & Schuster, 1988.
PBS NewsHour. "December 15, 2020." Directed by Chris Alexander.
Percy, Walker. "Why Are You a Catholic?" In *Signposts in a Strange Land: Essays*, edited by Patrick Samway, 304–5. New York: Farrar, Straus, & Giroux, 1991.
Perelman, Chaim. *The New Rhetoric and the Humanities: Essays on Rhetoric and its Applications*. Vol. 140. Berlin/Heidelberg: Springer Science & Business Media, 2012.
———. *The Realm of Rhetoric*. Notre Dame: Notre Dame University Press, 1982.
Perelman, Chaim, and Lucie Olbrechts-Tyteca. *The New Rhetoric: A Treatise on Argumentation*, translated by John Wilkinson and Purcell Weaver. Notre Dame: University of Notre Dame Press. 1969.
Pinn, Anthony B. *Making the Gospel Plain: The Writings of Bishop Reverdy C. Ransom*. London: Bloomsbury T. & T. Clark, 1999.
Plato. *Apology*. In *Plato: Collection*. Kindle ed. Edited by Benjamin Jowett. Copenhagen: Titan Read, n.d.
———. *Gorgias*. Public domain book.
———. *Phaedrus*. Translated by Benjamin Jowett. Glasgow: Good, 2019.
———. *The Republic*. Edited by G. R. F. Ferrari. Cambridge: Cambridge University Press, 2000.
Potok, Chaim. *The Chosen*. New York: Simon and Schuster, 1967.
Price, Reynolds. *A Serious Way of Wondering: The Ethics of Jesus Imagined*. New York: Simon and Schuster, 2003.
———. "Interview." In *The Christ-Haunted Landscape: Faith and Doubt in Southern Fiction*, edited by Susan Ketchin, 69–99. Oxford, MS: University Press of Mississippi, 1994.
Probyn, Elspeth. "A-ffect: Let Her RIP." *Media/Culture Journal* 8:6 (December 2005). http://journal.media-culture.org.au/0512/13-probyn.php.
———. "Teaching Bodies: Affects in the Classroom." *Body & Society* 10:4 (2004) 21–43.
Proctor, Samuel D. *"How Shall They Hear?": Effective Preaching for Vital Faith*. Valley Forge, PA: Judson, 2007.
Proctor, Samuel D., and William D. Watley, eds. *Sermons from the Black Pulpit*. King of Prussia, PA: Judson, 1984.
Read, Rupert. "What Is New in Our Time, The Truth in 'Post-Truth': A Response to Finlayson." *Nordic Wittgenstein Review* Special Issue (2019) 81–96.
Ramsey, G. Lee, Jr. *Preachers and Misfits, Prophets and Thieves: The Minister in Southern Fiction*. Kindle ed. Louisville: Westminster John Knox, 2008.
Randolph, David J. *The Renewal of Preaching*. Philadelphia: Fortress, 1969.
Ransom, Reverdy C. "Church That Shall Survive." In *Making the Gospel Plain: The Writings of Bishop Reverdy C. Ransom*, edited by Anthony B. Pinn. London: Bloomsbury T. & T. Clark, 1999.

BIBLIOGRAPHY

Recio, Belinda "One Thousand Words for Reindeer." *True North Gallery*, November 8, 2012. https://truenorthgallery.net/blogs/nature-culture/85246529-one-thousand-words-for-reindeer.

Rees, Martin. *Just Six Numbers: The Deep Forces that Shape the Universe.* London: Hachette UK, 2008.

Repucci, Sarah, and Amy Slipowitz. *Freedom in the World 2021: Democracy Under Siege.* New York: Freedom, 2021.

Reyes, G. Mitchell, and Kundai Chirindo. "Theorizing Race and Gender in the Anthropo-cene." *Women's Studies in Communication* 43:4 (2020) 429–42.

Richards, Ivor Armstrong, and Constable. John. *The Philosophy of Rhetoric.* Oxfordshire: Routledge, 2018.

Robinson, James H. *Adventurous Preaching.* Great Neck, NY: Channel, 1956.

Robinson, Ken, and John Rafter Lee. *Out of Our Minds.* New York: Tantor, 2011.

Rowe, C. Kavin. *World Upside Down: Reading Acts in the Graeco-Roman Age.* Oxford: Oxford University Press, 2009.

Sartre, Jean Paul. *Sketch for a Theory of the Emotions.* Translated by Mairet Philip. London: Methuen, 1962.

Scott, James C. *Weapons of the Weak: Everyday Forms of Peasant Resistance.* Kindle ed. New Haven: Yale University Press, 1985.

Schaefer, Donovan O. *Religious Affects.* Durham, NC: Duke University Press.

———. "Whiteness and Civilization: Shame, Race, and the Rhetoric of Donald Trump." *Communication and Critical/Cultural Studies* 17:1 (2020) 1–18.

Sedgwick, Eve Kosofsky. "Teaching/Depression." *The Scholar and Feminist Online* 4:2 (2006). http://sfonline.barnard.edu/heilbrun/sedgwick_01.htm.

Shepherd, J. Barrie. *Whatever Happened to Delight? Preaching the Gospel in Poetry and Parable.* Louisville: Westminster John Knox, 2006.

Skinnell, Ryan, ed. *Faking the News: What Rhetoric Can Teach Us About Donald J. Trump.* Societas. Exeter: Imprint Academic, 2018.

Smith, Dale M. *Poets Beyond the Barricades.* Tuscaloosa: University of Alabama Press, 2012.

Smith, David Livingstone. *Less Than Human: Why We Demean, Enslave, and Exterminate Others.* New York: St. Martin's, 2011.

Smith, James K. A. *How (Not) to Be Secular: Reading Charles Taylor.* Kindle ed. Grand Rapids: Eerdmans, 2014.

Snyder, Timothy. *On Tyranny: Twenty Lessons from the Twentieth Century.* New York: Tim Duggan, 2017.

Sozomenus, Salminius Hermias. *The Ecclesiastical History of Sozomen: Comprising a History of the Church from AD 323 to AD 425.* Vol. 1. "Book VIII, Chapter II: Education, Training, Conduct, and Wisdom of the Great John Chrysostom," 362–64. N.p.: Library of Alexandria, 2020.

Spinoza, Benedict. *Ethics.* Edited and translated by Edwin Curley. New York: Penguin, 1996.

Skinnell, Ryan. *Faking the News.* Exeter: Imprint Academic, 2018.

Stephens, Randall J., and Karl Giberson. *The Anointed: Evangelical Truth in a Secular Age.* Cambridge: Harvard University Press, 2011.

Strawn, Brent A. *The Old Testament Is Dying: A Diagnosis and Recommended Treatment.* Kindle ed. Grand Rapids: Baker Academic, 2017.

Tanaka, Hikaru. "Athanasius as Interpreter of the Psalms: His Letter to Marcellinus." *Pro Ecclesia* 21:4 (2012) 422–47.

Taylor, Barbara Brown. *When God is Silent*. Cambridge: Cowley, 1998.
Taylor, Charles. *A Secular Age*. Cambridge: Harvard University Press, 2007.
Taylor, Gardner C. *How Shall They Preach?* Elgin, IL: Progressive Baptist, 1977.
———. *The Scarlet Thread*. Progressive Baptist, 1981.
———. *The Words of Gardner Taylor: Quintessential Classics*. Vol. 3. Valley Forge, PA: Judson, 2000.
Thomas, Lewis. *Late Night Thoughts on Listening to Mahler's Ninth Symphony*. New York: Penguin, 1995.
Thompson Lisa. *Ingenuity: Preaching as an Outsider*. Nashville: Abingdon, 2018.
Tilley, Terrence W. *The Evils of Theodicy*. Eugene, OR: Wipf and Stock, 2000.
Tinder, Glenn. *The Political Meaning of Christianity: An Interpretation*. Eugene, OR: Wipf and Stock, 2000.
Tisdale, Leonora Tubbs. *Prophetic Preaching: A Pastoral Approach*. Louisville: Westminster John Knox, 2010.
Todorov, Tzvetan. *The Fantastic: A Structural Approach to a Literary Genre*. Translated by R. Howard. Ithaca, NY: Cornell University Press, 1975.
Toffler, Alvin. *The Third Wave: The Classic Study of Tomorrow*. New York: Bantam, 2022.
Tomkins, Silvan. *Affect Imagery Consciousness: The Complete Edition*. Edited by Bertram P. Karon. New York: Springer, 2008.
Tooley, Mark. "Stanley Hauerwas's America." *Juicy Ecumenism: The Institute on Religion and Democracy's Blog*, December 18, 2009. https://juicyecumenism.com/2009/12/18/stanley-hauerwass-america/#:~:text=%E2%80%9CWar%20is%20America%E2%80%99s%20central%20liturgical%20act%20onecessary%20to,nations%2C%E2%80%9D%20Hauerwas%20told%20students%20at%20Houghton%20in%20October.
Toulmin, Stephen. *The Philosophy of Science*. London: Hutchinson, 1953.
———. *The Uses of Argument*. Cambridge: Cambridge University Press, 2003.
Tracy, David. *The Analogical Imagination*. New York: Crossroads, 1998.
Tubbs-Tisdale, Leonora. *Prophetic Preaching: A Pastoral Approach*. Louisville: Westminster John Knox, 2010.
Updike, John. "Seven Stanzas at Easter." *Dialog: A Journal of Theology* 42:2 (2003) 110.
Von Rad, Gerhard. *Biblical Interpretations in Preaching*. Translated by John E. Steely. Nashville: Abingdon, 977.
Yoder, John Howard. *Original Revolution: Essays on Christian Pacifism*. Harrisonburg, VA: Menno Media, 2003.
Wallace, Karl R. "The Substance of Rhetoric: Good Reasons." *Quarterly Journal of Speech* 49:3 (1963) 239–49.
Wanzer-Serrano, Daniel. "Rhetoric's Rac(e/ist) Problems." *Quarterly Journal of Speech* 105 (2019) 465–76.
Watkins, Megan. "Desiring Recognition, Accumulating Affect." In *The Affect Theory Reader*, edited by Melissa Gregg and Gregory J. Seigworth, 269–85. Durham, NC: Duke University Press, 2010.
———. "Pedagogic Affect/Effect: Embodying a Desire to Learn." *Pedagogies: An International Journal* 1:4 (2006) 269–82.
———. "Thwarting Desire: Discursive Constraint and Pedagogic Practice." *International Journal of Qualitative Studies in Education* 20:3 (May–June 2007) 301–18.
Weaver, Richard M. *The Ethics of Rhetoric*. Oxfordshire: Routledge, 1995.

———. *Language Is Sermonic: Richard M. Weaver on the Nature of Rhetoric*. Edited by Richard L. Johannesen and Rennard Strickland. Baton Rouge: Louisiana State University Press, 1985.

———. *Life Without Prejudice, and Other Essays*. Washington, DC: H. Regnery, 1966.

Weil, Simone. *Need for Roots: Prelude to a Declaration Towards Mankind*. Oxfordshire: Routledge, 2002.

Weinberg, Steven "Without God." *The New York Review of Books* 55:14 (September 25, 2008). https://www.nybooks.com/articles/2008/09/25/without-god/.

West, Cornel. "Cornel West and the Fight to Save the Black Prophetic Tradition." *Truthdig*, September 9, 2013. https://www.truthdig.com/articles/cornel-west-and-the-fight-to-save-the-black-prophetic-tradition/.

———. *Democracy Matters: Winning the Fight against Imperialism*. London: Penguin, 2005.

Whitman, Walt. *Leaves of Grass: The First Edition + The Death Bed Experience of 1892*. e-artnow. N.p.: Kindle edition, 2021.

Williams, Rowan. *On Augustine*. London: Bloomsbury, 1987.

———. *Tokens of Trust: An Introduction to Christian Belief*. Louisville: Westminster John Knox, 2010.

Willner, Ann Ruth. *The Spellbinders: Charismatic Political Leadership*. New Haven: Yale University Press, 1985.

Wilson, Jessica Hooten. *Reading for the Love of God: How to Read as a Spiritual Practice*. Grand Rapids: Baker, 2023.

Wittgenstein, Ludwig. *Culture and Value*. Chicago: University of Chicago Press, 1984.

———. *Philosophical Investigations*. New York: Macmillan, 1952.

Wright Jeremiah A., Jr. "Words from the Pulpit: Faith in a Foreign Land." *Cross Currents*, 2007, 237–51.

Wright, N. T. *The New Testament and the People of God*. Minneapolis: Fortress, 1992.

Yoder, John Howard. *Original Revolution: Essays on Christian Pacifism*. Harrisonburg, VA: Menno Media, 2003.

www.ingramcontent.com/pod-product-compliance
Lightning Source LLC
Chambersburg PA
CBHW031358230426
43670CB00006B/578